Vulnerability and Resilience in Human Development

This book is ·
or before the ·

of related interest

Early Experience and the Life Path
Ann Clarke and Alan Clarke
ISBN 1 85302 858 4

Six Theories of Child Development
Revised Formulations and Current Issues
Edited by Ross Vasta
ISBN 1 85302 137 7

Child Development for Child Care and Protection Workers
Brigid Daniel, Sally Wassel and Robbie Gilligan
ISBN 1 85302 633 6

Psychology and Social Care
Edited by David Messer and Fiona Jones
ISBN 1 85302 762 6

Vulnerability and Resilience in Human Development

A Festschrift for Ann and Alan Clarke

Edited by Barbara Tizard and Ved Varma

Jessica Kingsley Publishers
London and Philadelphia

First published in the United Kingdom in 1992 by
Jessica Kingsley Publishers Ltd,
116 Pentonville Road, London
N1 9JB, England
and
325 Chestnut Street,
Philadelphia PA 19106, USA

www.jkp.com

This paperback edition published in 2000

© Copyright 1992 the contributors and Jessica Kingsley Publishers

British Library Cataloguing in Publication Data
Vulnerability and resilience in human development :
festschrift for Ann and Alan Clarke
1. Adults. Development
I. Tizard, Barbara II. Varma, Ved P. (Ved Prakash)
1931– III. Clarke, Ann IV. Clarke, Alan
155.6

ISBN 1 85302 877 0 ✓

Printed and Bound in Great Britain by
Athenaeum Press, Gateshead, Tyne and Wear

Contents

Introduction: Ann and Alan Clarke: an appreciation   7
Barbara Tizard

Part 1
New Perspectives on Nature and Nurture

1. Nature, nurture, and psychopathology:
   a new look at an old topic   21
   Michael Rutter

2. Early experience and the parent-child relationship: genetic
   and environmental interactions as developmental
   determinants   39
   H. Rudolph Schaffer

Part 2
Longitudinal Studies of Vulnerability and Resilience

3. Assets and deficits in the behaviour of people with Down's
   Syndrome - a longitudinal study   57
   Janet Carr

4. Interactions between offspring and parents in development   72
   Stella Chess and Alexander Thomas

5. Escaping from a bad start   88
   Doria Pilling

6. Vulnerability and resilience in adults who were classified
   as mildly mentally handicapped in childhood   102
   Stephen Richardson and Helen Koller

Part 3
Vulnerability, resilience, and rehabilitation from biological and psycho-social stress

7. Reducing mental and related handicaps:
    a biomedical perspective   123
    J. M. Berg

8. Rehabilitation of the dyspraxic dysphasic adult   137
    Robert and Margaret Fawcus

9. Vulnerability and resilience to early cerebral injury   151
    Edgar Miller

10. Educating children with severe learning difficulties:
    challenging vulnerability   163
    Peter Mittler

11. Resilience and vulnerability in child survivors of disasters 182
    William Yule

Part 4
Responses to Psychosocial Stress

12. A useful old age   201
    Don C. Charles

13. Troubled and troublesome: perspectives on adolescent hurt 217
    Masud Hoghughi

14. Implications of the Warsaw Study for Social
    and Educational Planning   233
    Ignacy Wald and Anna Firkowska-Mankiewicz

A Selection of the Clarkes' publications   244

Contributors   247

Introduction

Ann and Alan Clarke:
an appreciation

Barbara Tizard

This book is a tribute to Ann and Alan Clarke. All the contributors have been their colleagues, students or admirers, and all have felt the influence of their work and thinking. The book is centred round the theme of vulnerability and resilience. Whilst human beings are terribly vulnerable to psychological and physical damage,it is common knowledge that some emerge unscathed, or relatively unscathed, from situations that severely cripple others. And, as the Clarkes have demonstrated, some of those who are damaged may recover later. For many years psychologists were mainly concerned with vulnerability, no doubt in part because of the need to convince the public, and especially other professionals, that psychological damage is as real as physical damage. It took years of persuasion and argument, for example, before hospitals accepted the evidence that young children are likely to suffer if abruptly separated from their families and put in the care of a changing rota of staff. But attention is now shifting to attempts to understand the factors involved in the resilience of some people when exposed to stress and trauma. The topic is particularly appropriate for a Festschrift for the Clarkes, since much of their empirical and conceptual work has been concerned with the ability of human beings to overcome the influence of a hostile environment in early life.

Ann and Alan themselves had no such handicap to overcome. Both came from comfortable, cultured and loving middle class families. Ann Margaret Clarke (neé Gravely) was born in India in 1928, the daughter of a Quaker zoologist who was Director of the Madras Museum, and his Danish wife, who had come to India as a missionary. Ann was taught at home by her parents and a Danish governess, and later attended an American missionary school in the mountains of South India. In 1945 the family left for England, and settled in Reading, where Ann enrolled in the University at the age of 16, at that stage intending to be a teacher. In the autumn of 1946, when she entered the second year of the Honours course in psychology, the University was suddenly flooded with ex-Servicemen, of whom Alan was one. The Honours class consisted of six students, taught by Professor A. W. Wolters and Dr Magdalen Vernon, then embarking on a career as a university teacher after years of research in Cambridge.

Alan was born in 1922, the son of a well known solicitor, specialising in shipping law. His mother was one of eight children of an Aberdeen University lecturer. The family lived in Surrey, and Alan was sent to a private preparatory school, and then to a public school, Lancing College. His parents, unlike Ann's, were only nominal Christians, although his school was High Church, with compulsory chapel service twice daily. Alan became an agnostic by the age of 16, and on joining the army caused some commotion by refusing to go on Church parade. Nevertheless, what Ann and Alan had in common was a sense of the importance of integrity, duty and social obligation to those less fortunate than themselves, instilled in them both by their parents and their schools. These values, as we shall see, played an important role in shaping their careers. Alan's school career was undistinguished, but from the age of nine he developed a strong interest in geology, which led some six years later to his discovery of a previously unknown fossil coral, now in the Natural History Museum in London. At this stage he had no ambition for an academic career. He entered Reading University in 1940, intending to do a science degree, perhaps in Agricultural sciences, with a vague idea of going on to become a farmer. After one year, he joined the Royal Corps of Signals, was commissioned, and saw service in France, Belgium, and Germany. At the end of the European war he was posted to India for a year, where he was offered a career as an officer in the (now) Pakistani Army.

Meantime, however, his sister had married a psychologist, Monte Shapiro, and Monte's enthusiasm for applied psychology persuaded Alan to return to Reading University. In 1946 he joined the second year of the Honours psychology course, where Ann was a fellow student. Like many ex-service students, Alan was not interested in undergraduate social life, but determined to make the most of the two years of study ahead. To this end, he and a fellow ex-serviceman, George Granger, formed a self support study group to ensure that they would between them cover the syllabus, explain it to the other, and thus ensure success in their final examinations. Ann, although only 17, was allowed to join this group – no doubt her exceptional determination and capacity for hard work were already evident. All three graduated with first class honours in 1948, and Alan was offered a lectureship at Reading University.

However, Monte Shapiro had some years earlier joined Hans Eysenck at the Institute of Psychiatry, which was attached to the Maudsley Hospital in London, and he persuaded Alan that this was the pre-eminent centre of applied scientific psychology. Accordingly, all three members of the study group moved to London, and began their postgraduate research in the context of a large scale project directed by Hans Eysenck. The Institute of Psychiatry, directed by Sir Aubrey Lewis, was an exciting and intellectually stimulating, if demanding, place in which to work. There was a feeling that everything was possible within a framework which emphasised the hypo-thetico-deductive method. The atmosphere was intensely competitive, and the capacity for critical analysis was highly valued. Nevertheless, close friendships were formed, which often lasted a lifetime. In the case of the Clarkes, these friends included my late husband Jack, and Neil O'Connor, who were then working together on the staff of the Medical Research Council Social Psychiatry Unit, attached to the Institute. (At that time I was married to Jack, but a student in Burt's department at University College.)

In 1950 Ann, aged 21, and Alan, aged 28, were awarded their PhDs, got married, and started to look for jobs which would allow them to work together in a socially useful area. This was a tall order, since at that time jobs for psychologists were few and far between, and employers, including universities, were generally unwilling to appoint a married couple to their staff. One day Hans Eysenck told them that he had received a request from Dr MacMahon, the Physician Superintendent of the Manor Hospital, Epsom, for help in finding two clinical psychologists for his institution for the mentally deficient. Ann and Alan were advised by most of their friends not to apply, on the grounds that nothing could be done for such 'patients', and that accepting the jobs, which would inevitably consist mainly of routine IQ testing, might irrevocably damage their careers as researchers and academics. However, since nothing else offered, and since Dr MacMahon seemed keen for them to do some research, they decided to try it for a year or two. In the event, they stayed for 12 years, during which time they made a major contribution to the scientific study of mental retardation.

The Manor Hospital held at that time approximately 1,500 people, all compulsorily detained under the Mental Deficiency Act of 1913, with strict segregation of the sexes, and a budget of £5 per patient per week to cover everything from staff salaries to new bed linen. Approximately 70% of this population were deemed to be 'feebleminded' (i.e. mildly retarded). Many were not mentally retarded at all. As disturbed, scholastically backward children from problem families they had been sent to residential special schools, and gone on to mental deficiency hospitals. From there, release was difficult. The best that could be hoped for by the 'higher grade' inmates was trial in often unsuitable jobs under licence in the community, and then, with luck, eventual discharge from 'care.' Institutionalisation was the preferred mode of containment, since the inmates were regarded as incapable of supporting themselves, and as a danger to the community because of their propensity for crime and immorality. It was believed that if they were allowed to reproduce, crime and other social problems would multiply. Compulsory detention was thus thought to protect both society and themselves. At the Manor Hospital some were kept occupied in extensive, very old fashioned workshops, where brooms and the like were handmade for use in institutions. Others worked in the hospital as gardeners or as maids, with the aim of getting similar jobs in the community if they were eventually discharged from care. New arrivals came every month, often with pathetic records of school failure, theft, and sexual promiscuity, and a background of parental poverty, cruelty and neglect. The hospital was overcrowded and understaffed, a place without much hope, where nothing new ever happened.

In 'colonies' of this kind most professionals soon became apathetic and institutionalised themselves. If any research was undertaken, it was of a purely descriptive nature. However, for the Clarkes, with their strong sense of social obligation and their intellectual energy, such a setting provided a challenge. They were aware that a wind of change was beginning to stir. Jack Tizard and Neil O'Connor, from the basis of a Medical Research Council Unit, were starting to train mildly handicapped young men for industrial employment, and the National Council for Civil Liberties was planning a campaign for the release of such patients from mental deficiency hospitals. The Clarkes, with their customary enthusiasm, saw that the situation offered them great opportunities.

What they did was to look anew at the skills and potentials of the inmates, first of the 'higher grade' patients, and then at those at the time called imbeciles, who would now be described as having moderate learning difficulties, and who were then considered completely untrainable. Their research showed that such people could not be adequately assessed by a one-shot, once and for all assessment; that initial skill level on a task was no guide to the level that could be reached with training; and that, although this training might have to be lengthy, those who received it were capable of work which could enable them to be employed under sheltered conditions.

One of their most important contributions, which was to influence much of their subsequent thinking, was to demonstrate that those young people of 'higher grade' who came from particularly unfavourable social backgrounds had relatively good prognoses as far as rehabilitation was concerned. Even the unstimulating but orderly life of the hospital ward and workshop was an improvement on their previous environment, and brought about substantial IQ gains. Within three years of arriving at the hospital the Clarkes were able to publish an article in the *Lancet* entitled 'How constant is the IQ?' (1953). This challenged the traditional wisdom of the time, by providing evidence of IQ changes, and by demonstrating the resilience and potentiality for change of many people when early severe deprivation is relieved. An editorial in the same issue discussed their work. The publication was a watershed in their lives, bringing public recognition of their work.

Another important landmark was the publication in 1955, again in the *Lancet*, of a paper by Alan Clarke and Beate Hermelin, entitled 'Adult Imbeciles: their abilities and trainability.' It reported experimental work, which demonstrated that young men with IQs in the 30s could, with appropriate training, perform fairly complex industrial tasks. In the condition of 'over-full' employment in the 1950s the implications were profound, both in Britain, and later in the USA.

The Clarkes' programme of research and their new outlook on mental retardation had an enormous influence on the Manor hospital, as well as elsewhere. It amounted to a demedicalisation of mental deficiency, a demonstration that the patients' problems were in dealing with their lives, and in learning, and were primarily the province of psychologists rather than medical doctors. Inevitably, bringing about the changes they wanted in their own hospital was never easy. They met the prejudices and increasing jealousy of some of their medical colleagues, who, in the eyes of the law, had the sole responsibility for treatment and training, and who would have preferred to confine the Clarkes to the role of testers. Fortunately, they had an excellent relationship with the Physician Superintendent, Dr MacMahon, an exceedingly intelligent, somewhat introverted Irish bachelor, who purported to scorn conventional wisdom, and had a passionate interest in methodologically sound research findings, though he did not publish himself. He backed any proposals which the Clarkes could 'scientifically prove', and promoted and guarded their research with as much devotion as if he had been their father. Further support came from Jack Tizard, Neil O'Connor, and their students, who were granted facilities for research in the Manor Hospital. But above all, the Clarkes stimulated and supported each other, together reading, debating, and seeking solutions to the problems they met.

During this period Alan began his long and influential involvement with the British Psychological Society, of which he was later to become President. He gave evidence on its behalf to the Royal Commission on Mental Deficiency and Mental Illness, arguing that any definition of 'mental subnormality' needed to include 'subnormality of intelligence', defined and assessed in terms of standardised tests. (This was important to prevent certification and incarceration solely on social grounds, e.g. delinquency or sexual promiscuity.) Although the Royal Commission did not accept the advice, the definition was later incorporated into the 1959 Mental Health Act, which also signalled a major shift of emphasis from hospital to community based services.

Alan also interested himself in the professional development of teachers and other staff working with the mentally retarded – in 1962 the Scott Committee reported that only 12% of the staff of Occupation (training) Centres had any formal qualification. Alan later became Chairman of the Training Council for Teachers of the Mentally Handicapped, from 1969–74, and it was partly for this work that he was appointed CBE in 1974. The Clarkes initial interest in psychology was to study a science with a view to 'doing something useful', and throughout their lives they have striven to bring scientific knowledge to bear on public policy.

In 1958 the Clarkes' multi-authored magnum opus *Mental Deficiency: The Changing Outlook* was launched as a research-based textbook. It was quickly acknowledged to be the most authoritative statement of current knowledge in the field. Three subsequent editions, culminating in the 1985 (4th) edition, maintained the very high standard set by the first. The energy and scholarship which the Clarkes brought to the task of editing these massive volumes, in the midst of their other activities, was formidable.

By the late fifties their research and rehabilitation projects were becoming well known. In 1960 the Spastics Society commissioned a documentary film, *Learning in Slow Motion*, which recorded their findings and was widely circulated. In the same year the first international multidisciplinary conference on mental retardation took place in London, with Alan as one of the three main organisers. This was an exciting occasion (see *Journal of Mental Deficiency Research*, February, 1991, for an account) at which lifelong friendships were forged. It led, four years later, to the formation of the International Association for the Scientific Study of Mental Deficiency, of which Alan became successively Secretary, President, and Honorary Life President. In his international work, as elsewhere, Alan worked to develop an active integration between scientific and service objectives.

By 1962 the Clarkes were looking for a change. Their work in the field of rehabilitation was well known, as was their theoretical contribution, but in a sense they had been too successful – the excitement of the earlier challenges had gone. Alan now felt he would like to try the challenge of academic life, and Ann felt she would like to spend more time looking after their two sons, by now aged 18 months and six. Very unusually for the period, she had worked fulltime up to this point, apart from a year off when their first child was born. This was not because she held feminist beliefs in advance of her time, but because of the closeness of her partnership with Alan, and her passionate interest in their work. A Chair in psychology in Hull was advertised, and whilst at that time no psychologist had ever been appointed to a University Chair from a clinical post in an institution, let alone an institution for the retarded, Alan applied, and was appointed. In 1966 he became Dean of the Faculty of Science, and from 1968–71 he was the sole Pro-Vice-Chancellor at Hull.

Meantime Ann's ambition to devote herself to her children did not last long. President Kennedy's sister, Eunice Kennedy Shriver, visited Britain during the Clarkes' first year in Hull. The Kennedy family had a personal interest in mental retardation, and during an interview published in the *Observer* newspaper Eunice heaped praise on the Clarkes' work. This led to research funds being made available to them by the Nuffield Foundation and later the Association for the Aid of Crippled Children. Ann found herself leading a team of research assistants in an exploration of concept formation and transfer of learning in young severely subnormal adults and pre-school children. This work was later reviewed at length in the *Annual Review of Psychology*, 1972, in a chapter on Instructional Skills. Alan was, of course, co-director of the research, but his teaching and ever increasing administrative responsibilities militated against very active participation.

By 1970 the burden of empirical work, research direction, and domestic responsibilities was taking a toll on Ann, and she again decided to give up paid employment and spend more time with her family, whilst also writing up the products of seven years research. But again a new challenge proved irresistible, and her semi-retirement did not last long. In 1972 the department of Educational Studies at Hull University required a lecturer in Psychology at short notice, and shortly before her forty-fourth birthday Ann began a new career in Education. This led her for the first time to collaborate with colleagues other than Alan, and precipitated her involvement in the unmasking of Sir Cyril Burt's scientific fraud. In the course of preparing a review with Michael McAskie of theories and evidence on parent-offspring resemblances in intelligence the unsatisfactory nature of Burt's reporting of his empirical data became increasingly apparent. The Clarkes had already begun to look in detail at two of Burt's seminal research papers during 1971/2, whilst preparing the 1974 edition of *Mental Deficiency: The Changing Outlook*, and had concluded that they contained puzzling features, and that there were results which appeared suspiciously perfect.

The Clarkes did not at this time suspect fraud, but they did conclude that Burt's methods were shoddy, and involved cutting corners in an unacceptably subjective way. However, as Ann collaborated with Michael McAskie on a detailed analysis of several of Burt's studies, their suspicions grew. To quote their paper (McAskie and Clarke, 1976) 'Careful inspection reveals a grossly inadequate description of the material and how it was collected. References to further details in other papers proved empty and the trail through a number of publications led nowhere. . . . The 1943 paper proclaimed a mean IQ of 153.2 for his higher professional group, which exceeds that of the Terman gifted group . . . By 1961 the mean IQ of the professional group had miraculously shrunk to 139.7, but the range for the offspring underwent no change during this period.'

At about the same time Jack Tizard was also puzzling over Burt's data. He decided to try to locate two of Burt's collaborators, Miss Howard and Miss Conway, using the resources available to him as President of the British Psychological Society, to see if they could resolve the problems. No trace of their past or present whereabouts could be found. Jack discussed his suspicion that they did not exist with a science journalist, Dr Oliver Gillie, who decided to make further attempts to find them. There was no record of them as students or staff of the University, or as employees of the LCC, or as members of the BPS. When Dr Gillie, at Jack's suggestion, visited the Clarkes, and told them that he and Jack had met with a total lack of success in their search, the Clarkes felt that a turning point had been reached. With considerable courage they decided to make their doubts public, and it was with their support that Oliver Gillie published a long article in the *Sunday Times* in October 1976, suggesting for the first time publicly that Burt's work was fraudulent. Further evidence of extensive malpractice which subsequently came to the Clarkes' notice served to confirm their views. For example, careful bibliographic research by Ann on the alleged activities of Miss Conway, who was credited with testing in the fifties Burt's unique sample of monozygotic twins reared apart, and who published alone from University College, provided substantial evidence of fraud. Whilst Hearnshaw, Burt's biographer, believed that Burt's misdemeanours started at around the age of 57, and were due to current personal problems, the Clarkes thought it was more likely, that, with his charisma and charm, he had been a successful confidence trickster from an early age. The Clarkes have held to their position strongly, in the face of considerable controversy. Their position was set out in a letter to the *Bulletin* of the British Psychological Society in 1977, an article in a supplement to the *Bulletin* in 1980, and a letter to *The Psychologist* in 1990. It is often supposed that their motivation in exposing Burt was political or ideological, or arose from a commitment to environmentalism, but this was not the case. On the contrary, the Clarkes have always given some weight to genetic influences on development, and their views on the heritability of intelligence and on educational policy are in many ways similar to, though less extreme than, Burt's. They were simply shocked that an eminent psychologist should deceive his colleagues and bring disrepute on the profession by departing so far from standards of scientific integrity.

An event of greater importance in the same year was the publication of their seminal book, *Early Experience: Myth and Evidence* (1976). The story of how it came to be written is worth telling, because of the light it throws on the Clarkes' intellectual rigour and persistence. Its genesis went back a long way. Whilst working in the Manor Hospital in the early fifties, they noticed that some mildly retarded adolescents and young adults were showing significant gains in IQ and social competence. This was against the received wisdom of the day, so the Clarkes set out to find what factors were associated with these gains. Only one of the hypotheses they explored was supported. A record of early, severe, and prolonged social adversity predicted later gains, whilst milder adversity did not. After a pilot study, they set up a 'clean' series of experiments, in which the assessment of the young people was carried out independently by a colleague without knowledge of their social history or earlier test scores, whilst another independent researcher, without knowledge of the individuals or their test scores, rated the childhood history of the young people for degree of adversity. A control group of consecutive new admissions, reassessed after three months, enabled them to estimate the greatest possible effects of test practice, and of regression towards the mean. On average these factors accounted for at the most a quarter of the increments. Over six years, 78% of the severely deprived group showed increments of 15 or more IQ points, compared with 25% of the less deprived group. These changes were not related to any rehabilitative programme but seemed to represent a fading of the effects of earlier adversity in the relatively benign environment of the institution – a self-righting tendency.

The studies were subsequently replicated several times elsewhere. The findings challenged the notion of developmental constancy, a view which had dominated developmental theory for most of the century. They also challenged the idea, then very prevalent, that the first few years of life constitute a critical period in development, when events have a crucially formative influence on later development. This theory seemed to be supported by a good deal of animal experimentation and clinical data from child psychologists and psychiatrists. A very important exponent of the theory was John Bowlby, who argued that maternal deprivation in the first three years of life 'may entirely cripple the capacity to make relationships with other people'. This belief rapidly became widely accepted, and influenced public policy on women's employment and childcare. However, the Clarkes were soon greatly encouraged by news of the identification of the 'catch up' phenomenon in physical growth, following illness or mild malnutrition. This seemed analogous to the intellectual 'catch up' they had observed, and raised the possibility that their ideas might have a more general applicability. Their publishers suggested that they write a book on recovery from deprivation, and issued a contract for it in 1959. But as they began to write, they realised that the extensive evidence they needed was not available, and it was another 15 years before they felt ready to start on the book again. During the sixties most of the published evidence on the influence of early experience on development, especially from ethologists and animal psychologists, seemed to be against their hypothesis. The Clarkes were critical of the ease with which the results of animal experiments and observations, e.g. on imprinting, were extrapolated to human beings. They were also critical of the failure of animal experimenters at that time to see whether the emotional and social damage they had caused in deprivation experiments was reversible, evidence which would have had a crucial bearing on the critical period theory of development. Characteristically, their interest was not only in the scientific issues, but in the implication of the theories for social policy.

In 1967 Alan was invited to give the 42nd Maudsley lecture, and used the occasion to voice many of these points. By 1975 the Clarkes decided that there was enough evidence available to make out a sustained case for a greater degree of potential open-endedness in human development than until then had been accepted. The book that resulted, *Early Experience, Myth and Evidence*, was made up of contributions from a number of distinguished scientists, including Rutter, Kagan, and Bronfenbrenner, as well as five chapters by the Clarkes. They argued that the prevalent belief in the crucial importance of the early years is rendered plausible by the fact that most children do not experience drastic environmental change – one fortunate or unfortunate event is likely to be followed by a similar one. But in the unusual situation where a drastic environmental change has occurred, the evidence suggests that early experience will not *per se* have a long term influence on adult behaviour. Whether it does or not will depend on the degree of environmental change, and also on constitutional factors in the child. There is no known psychosocial adversity, they argued, from which at least some children have not recovered if their circumstances improved. They argued that the evidence does not support the theory of critical periods in human development. Instead, it suggests that the whole of the life path provides a potential for change, although they acknowledged that this potential was 'wedge shaped', with the potential for change decreasing at the thin, older age of the 'wedge'. This may be because personal characteristics achieve autonomy and self perpetuation as development proceeds, perhaps because of changes intrinsic to the aging process. However, they argued that the thick end of the wedge extends well into early adult life. They now see development as a series of linkages, in which characteristics in each period have a probability of linking with those in another period. Such probabilities are not certainties, and deflections are possible, but always within limits imposed by genetic, constitutional, and social trajectories.

The immediate impact of the book was considerable. It challenged widely held and taken for granted assumptions, and offered an alternative, and much more optimistic model of development, solidly grounded in evidence. But like all seminal books it also had a long term impact, the ideas gradually filtering through to an ever wider audience, often mediated by the writing of other researchers, who themselves had been influenced by the Clarkes. During the eighties there has been considerable research on the factors in the child and its environment that are related to vulnerability and resilience. Evidence from important longitudinal studies, some by contributors to this volume, is beginning to throw light on the circumstances, both genetic and environmental, in which 'self-righting tendencies' can indeed occur throughout childhood and into adult life. To his credit, John Bowlby, who had been the arch proponent of the theory that early mother-child relationships had a crucial and irreversible influence on adult development later modified his views. When in his eighties he wrote 'the central task . . . is to study the endless interactions of internal and external, and how the one is influencing the other not only during childhood but during adolescence and adult life as well . . . Present knowledge requires that a theory of developmental pathways should replace theories that invoke specific phases of development in which it is postulated that a person may become fixated and/or to which he may regress' (Developmental Psychiatry comes of Age, *American Journal of Psychiatry*, 1988, 145, 1–10).

One of the strengths of the Clarkes is that they have pursued their ideas over a long period of time, so that they bring an immense amount of knowledge and experience to each new consideration of a theme. *Early Experience: Myth and Evidence*, for example, was followed by a careful analytic critique *Sleeper Effects in Development: Fact or Artifact?* (Clarke and Clarke, 1981). Alan has contributed admirably short and succinct 'State of the Art' summaries on mental retardation over the years, of which 'Recent Advances in the study of Mental Subnormality', NAMH, 1975, was a notable example.

The Clarkes have been invited to lecture in the USA, Canada, India, New Zealand, Australia, and many countries in Europe. Over the years, numerous honours have come their way. In 1974 Alan was appointed a CBE for his work on public bodies. From 1977–78 he was President of the British Psychological Association, and from 1973–79 he was editor of the *British Journal of Psychology*. In 1977 the Clarkes were jointly given the Annual Research Award of the American Association on Mental Deficiency, and in 1982 each received the Distinguished Achievement Award for Scientific Literature from the International Association for the Scientific Study of Mental Deficiency. In 1985 Ann was appointed to a Personal Chair in the University of Hull. In 1986 Alan's services to the University of Hull were recognised by the conferment of an honorary Doctorate of Science, and in 1989 he was elected an Honorary Fellow of the Royal College of Psychiatrists.

In the nineteen-eighties, British universities suffered a severe financial onslaught from the Government. In 1984, along with 200 others on the teaching staff at Hull, Alan felt that he had to volunteer early retirement and

Ann followed a few years later. Alan has continued to teach voluntarily in the University. His ex-students, two of whom are contributors to this book, testify to the strength of his influence. What impressed them was his demonstration of the possibility of applying scientific psychology to clinical problems, his combination of a strong methodological rigour with compassion and humanity, and his personal kindness and generosity. The special quality of both the Clarkes is undoubtedly their combination of a rigorous and scholarly scientific approach with a determination to use psychology for the public benefit. To this task they have brought immense energy and intellectual persistence, and the strength derived from their close and harmonious partnership. Both Ann and Alan continue to publish, and this chapter should be regarded as an interim, not a final report on their work.

This Festschrift, centred round the theme of Vulnerability and Resilience, includes critical reviews of the current status of aspects of the nature-nurture debate, reports of important new evidence from longitudinal studies on factors affecting young people's vulnerability and resilience to stress, and accounts of responses to, and rehabilitation from, both bio-medical and psycho-social stress. These are all debates to which the Clarke's have made important contributions.

Part 1

New Perspectives on Nature and Nurture

Nature, nurture and psychopathology: a new look at an old topic

Michael Rutter CBE, MD, FRS

Through their empirical research and their incisively critical reviews of concepts and of empirical evidence, Ann and Alan Clarke have shed much needed light on so many important and controversial issues that there has been an embarrassment of riches in the decision on which topic to choose for this chapter. I wanted a subject that was of interest to them (that gave an extremely wide choice); one on which I might have something fresh to say that had not been already stated more eloquently and decisively by one or other of them (that narrowed the field in a drastic fashion); and also one on which my own thinking had been shaped in an important way by discussions with them or by their writings (that included most things that I know anything about). They have been enormously helpful on numerous occasions, combining warm supportiveness with sharp critical appraisal and it is a pleasure to express my thanks to them here. My indebtedness has been particularly great in the fields of lifespan development, intergenerational continuities, and psychosocial influences, as my acknowledgements in papers and books on these topics indicate (Rutter, 1985; Rutter and Madge, 1976). It seemed desirable to move onto different territories for this review, if a new perspective was to be presented. Genetic issues seemed an obvious choice as they are so frequently misunderstood, and because the Clarkes' writings on the topic show so well the mastery of the technical issues and the balanced appraisal, with a concern for the social implications, that are the hallmarks of their scientific contributions (see e.g. McAskie and Clarke, 1976; Clarke, 1985; Clarke and Clarke, 1978).

As the Clarkes noted in their 1978 review, scientists have argued with passion over the relative importance of nature and of nurture on human psychological characteristics and on mental disorders of different types. During the 1960s and 1970s, many people came to dismiss the role of genetic factors and to emphasize the power of environmental influences. This dismissal came about for four main reasons: a concern to improve the outlook for disadvantaged children; a fatalistic view that we could not do anything about genetic effects; a distrust of the genetic evidence; and a distaste arising from the misuse of genetics in support of racist and eugenic policies. All of that has changed in the last decade and genetic research constitutes one of the major growth areas in psychiatry and psychology. The change has come about, first, because improvements in traditional genetic research strategies led to convincing evidence on the importance of genetic factors in a wide range of human behaviour, normal and abnormal; second, because it came to be appreciated that a fatalistic view of genetics was seriously misleading; and thirdly, because a revolution in molecular biology has allowed the precise localization and identification of individual genes (Bock and Collins, 1987; Chadwick, Bock, and Whelan, 1990).

The technical issues and methodological advances have been discussed previously (Rutter, Bolton, Harrington, Le Couteur, Macdonald, and Simonoff, 1990a; Rutter, Macdonald, Le Couteur, Harrington, Bolton, and Bailey, 1990b) and will be noted only briefly. The aim here is to consider some of the new concepts and implications in terms of their general implications for non-geneticists in the field of developmental psychopathology.

Advances in psychiatric and behavioural genetics

The main methodological advances that have implications for the study of psychopathology may be summarized briefly under three main headings. First, there are those that apply to the traditional genetic strategies that allow an estimate of the strength of genetic influences by being able to separate nature and nurture.

The longest established traditional genetic strategy is that of comparing monozygotic, or identical, twin-pairs who have all their genes in common with dizygotic, or fraternal, twin-pairs who (on average) share only half their genes. The comparison of levels of concordance, or within-pair correlations, in monozygotic and dyzogotic pairs allows an estimate of the extent to which genetic factors account for individual variations in the occurrence of either some form of disorder or the manifestation of some trait or characteristic. This remains a good research method but it has been much strengthened by extensions of the twin design. Thus, for example, additional leverage has been obtained by the examination of monozygotic pairs in which the twins have been separated in infancy and brought up in rather different environments; by the study of discordant monozygotic pairs; and by investigation of the offspring of monozygotic and dizygotic twin pairs (in which the former are the equivalent of half sibs because the twin parents are genetically identical, whereas the latter are simply ordinary cousins). In addition to the strengthening of the strategies, twin research has been improved by the more accurate identification of zygosity (the use of DNA probes now enables virtually certain identification – Spence, Corey, Nance, Marazita, Kendler, and Schieken 1988), better measurement of traits, and the several advantages that follow from the use of longitudinal research designs.

Particularly in recent years, twin studies have been complemented by the study of adopted children who provide the opportunity to compare biological parentage with the parentage of rearing, and hence to contrast nature and nurture. Once more, there are a range of different designs using this basic strategy. For example, there is the straightforward comparison of rates of disorder in biological and adoptive relatives. However, rather stronger evidence is provided by the comparison of sibs reared by the biological parents and sibs who have been adopted in infancy away from the biological family. There are also various kinds of cross-fostering designs in which the outcomes can be compared according to the characteristics of both the biological and adopting parents. Alternatively, there is the adopted sibling design, in which comparisons are made between the correlations or concordance between genetically related pairs of adoptees who have been reared separately, and genetically unrelated pairs of adoptees who have been reared together. The former reflects genetic mediation and the latter environmental mediation.

In a sense, though, the most important advance has come from an appreciation that each of these different genetic strategies has a rather different pattern of advantages and disadvantages. The consequence is that there is huge value in combining twin, adoptee and family genetic methodologies. Conclusions are very much stronger when each of these strategies leads to a similar conclusion. Conversely, when the findings do not agree, there needs to be caution, and an appreciation that artefacts of one kind or another may be leading to misleading inferences. What have been encouraging are the several well-replicated examples in which different strategies do lead to the same conclusion.

A second, rather different, type of advance is that provided by the very important developments in quantitative mathematical techniques (Eaves, Eysenck, and Martin 1989; Hahn, Hewitt, Henderson, and Benno 1990; and Plomin, DeFries, and Fulker, 1988). These have come about both through a better appreciation of the concepts and of the ways in which these may be tested through quantitative techniques, and also through advances in computer technology which have made it possible to deal with the complex algebra entailed. The results of these developments have meant that much more accurate modelling of genetic and environmental effects is possible; that there are improved means of testing competing genetic models; that there is a better testing of gene-environment interactions; that problems of heterogeneity and comorbidity can be tackled using genetic influences as a way of testing diagnostic distinctions, and that it is possible to test whether extremes of psychopathology are genetically separate from variations within the normal distribution or whether they have the same genetic basis.

Thirdly, there are the most exciting advances in cytogenetics and molecular genetics that have come to be termed 'the new genetics'. The cytogenetic advances have been less dramatic but they are nonetheless quite important (Pembrey, 1991). These include techniques to detect the banding patterns on individual chromosomes, techniques to determine which of the two X chromosomes has been inactivated (because only one functions actively), and the concept and means of study of chromosomal 'imprinting'. The last of these, 'imprinting', refers to the discovery of effects associated with whether a chromosome comes from the father or the mother. This promises to throw light on some of the unusual patterns of inheritance that are being found, for example, with the fragile X anomaly, as well as with the quite different clinical disorders associated with deletion of chromosome 15 according to whether it comes from the father or mother. What have become rather better known are the advances in molecular genetic techniques – especially the identification of a large number of highly polymorphic DNA fragments, so called restriction fragment length polymorphisms or RFLPs, which serve as genetic markers. As any regular reader of newspapers will be aware, there is now a huge research investment in mapping the human genome. Potentially, through this advance, genetics need no longer be a 'black box'; instead specific genetic factors potentially can be localized and identified. Of course, science is only just beginning to proceed down this path, but progress has already been rapid in many branches of medicine.

A sceptic might still query whether this growth of knowledge has any practical value, other than in allowing parents who carry genes for seriously handicapping disorders to decide whether or not to have children, and in allowing affected fetuses to be identified in the womb so that decisions on termination of pregnancy may be taken. However, there are many other implications, quite apart from the long term potential of the 'star wars' technology of gene therapy. These are most easily highlighted by considering them in terms of a series of misconceptions or mistaken views held by some non-geneticists.

Misconceptions

Misconception 1. Strong genetic effects mean that environmental influences must be unimportant

The first mistaken view is that if a characteristic is strongly genetic, environmental influences must be rather *un*important. In fact this is not so. There are two main reasons why the assumption is wrong. Firstly, estimates of heritability apply only to the specific populations on which they are based. If environments change, estimates of the strength of genetic effect will also necessarily alter. Secondly, environmental influences may affect the average population *level* of a trait without necessarily altering genetic effects on *individual differences* within it. Estimates of heritability are concerned with population variance as it applies to individual differences, and it is quite possible for environmental factors to make a major impact on the *level* of a trait even if there is less effect on variations between people.

For example, height is very strongly genetically determined, but nutritional factors make a big difference to growth. The data brought together by Tizard (1975) on the increase in the height of London boys aged 7–12 years across the time period spanning 1909–1959 showed that the average height rose by about 10 cms during this 50 years – almost certainly as a result of improvements in diet (Tizard, 1975). The heritability of height in the UK has been high whenever it has been studied but the major difference in average height between time periods is likely to have been brought about by environmental factors. The genes have not changed during this century, but people today are much taller than they were in previous generations.

Misconception 2. Genes provide a limit to potential

This leads on to the second, at least partially, mistaken view; namely, that genes provide a limit to potential. If environments change, so will the potential alter. The height example illustrates that effect but so do the contrasted environments adoption study findings on intelligence (Locurto, 1990).

A French study undertaken by Schiff and Lewontin (1986) showed that children born to socially disadvantaged mothers and fathers, who had then been adopted into privileged homes, had an IQ some 12 points higher than those reared by their disadvantaged biological parents. Siblings who were adopted into middle class homes had a mean IQ of just over 106 (well above the population average of 99), compared with the mean IQ of 95 (appreciably below the population average) for those reared by their biological mothers in disadvantaged circumstances.

Another study, undertaken in France by Capron and Duyme (1989), used a cross-fostering design based on a sample of adopted children where there was a marked disparity between the social level of the biological and adoptive parents. The findings showed a major effect, of both nature and nurture, of approximately similar degree. In each case the children born to, or reared by, socially advantaged parents had a mean IQ some dozen points above those from a lower social level background. In other words, a favourable rearing environment can have a substantial effect in raising intellectual performance. Genetic factors *do* affect individual levels of attainment (or 'reaction range' – Gottesman, 1963) in any given environment, but with the exception of single major genes causing gross handicap, they do not limit potential in any absolute sense. If environments change, so does potential (Scarr and Kidd, 1983).

Misconception 3. Genetic strategies are of no value for studying environmental influences

However, these adoptee studies of IQ underline the very important fact that genetic research strategies are particularly powerful for testing, and demonstrating, the influence of environmental factors. The notion that these strategies are of no value to investigators interested in environmental influences is quite mistaken. That is because only genetic strategies can allow determination of which effects are truly environmental, and because genetic strategies can be used to discriminate between different types of environmental influences. The key practical implication that follows is that genetic strategies are crucial, not just in showing the operation of environmental factors, but more importantly in identifying *which* environmental factors make most impact. For example, genetic research has been important in differentiating between 'shared' and 'non-shared' environmental influences (Plomin and Daniels, 1987).

In brief, shared influences are those that impinge similarly on all children in the same family. For example, that would be the case with features such as overcrowding in the home or family discord or poverty. By contrast, non-shared environmental influences are those that impinge differently on different children in the same family (Dunn and Plomin, 1990). This would apply not only to experiences outside the home but also to features of upbringing that are not the same for all children in the family. In the past, most environmental research has focused on shared influences. However, genetic findings indicate that for most psychological characteristics within the normal range, as shown by individuals reared in non-extreme environments, non-shared influences are probably much more important. This is indicated by the lack of similarities between individuals, especially non-related individuals, raised in the same family. That is indeed the usual state of affairs. It is obvious that children within the same family frequently differ markedly in temperament, in their athletic prowess, and in their patterns and levels of cognitive ability.

Shared influences are suggested when siblings within the same family are very similar in their characteristics; that is, when within-family differences are small compared with between-family differences. That is the case with respect to delinquency and it is also the case with IQ and educational attainments when examined in relation to extreme differences in environment (although not within the middle of the environmental range).

In other words, genetic research has indicated that, for many psychological characteristics, factors that impinge on just one child in the family tend to be more influential than family-wide factors that impinge on everyone in the home. This finding has very important implications in focusing attention on experiences in and outside the home that are *specific* to individual children. Thus it matters that one child tends to be favoured and another scapegoated; that one has suffered repeated hospital admission or been exposed to stressful separations, and that one has good experiences at school whereas another has not.

Misconception 4. Nature and nurture are separate

The next mistaken stereotype is that nature and nurture are polarized and separate. It is clear now that they are not. In the first place, some genes operate mainly through their effect on susceptibility to environmental influences. This is most obvious in relation to certain medical diseases. For example, the genetically determined metabolic disease, phenylketonuria, causes mental handicap only if the children have phenylalanine in their diet. That substance is part of all ordinary diets but the genetic effects on IQ can be virtually eliminated through the simple expedient of removing the offending substance from the diet (Fuggle and Graham, 1991). It is not yet known for sure whether similar effects operate in psychiatry and psychology, but it seems likely that they may do so. Thus, physiological responsivity to stress seems to be genetically determined to an important extent (Matheny, 1989) and adoptee studies suggest that the genetic influences associated with criminality may operate in part though an effect on vulnerability to psychosocial adversities and hazards (Cadoret, 1985). If this ultimately proves to be the case, it will be important in indicating that genetically at-risk children are those most liable to be damaged by adverse environments.

A second way in which nature and nurture are not as separate as seems at first sight is that people both select and shape their environments (Plomin and Bergeman, in press; Scarr and McCartney, 1983). This means that, to an important extent, genes are likely to determine the kinds of experiences that people have. Initially, this seems a surprising suggestion but, in reality, it is not. Environments are not randomly distributed and each of us has a degree of choice in what happens to us. We 'choose' whom we marry, what job we do, where we live, whether we will be sociable party-goers or reclusive loners. By 'choice', of course, I do not mean to suggest that these are necessarily conscious decisions, nor indeed that they are wholly, or even largely, within our control. But that is the point. Characteristics that are to a substantial extent determined genetically will influence this selection and shaping of environments. Thus, this will apply to characteristics such as sex, IQ, and temperament.

It also applies to behaviour disorders. For example, aggressive delinquent children tend to have discordant relationships with other people; as a consequence they will experience more rebuffs, rejections and broken friendships (or marriages) than other people. That is, the adverse environments that later stress them are in part brought about by their own behaviour. This was shown, for example, in the findings from Lee Robins' (1966) classical long-term follow-up study of children who attended a child guidance clinic and a comparison group from the general population. The antisocial boys were very much more likely to experience a whole range of psychosocial stressors and adversities in adult life. Thus, three times as many experienced divorce, more than twice as many married a deviant spouse, ten times as many were unemployed, very frequent job changes were much more frequent, the antisocial boys were twice as likely to be in a non-skilled or semi-skilled job, and four times as many were virtually without friends in adult life. The data make clear that the characteristics of the antisocial boys predispose them to a very much increased risk of adverse environments. I should underline that this does *not* mean that the environmental stressors are not the causes of later problems. People choose whether or not they smoke cigarettes, but the fact that they choose to expose themselves to a carcinogenic environment does not alter the fact that smoking plays a key role in the development of lung cancer. It is important to appreciate that people select and shape their environments because it focuses attention on an influence which must be taken into account in our attempts to improve environmental circumstances and conditions.

Misconception 5. Genes for serious diseases are necessarily bad

The next mistaken view is that genes for serious diseases are necessarily bad. It seems obvious that this must be the case but it is not so, for two reasons. First, having the gene and having the disease are not the same thing. Most healthy people carry genes that they know nothing about; this happens because many diseases require the presence of two or more genes (either because the gene is recessive or because two different genes are needed for the disease to be manifest). In other words, *genes* for disease are much more common than the diseases they cause. The second reason is that genes that cause one disease may *protect* the person against some other disease (Rotter and Diamond, 1987). The best known example is the protection against malaria associated with heterozygote status sickle cell disease, but there are others, albeit less well documented. Such effects have long been suspected in psychiatry, but they have yet to be proven. However, it may be that families at risk for certain kinds of mental disorder include an unusually high proportion of gifted, creative or talented individuals. It seems that, sometimes, genes associated with serious diseases may also carry benefits.

Misconception 6. Diseases have nothing to do with normal variation

It is commonly supposed that diseases have nothing to do with normal variations in the general population and, hence, that genetic findings on the one hand will have no implications for the other. However, with many psychiatric disorders this is not the case. The issue used to be a matter for armchair debate, but mathematical techniques are now available to put the matter to empirical test (DeFries and Fulker, 1985; 1988). The computations are complex, but the principle is in essence quite simple. It relies on determining whether the distribution of the trait or disorder under consideration in family members fits in with the expectations that would follow if the psychopathological disorder functioned as an extension of the normal distribution. In so far as it does *not*, it indicates that there must be a discontinuity between the disorder and normal variation. Where, however, it does act like an extension of the normal distribution, it may well be that the two have the same genetically influenced risk liability. The contrast is most easily illustrated by a specific example from the study by Nichols (Plomin, Rende, and Rutter, 1991).

Nichols (1984) studied the IQ and rate of mental retardation in the sibs of white individuals with severe and with mild mental handicap. The sibs of mentally retarded probands differed from the general population in the same direction as the probands, but did so to a lesser degree. This is what would be expected if mild mental retardation often represented an extreme of the normal distribution. By sharp contrast, the data for severe mental handicap were quite different. Although, by definition, the mean IQ of the probands was much lower, the sibs did not differ from the general population. Their mean IQ was just average and there was no increase in the rate of retardation. It may be concluded that severe mental retardation is genetically distinct from normality whereas mild retardation often represents the extreme of the normal distribution of IQ and is *not* a qualitatively different disease. This inference from the Nichols data is, of course, in line with Lewis' (1933) broad distinction many years ago between 'pathological' and 'subcultural' retardation, as well as with the findings from other empirical population studies (see Johnson, Ahern, and Johnson, 1976). It seems probable that many of the more common emotional and conduct disorders of childhood also represent extremes of normality arising from a complex interplay of risk factors rather than genetically distinct diseases, although that is not yet known for certain. In so far as this is the case, it is likely that genetic influences will be found to stem from many genes with small effects, rather than from one major gene causing a specific disorder (Plomin, 1991).

Misconception 7. Genetic findings won't help identify diseases

Another mistaken view is that genetic studies will not help to identify diseases; they can be undertaken only when we know already how to diagnose the condition. This concept, too, is at least partially mistaken. Of course, genetic research requires a prior specification of the disorder to be investigated. However, there are many examples in medicine in which genetic findings have led to a reconceptualization of the condition (McKusick, 1969 and 1983). Sometimes what has been thought to be one disease turns out to include several different genetic conditions (as is the case, for example, with 'gargoylism' and retinitis pigmentosa); conversely, what have been thought to be separate disorders sometimes prove to be genetically the same (as may be the case with Tourette's syndrome and some types of obsessive-compulsive disorder – Paul, Towbin, Leckman, Zahner, and Cohen, 1986). For instance, in child psychiatry, genetic data suggest that autism actually includes a range of cognitive (especially language) and social deficits.

This was evident from the pooled data from our own two population-based twin studies of autism (Folstein and Rutter, 1977; Le Couteur, Bailey, Rutter, and Gottesman 1989). About half the monozygotic twin pairs were concordant for autism (the precise figure depending somewhat on the stringency of the diagnostic criteria), whereas none of the dizygotic pairs were. This suggests that autism has a strong genetic basis (see below). However, the point that also emerges from the twin study is that most of the monozygotic cotwins who did not have autism *did* have some form of cognitive deficit, usually a specific language disorder. By contrast, this was so for less than one in 10 of the dizygotic pairs. The implication is that what is inherited extends beyond the traditional diagnosis of autism.

Initially, it seemed that this extension mainly involved cognitive problems, but a follow-up of the first twin sample showed that in almost all cases the disorder was accompanied by persisting problems in close social relationships.

Although, in most cases, the non-autistic cotwins in discordant MZ pairs in the Folstein and Rutter twin sample outgrew their early language problems, they continued to have substantial difficulties in the development of close friendships and love relationships. The implication is that the concept of autism needs to be widened to include a pattern of cognitive and social deficits of a type that is quite similar to that found in autism but markedly different in degree, and not associated with several aspects that have in the past been regarded as essential for diagnosis.

The same conclusion derives from family data (Macdonald, Rutter, Rios, and Bolton 1989). Cognitive and social deficits were much more frequent in sibs within families of autistic probands than in the sibs of Down's syndrome subjects. Once again, the implication is that, genetically speaking, autism comprises patterns of cognitive and social deficits found in individuals of normal intelligence who are not obviously handicapped in the way that has traditionally been associated with autism. Probably, too, the phenotype includes some cases with social or cognitive deficits alone, although this is much less certain. It is becoming apparent that one of the important results of genetic research is an improved understanding of how to define psychiatric conditions and of how to separate one psychiatric disorder from another.

Misconception 8. Genetic influences diminish with age

Most people take it for granted that genetic effects are maximal at birth and that, as we grow older, environmental factors have a cumulatively greater impact on how we function. It might seem obvious that this ought to be the case, but it is now evident that it is not generally so (Plomin, 1986). The evidence indicates that, for variables such as height and weight, dizygotic twins are more alike at birth than are monozygotic twins, but that, with increasing age, DZ twins grow apart whereas MZ twins do not, at least not to the same extent (Matheny, 1990). This pattern applies also to intelligence, although with temperamental characteristics both types of twins tend to grow apart (McCartney, Harris, and Bernieri, 1990). Obviously, all the genes are *present* at birth, but they may not exert their main effect until much later. There are several reasons why this is the case. First, the finding that DZ twins grow apart to a greater extent than MZ twins suggests that there is an interplay between genetic and environmental influences such that the effects of the latter are being shaped by the former. This could be the result of either gene-environment correlations (so that genes are influencing the likelihood of exposure to particular environments) or gene-environment interactions (with genes affecting susceptibility to particular environments). Second, the finding that MZ twins are more different at birth than are DZ twins suggests an effect of intrauterine influences; an effect that diminishes with time. Third, some psychological characteristics that are strongly genetically determined take time to become manifest. This is obviously so with respect to language, but it also applies to a wider range of cognitive skills. Fourth, although the genes are present at birth, some of their effects do not, as it were, 'switch on' until later in life. It is well known that this is so with various hereditary diseases that only appear for the first time in middle age; for example, the dementia associated with Huntington's disease. However, the phenomenon is much more widespread than that; for example, the timing of the menarchè is genetically determined to an important extent and yet it does not occur until adolescence.

The increase in genetic effects as children grow older may be illustrated by considering the proportion of variance explained by genetic factors with respect to measures of cognitive functioning at different ages. Plomin (1986) summarized the findings from a range of studies. The heritability estimates for cognitive functioning during the infancy period were quite low – about the 20% level. Genetic factors became much more important during childhood, with estimates at around 40%, and were stronger still in adolescence, with a heritability at that age of about 50%. The data are less extensive on other aspects of psychological functioning, but the pattern is much the same for at least some other traits. Whatever the full explanation, research findings suggest that, for many psychological features, genetic effects *increase* as children grow older, at least up to middle childhood.

Misconception 9. Disorders that run in families must be genetic

Another mistaken stereotype is that disorders that run in families must be, or at least are highly likely to be, genetic in origin. A moment's thought indicates that there are many other reasons why conditions may aggregate in families. Thus, they may be due to infectious agents transmitted through close contact, or due to dietary factors (because families usually share the same meals). Also, of course, normal behaviour and attitudes run in families for cultural reasons and from a shared pattern of upbringing. This is probably the case with religious and political beliefs, for instance. There are genetic influences on the *degree* of religiosity (Waller, Kojetin, Bouchard, Lykken, and Tellegen, 1990) but cultural factors are likely to be more important in determining whether the religion is Christianity, Islam or Buddhism. Specific genetic strategies, as provided by twin and adoptee designs, are needed to separate genetic and environmental reasons for the familial loading.

Juvenile delinquency and conduct disorders in childhood seem to constitute an interesting example of patterns of behaviour with a very strong tendency to run in families but with more of an environmental, rather than genetic, explanation. This is shown by the very high proportion of cases in which both twins in any pair, whether identical *or* non-identical, show similar behaviour (McGuffin and Gottesman, 1985). There is a slight difference in the pair-wise concordance for monozygotic and dizygotic pairs, but the difference is quite small and suggests a rather modest genetic component. The fact that nearly three quarters of dizygotic pairs are concordant needs to be attributed in large part to environmental influences. The available data are based on rather old twin studies, but the findings are broadly in keeping with the widespread observation that when one child in a family is delinquent, it is very common to find that others show somewhat similar antisocial behaviour. Disturbances of conduct and delinquency are associated with family discord and disorganization and with other family disadvantages, and it appears that they operate largely through environmental mechanisms. The particular interest in these data from childhood stems from the parallel finding that genetic factors are rather more important in adult criminality and personality disorders. The implication seems to be that those varieties of conduct disturbance that persist into adult life are more likely to have a substantial genetic component; the task now is to put this suggestion to the test and to identify the features that differentiate the more genetic from the largely environmental varieties.

Misconception 10. Disorders that seem not to run in families cannot be genetic

The next mistaken view is the notion that disorders that seem *not* to run in families to any marked extent cannot be genetic. This, too, is wrong for two rather different reasons. First, conditions can be genetic but yet not hereditary. This is the case with Down's syndrome or mongolism, for example. The cause is a chromosome anomaly, but in the great majority of instances this is not transmitted as such from either parent – rather, it is something that went wrong at the beginning of development. The second reason is that rare disorders may run in families but yet not appear to do so because the absolute rate is very low, even though it is many times higher than that in the general population. That is the case with the psychiatric condition of autism.

Autism is a rather rare disorder, with a prevalence in the general population of about four per 10,000 – in other words 0.04%. The rate in sibs (including dizygotic twins), as estimated from the pooling of data from our own extensive family studies, was 3%. This is closely in line with the results of other investigations (Smalley, Asarnow, and Spence, 1988). This is quite a low percentage but it is about 75 times the base rate in the general population. This is a huge increase in relative risk. The rate in monozygotic cotwins was about 50% in our pooled twin studies: an increase of 1,250 times the base rate. When these rates are translated into tetrachoric correlations, this produces an estimate of 97% heritability on a multifactorial model. The precise estimate depends on a variety of assumptions about the mode of genetic transmission, and not too much weight should be attached to the particular percentage figure. However, what is abundantly clear is that there is an extremely powerful genetic effect. There is almost no other psychiatric condition that is so strongly genetic (Rutter, 1991). This is so in spite of the fact that the rate of autism in sibs, namely 3%, is so low that for a long time people assumed that autism did not run in families and could not be genetic.

However, there are several curious and interesting aspects to the genetic findings, of which I shall mention just two. First, this concordance pattern strongly points to the operation of several genes acting in combination – a finding that is highly unusual for rare genetic disorders (which are usually due to just one major gene) but which may be more characteristic of disorders of development. Second, the social handicaps associated with autism are such that it is extremely uncommon for autistic individuals to marry and have children. The question that arises, then, is why doesn't it die out? We do not know the answer as yet but the likelihood is that the genes are carried by many people who do not appear autistic (perhaps because several genes are involved) and /or that lesser varieties of autism (which are not recognized as such at the moment) carry benefits.

Misconception 11. Single major genes lead only to specific rare diseases that follow a Mendelian pattern

The last mistaken view to mention is the assumption that single major genes lead only to specific rare diseases that follow a Mendelian pattern. It is, of course, well known and well demonstrated that there are a variety of diseases where this is the case, and where the pattern of the disease in family members follow the Mendelian expectations of dominant, autosomal or sex-linked recessive inheritance. Thus, people are well familiar with the genetic diseases of colour blindness (which follows a sex-linked recessive pattern) or Huntington's disease (which is due to an autosomal dominant gene). The usual contrast has been between these single major gene disorders and polygenic transmission as part of a multifactorial liability in which environmental influences are also very important. This latter mode is clearly the way that genes operate in relation to normally distributed human characteristics, such as height and intelligence. Until recently it has been assumed that it also applies to common diseases that run in families but which do not follow any of the Mendelian patterns. However, recent research has indicated that this traditional demarcation between two quite different sorts of genetic mechanisms is an oversimplification (Bock and Collins, 1987: Chadwick, Bock and Whelan, 1990). There are medical disorders in which genetic factors play only a contributory role, along with a range of environmental factors, but in which single major genes have been demonstrated to play an important part in the liability to disease. For example, this seems to be the case with insulin dependent diabetes mellitus (i.e., the form that usually develops in child-hood). This form of diabetes is less strongly genetic than diabetes of late onset, but it has been found that the major contribution to the moderate genetic effect comes from a gene or genes on the short arm of chromosome six (Todd, Bell and McDevitt, 1987; Hitman and Niven, 1989). Something similar probably also applies to the genetics of variability in the risk or liability to coronary artery disease (Sing and Moll, 1989). The implication is that the new DNA technology offered by the advances in molecular genetics may well be applicable to the elucidation of genetic influences in common multifactorial disorders, as well as in rare Mendelian diseases (Pembrey, 1989). The possibility that this also applies to many psychiatric conditions has yet to be explored but it is apparent that this remains a fruitful avenue likely to reward systematic study (Cloninger, Reich, Suarez, Rice, and Got-tesman 1985).

Conclusions

We have come a long way since genetic questions were posed in terms of the simple alternative of whether some behaviour or some disorder was due to nature or nurture. The field of genetics has become more complex but, as is the way of science, the growing understanding of how genetic processes operate has simplified some issues that seemed puzzling in the past and has opened up new vistas that are exciting to researchers, and which are likely to prove useful in improving the outlook for children in the future.

Acknowledgements

Based on a paper with the same title previously published in 'Development and Psychopathology' in 1991, Vol 3, pages 125–136. Partial support on NIMH MH45268 is greatly acknowledged.

References

Bock, G., and Collins, G. M. (eds) (1987) *Molecular approaches to human polygenic diseases.* Ciba Foundation Symposium No. 130. Chichester: Wiley.

Cadoret, R. J. (1985) 'Genes, environment and their interaction in the development of psycho-pathology', in Sakai, T., and Tsuboi, T. (eds), *Genetic aspects of human behaviour.* 165–175. Tokyo: Igaku-Shoin.

Capron, C., and Duyme, M. (1989), 'Assessment of effects of socio-economic status on IQ in a full cross-fostering study'. *Nature,* (340) 552–554.

Chadwick, D., Bock, G., and Whelan, J. (1990) *Human genetic information: Science, law and ethics.* Ciba Foundation Symposium 149. Chichester: Wiley.

Clarke, A. M. (1985). 'Polygenic and environmental interactions'. In Clarke, A. M., Clarke A. D. B. and Berg, J. M. (Eds) *Mental Deficiency: The Changing Outlook*. 267–290. London: Methuen.

Clarke, A. M. and Clarke A. D. B. (1978), 'Genetic-environmental interactions in cognitive development', in Clarke A. M. and Clarke A. D. B. (Eds) *Readings from Mental Deficiency: The Changing Outlook*. 72–113. London: Methuen.

Cloninger, R. C., Reich, T., Suarez, B. K., Rice, J. P., and Gottesman, I. I. (1985) 'The principles of genetics in relation to psychiatry', in Shepherd M. (ed), *Handbook of psychiatry. The scientific foundations of psychiatry*, (5) 34–66. Cambridge: Cambridge University Press.

DeFries, J. C., and Fulker, D. W. (1985), 'Multiple regression analysis of twin data'. *Behaviour Genetics*, (15) 467–473.

DeFries, J. C., and Fulker, D. W. (1988), 'Multiple regression analysis of twin data: Etiology of deviant scores versus individual differences'. *Acta Geneticae Medicae et Gemellologiae*, (37) 205–216.

Dunn, J., and Plomin, R. (eds), (1990) *Separate lives: Why siblings are so different*. New York: Basic Books.

Eaves, L. J., Eysenck, H. J., and Martin, N. G. (eds), (1989) *Genes, culture and personality: An empirical approach*. London: Academic Press.

Folstein, S., and Rutter, M. (1977), 'Infantile autism: A genetic study of 21 twin pairs'. *Journal of Child Psychology and Psychiatry*, (18) 297–321.

Fuggle, P., and Graham, P. (1991) 'Metabolic/endocrine disorders and psychological functioning' in Rutter, M. and Casaer, P. (eds), *Biological risk factors for psychosocial disorders*. Cambridge: Cambridge University Press.

Gottesman, I. I. (1963) 'Genetic aspects of intelligent behaviour', in Ellis, N. (ed), *Handbook of mental deficiency*. New York: McGraw Hill.

Hahn, M. E., Hewitt, J. K., Henderson, N. D., and Benno, R. H. (eds) (1990) *Developmental behaviour genetics: Neural, biometrical and evolutionary approaches*. Oxford: Oxford University Press.

Hitman, G. A., and Niven, M. J. (1989), 'Genes and diabetes mellitus'. *British Medical Bulletin*, (45) 191–205.

Johnson, C. A., Ahern, F. M., and Johnson, R. C. (1976), 'Levels of functioning of siblings and parents of probands of varying degrees of retardation'. *Behavioural Genetics*, (6) 473–477.

Le Couteur, A., Bailey, A., Rutter, M., and Gottesman, I. (1989). 'Epidemiologically based twin study of autism'. Paper presented at the First World Congress of Psychiatric Genetics, Churchill College, Cambridge, August 1989.

Lewis, E. O. (1933), 'Types of mental deficiency and their social significance'. *Journal of Mental Science*, (79) 298–304.

Locurto, C. (1990), 'The malleability of IQ as judged from adoption studies'. *Intelligence*, (14) 275–290.

Macdonald, H., Rutter, M., Rios, P., and Bolton, P. (1989), 'Cognitive and social abnormalities in the siblings of autistic and Down's syndrome probands'. Paper given at the First World Congress on Psychiatric Genetics, Churchill College, Cambridge, 3–5 August 1989.

Matheny, A. P. (1989), 'Children's behavioural inhibition over age and across situations: Genetic similarity for a trait during change'. *Journal of Personality*, (57) 215–235.

Matheny, A. P. (1990), 'Developmental behaviour genetics: Contributions from the Louisville twin study', in Hahn, M. E., Hewitt, J. K., Henderson, N. D., and Benno, R. H. (eds), *Developmental behaviour genetics: Neural, biometrical and evolutionary approaches*. pp 25–39. Oxford: Oxford University Press.

McAskie, M. and Clarke, A. M. (1976). 'Parent-offspring resemblances in intelligence: theories and evidence', *British Journal of Psychology*, (67) 243–273.

McCartney, K., Harris, M. J., and Bernieri, F. (1990), 'Growing up and growing apart: A developmental meta-analysis of twin studies'. *Psychological Bulletin*, (107) 226–237.

McGuffin, P., and Gottesman, I. I. (1985). 'Genetic influences on normal and abnormal development', in Rutter, M. and Hersov, L. (eds), *Child and adolescent psychiatry: Modern approaches* (second edition). Oxford: Blackwell Scientific.

McKusick, V. A. (ed) (1969) *Human genetics*. Englewood Cliffs, New Jersey: Prentice-Hall.

McKusick, V. A. (1983) 'Mendelian inheritance in man'. *Catalogs of autosomal dominant, autosmal recessive and X-linked phenotypes* (sixth edition). Baltimore: John Hopkins University Press.

Nichols, P. L. (1984), 'Familial mental retardation'. *Behaviour Genetics*, (14) 161–170.

Paul, D. L., Towbin, K. E., Leckman, J. F., Zahner, G. E. P., and Cohen, D. J. (1986), 'Evidence supporting an etiological relationship between Gilles de la Tourette syndrome and obsessive compulsive disorder'. *Archives of General Psychiatry*, (43) 1180–1182

Pembrey, M. (1989), 'Advances in genetic prediction and diagnosis', in Doxiadis, S. (ed), *Early influences shaping the individual*. New York: Plenum Press.

Pembrey, M. (1991), 'Chromosomal abnormalities', in Rutter, M. and Casaer, P. (eds), *Biological risk factors for psychosocial disorders*. Cambridge: Cambridge University Press.

Plomin, R. (1986). *Development, genetics and psychology*. Hilldale, NJ: Lawrence Erlbaum.

Plomin, R. (1991), 'Genetic risk and psychological disorders: Links between the normal and abnormal', in Rutter, M. and Casaer, P. (eds), *Biological risk factors for psychosocial disorders*. Cambridge: Cambridge University Press.

Plomin, R., and Bergeman, C. S. (1991), 'The nature of nurture: Genetic influences on "environmental" measures'. *Behavioural and Brain Sciences*, (14) 373–386.

Plomin, R., and Daniels, D. (1987), 'Why are children in the same family so different from one another?' *Behavioural and Brain Sciences*, (10) 1–15.

Plomin, R., DeFries, J. C., and Fulker, D. W. (1988) *Nature and nurture during infancy and early childhood*. Cambridge: Cambridge University Press.

Plomin, R., Rende, R. D., Rutter, M. (1991), 'Quantitative genetics and developmental psychopathology', in Cicchetti, D. and Tover, S. (eds) *Rochester Symposium on Developmental Psychopathology*, Vol. 2: Internalizing and Externalizing Expressions of Dysfunction, Hillsdale, NJ: Lawrence Erlbaum.

Robins, L. N. (1966). *Deviant children grown up*. Baltimore: Williams and Wilkins. (Reprinted 1973, Krieger, Melbourne, FA.)

Rotter, J. I., and Diamond, J. M. (1987) 'What maintains the frequencies of human genetic diseases?' *Nature*, (329) 289–290.

Rutter, M. (1985). 'Family and School Influences on Cognitive Development'. *Journal of Child Psychology and Psychiatry*, (26) 683–704.

Rutter, M. (1991), 'Autism as a genetic disorder' in McGuffin, P. and Murray, R. (eds), *The new genetics of mental illness*. Oxford: Heinemann Medical.

Rutter, M., Bolton, P., Harrington, R., Le Couteur, A., MacDonald, H., and Simonoff, E. (1990a), 'Genetic factors in child psychiatric disorders – I. A review of research strategies'. *Journal of Child Psychology and Psychiatry*, (31) 3–37.

Rutter, M., Macdonald, H., Le Couteur, A., Harrington, R., Bolton, P., and Bailey, A. (1990b), 'Genetic factors in child psychiatric disorders – II. Empirical findings'. *Journal of Child Psychology and Psychiatry*, (31) 39–83.

Rutter, M. and Madge, N. (1976) *Cycles of Disadvantage: A Review of Research*. London: Heinemann.

Scarr, S., and Kidd, K. K. (1983), 'Developmental behaviour genetics' in N. M. Haith and J. J. Campos (eds) *Infsncy and Developmental Psychobiology*, (2),*Mussen's Handbook of child psychology*, (4) 345–433. New York: Wiley.

Scarr, S., and McCartney, K. (1983). 'How people make their own environments: A theory of genotype-environmental effects'. *Child Development*, (54) 424–435.

Schiff, M., and Lewontin, R. (1986). *Education and class: The irrelevance of IQ genetic studies*. Oxford: Clarendon.

Sing, C. F., and Moll, P. P. (1989). 'Genetics of variability of CHD risk'. *International Journal of Epidemiology*, (18) 183–195.

Smalley, S. L., Asarnow, R. F., and Spence, M. A. (1988), 'Autism and genetics: A decade of research'. *Archives of General Psychiatry*, (45) 953–961.

Spence, J. E., Corey, L. A., Nance, W. E., Marazita, M. L., Kendler, K. S., and Schieken, R. M. (1988), 'Molecular analysis of twin zygosity using VNTR DNA probes'. *American Journal of Human Genetics*, (43) A159 (Abstract).

Tizard, J. (1975), 'Race and IQ: The limits of probability'. *New Behaviour*, (1) 6–9.

Todd, J. A., Bell, J. I., and McDevitt, H. O. (1987). 'HLA-DQB gene contributes to susceptibility and resistance to insulin-dependent diabetes mellitus'. *Nature*, (329) 599–604.

Waller, N. G., Kojetin, B. A., Bouchard, T. J., Lykken, D. T., and Tellegen, A. (1990). 'Genetic and environmental influences on religious interests, attitudes, and values: A study of twins reared apart and together'. *Psychological Science*, (1) 138–142.

number and also directed at the mothers. Secondly, it was assumed that there are direct causal links between the mothers' rearing practices and the behaviour of their children, thus expressing the prevailing unilateral view of the relationship and the belief that child outcome is wholly explicable by maternal input. And finally there was the assumption that later personality characteristics are extensions of the effects of early experience and that the findings therefore had implications for understanding not only current but subsequent behaviour. In short, the study reflected the general consensus at the time that child development is largely to be explained by whatever it is that mothers do to children.

As we have learned since, these assumptions are invalid. Much of the research in the following decades was initially devoted to extending the list of potential socialising agents. 'Matricentric thinking' (as Lamb, 1978, called it) had to give way to the realisation that children from the beginning are embedded in a network of social relationships involving a diversity of individuals, each of whom has to be recognised as exerting some sort of influence on the course of the child's development. The notion, embodied in Bowlby's (1969) concept of *monotropism*, that children are initially incapable of forming more than one emotionally meaningful attachment, that this will normally be formed with the mother and that all other attachments will only emerge subsequently and always be of minor importance, has not been borne out by empirical research (Schaffer and Emerson, 1964; Cohen and Campos, 1974). Children, it appears, are capable of forming multiple relationships even in infancy; there are no biological constraints that make the bond to the mother an exclusive one. For that matter the feeding situation, which is generally managed by mothers, is now no longer regarded as playing the crucial role attributed to it by psychoanalysts and Hullian learning theorists; the way is thus open to any individual with whom the child comes into regular contact, whatever the context, to qualify as an attachment object and to become a source of influence in the child's world. Fathers, siblings, peers, grandparents and others thus all entered the picture as far as socialisation research was concerned.

The 1970s in particular became the decade of the father. To some extent this was a recognition by psychologists of the social changes that had been taking place around them for some time – changes in the role definitions of males and females and the consequently far greater participation of fathers in child rearing. Fathers, it became evident, tend to be just as responsive to their children's signals as mothers (Frodi et al., 1978); although they may differ in their style of interaction by being more vigorous and physical, there is no indication that they are less competent as caregivers (Parke, 1981). The notion that women, by virtue of their biological make-up, are inevitably better prepared for parenting than men has had to be re-examined; whatever sex differences do exist in parental competence can probably be better explained by social convention than innate endowment, as seen in studies of men who have assumed the role of primary caretaker in the family (Field, 1978). In short, fathers cannot be neglected as direct sources of influence on children's development, and particularly not at a time of sex role flexibility and high maternal employment outside the home.

Siblings have also come to be recognised as potentially important sources of influence (Dunn and Kendrick, 1982). The influence is, in the first place, an indirect one: the very fact that there are two (or more) children to be cared for by the parents transforms the relationship between parent and any one child – a point particularly well illustrated by studies of twins whose opportunities for one-to-one interaction with the mother tend to be sharply reduced because of the mother's need to distribute her attention among both children, with sometimes marked consequences for development (Tomasello et al., 1986). The direct effects stem from the great opportunities siblings have to acquire, through their mutual interaction, an understanding of their social world and the rules which regulate that world. Conflicts and arguments, shared fantasy play, the activities of one child that may serve as a model for the other – these and other interactional situations serve as the contexts wherein siblings can, in diverse and often emotionally intense ways, affect each other's psychological development.

The emotional intensity may not be as great in interactions outside the family, yet the increase in the number of even quite young children attending daycare has drawn attention to the possibility of behaviour change brought about by encounters with peers. As Hartup (1983) has shown, there is a great deal of evidence indicating that peer interaction can be a powerful means of exerting socialising pressures at all stages of development beyond infancy. The idea that only adults are responsible for socialisation is certainly not tenable. For that matter the notion, also widely maintained at one time, that the only socialisation context to be taken seriously is the child's family must also be challenged; research, for instance, on the school setting as a source of influence (Rutter et al., 1984) has shown this vividly. Indeed the list of potential socialising agents is continuing to grow: grandparents (Tinsley and Parke, 1984), daycare staff (Hess et al., 1980), individuals such as neighbours comprising social support systems outside the family (Crittenden, 1985), and also such inanimate sources as television (Singer and Singer, 1983) have come to attract the attention of research workers in recent years and shown that they too need to be taken into account if one is to understand the final product.

Separate influences and their joint impact on the child

The list of socialising agents has grown considerably, but what has also become apparent is that these different sources do not act on the child in a simple additive fashion, each functioning independently of all the others. One may, for instance, investigate father-child relationships as well as mother-child relationships, comparing and contrasting the two and considering both as relevant to personality development and yet, because each dyad is treated as a separate unit, one may thereby fail to do justice to the *joint* influence that the parents have on the child (Schaffer, 1984).

The fact that mother and father do not impinge on the child separately, with additive effects, but have a combined influence that thus constitutes the child's family environment, is illustrated by the work done on second-order (or indirect) effects. This work has demonstrated that whatever transpires between the members of a given dyad (say mother and child) is likely to be affected by the relationship that each of these individuals has with a third person (say the father). The mere presence or absence of the father changes what goes on between mother and child in terms of both the quantity and the nature of dyadic exchanges (e.g. Belksy, 1979). The same applies, of course, to other second-order effects such as those involving a mother and her two children: as Dunn and Kendrick (1982) have shown, the arrival of a new child in a family brings about a marked *decrease* in the mother's attention to the older child but also a considerable *increase* in confrontation and prohibition. Parent-child interaction cannot therefore be understood by merely examining the separate parent-child dyads.

What applies to behavioural interaction is also applicable to more general child rearing attitudes and practices. As Block et al. (1981) have argued, it is less a matter of what mother and father do separately than the extent to which they agree or disagree as to what should be done with the child. Each parent's report on his or her practices and values in bringing up the child was found by them to be of less use in predicting developmental problems than the *joint* impact of their separate sets of influence. Again it is shown that to take into account the various individuals whom a child encounters is not sufficient if one fails to consider them in combination.

The same conclusion emerges from more recent work on attachment relationships, for here too researchers are increasingly paying attention not just to single relationships (usually with the mother, of course) but to the multiplicity of the child's relationships. Here too there was initially the tendency to treat the various attachments independently (e.g. in terms of the number of children falling into the various security categories vis à vis mother and father respectively, Lamb, 1977). However, the usefulness of taking the next step is well illustrated by Howes et al. (1988), who showed that children's behaviour in daycare settings is a joint function of the attachment to the mother *and* to the caregiver. Children with secure relationships to both adults were found to be the most competent in play and social interactions, while those with insecure relationships to both were least competent. However, those with an insecure attachment to the mother but a secure attachment to the caregiver were somewhere in between, suggesting that a good relationship can, at least in part, compensate for the deleterious effects of a poor relationship, even with the mother. Once again we see that it is the totality of a child's relationships, but in particular their concordance, that must be taken into account.

This conclusion also emerges from studies which have examined the influence of particular *settings* on children. Beatrice Whiting (1980) once provocatively suggested that parents exert their influence not so much directly as through their choice of settings to which they expose and assign children. However that may be, settings such as daycare and the influence they exert on children have attracted an enormous amount of research in recent years. Most of this work, however, has examined daycare characteristics in isolation as a possible source of influence, without taking into account the fact that children live simultaneously in at least two different worlds, namely at home as well as in the daycare centre, and so disregarding the possibility that it is neither one alone nor, for that matter, both added together that have predictive power, but rather the relationship between the two.

As yet we have very little data that address this issue. One relevant study is that by Liddell and Kruger (1987, 1989), conducted in a nursery in a South African black township. By Western standards, conditions in that nursery were extremely bad, as indicated by a number of measures but in particular by indices of overcrowding (five square feet per child). In line with findings from studies conducted in the West on the effects of overcrowding on children, one would expect the quality of children's behaviour drastically to deteriorate in such an environment, yet this was not found. Levels of play and social interaction were highly similar to those found in children in high-grade nurseries in First World countries: overall rates of behaviour and ability to form playmate bonds showed no difference compared with data reported by studies conducted in settings of 'optimal' densities. The reason for this may, according to the authors, lie in the children's experience *outside* the nursery, for all came from homes that were similarly overcrowded and in which they had presumably acquired the necessary coping skills. As a result the children experienced no disparity in the nursery in relation to their base level. Thresholds for density effects as observed in nurseries cannot therefore be construed as absolute, but must be seen in relation to the everyday levels of crowding to which children are exposed.

This explanation is admittedly speculative and in need of confirmation. It does, however, make the important point that, in attempting to understand the influence of one particular setting on a child, one cannot detach that influence from all others and treat it as though it exists in isolation – just as the influence of individual caretakers cannot be understood separately. Thus research on daycare has, with only a few notable exceptions (e.g. Powell, 1980, Long and Garduque, 1987), disregarded the fact that children at admission are not formless and naive but have instead built up a set of expectations as a result of previous family life – a life which, for that matter, continues to exist side by side with their experience of daycare. The effects of the latter are thus filtered through structures built up as a result of their encounters with the former. There may well be marked discrepancies between teachers on the one hand and parents on the other in such matters as attitudes to aggression or to sexism or to racism; there may also be differences in child-rearing practices and disciplinary techniques – all with possibly quite marked implications for children who are learning to live in both worlds simultaneously and obliged to adjust to several diverse sets of social demands.

The whole issue of continuity or discontinuity of care is in fact a most important topic, but one which has so far been badly under-researched (Peters and Kontos, 1987). Discontinuity tends to have negative connotations: children are supposed to require stability and consistency, and therefore the more one can provide of such qualities the better for the child. However, whether the highest possible degree of continuity across settings is in fact desirable or whether there may not be certain optimal degrees of discontinuity that have positive effects on children's social learning possibilities is just one of the questions in this area that remains to be answered. First, however, there is a need for definitional clarity as to what we mean by continuity: are we talking of continuity in the sense of identity, or of consistency, or of complement, or of congruity, or what? It may well be that the concept of continuity is not a unitary one and that a lot more conceptual analysis is required before one can proceed with further research in this area. The essential point remains: it is the relationships between different sets of experiences that one must attend to and not just each separate set in isolation.

Nature and role of child effects

The multiplicity of socialising agents, plus the multiple settings to which they expose children, plus the highly intricate interactions among different agents and settings – all this adds up to a far more complex view of socialisation that we now need to adopt. But over and above there is one other set of influences that we must also take into account; namely, influences stemming from the child. In principle the notion of child effects is now widely accepted and the implications for the reciprocal nature of social interactions involving even the very youngest infant are generally recognised. In practice, however, the nature of child effects has mostly been treated in somewhat crude terms (of age differences, pathology status and so forth) and only the attempts to isolate temperamental characteristics constitute a rather more refined approach to this problem.

It is here, however, that the recent work in behaviour genetics becomes so relevant. From that work emerges the important argument (spelled out in detail by Scarr and Kidd (1983) that it is not only a matter of *parents* assigning children to settings; *children*, too, actively select and shape those environments that are appropriate to their own characteristics. Children themselves, that is, seek out and construct compatible environments and in this way help to determine which settings will have an opportunity to influence their own development – surely a much more dynamic and truly reciprocal view of the social influence process. As Bolger et al.(1988) have pointed out, this also means a reversal of the usual research paradigm: the individual is now cast in the role of the *independent* variable and the environment in the role of the *dependent* variable.

More important, however, is the implication that individual and environment are not as independent as has been held by psychologists brought up in the stimulus-response tradition (Plomin and Bergeman, in press). According to that tradition, parents are powerful environmental forces that impinge on children and shape and transform their behavioural development. According to the findings of the behaviour geneticists, however, measures of parental influence invariably reflect child characteristics too: the construct of parental responsiveness, for instance, does not exist as an independent entity but is perfused with characteristics of the parent's child. One cannot therefore conceptualise the socialisation process in terms of parent input-child output relationships; correlations between parental and child measures are open to other interpretations, especially so in view of the fact that characteristics are transmitted genetically as well as through behavioural interaction. No wonder that Sandra Scarr (1988) felt impelled to point out that virtually all research on parent-child socialisation is uninterpretable because parents provide both genes and environment, making it impossible to interpret either direction or cause of effects as observed in parent-child interaction within biologically related families.

It therefore becomes all the more important to examine the findings from studies of adopted children, twins reared apart and other such designs used to disentangle environmental and genetic effects. To take an example, Plomin et al. (1985) compared parent-child correlations in adoptive and non-adoptive families on a range of measures and found, first of all, that such correlations can to a substantial extent be genetically mediated and therefore cannot invariably be regarded as environmentally determined, and secondly that the genetic effect is stronger for some relationships than for others: infant soothability, for example, was found to show a largely genetically based relationship to various parental practices and not, as is so often automatically assumed, an environmentally determined relationship. Implications for intervention efforts must follow such results, in so far as knowledge about the basis for observed parent-child correlations has different consequences depending on the way in which they are produced.

The blinkered attitude whereby all parent-child correlations are interpreted in environmental terms thus needs to give way to a willingness to consider genetic mediating influences as well, and once that step has been taken, some rather surprising possibilities emerge. Take children's television viewing: the amount of time spent on that is usually thought of as depending on parents' permissiveness-restrictiveness, so that individual differences among children in viewing time are attributed primarily to parental practice. However, one of the findings of the Colorado Adoption Project (Plomin et al., in press) was that the correlation for amount of television viewing among biologically related siblings was nearly twice as great as among adoptive siblings (.48 and .26 respectively). It is suggested, in other words, that a substantial genetic influence is evident even in this type of activity; differences among children are not inevitably and wholly brought about by what parents actually do to their children.

Parent as cause: child as effect

The idea of total parental responsibility for the nature of the developmental course taken by individual children continues to have a powerful hold on the general public, as seen for instance in the proposal, advanced by some politicians, that parents should be called to account for the delinquency, truancy, addiction and other problem behaviours of their offspring. Developmental change in psychological functioning, it is assumed, must be due to parental input: it is this which is the major, if not the sole, determinant of individuality. For instance, if children become less impulsive as they grow older it must be because of their caretakers' controlling and restraining influence, and if some children fail to develop impulse control it must be attributed to socialising failure on the part of their parents. Similarly with altruism, compliance, autonomy, cooperation and so forth – the reasons for success or failure are to be found in parental socialisation practices.

Yet, as Eleanor Maccoby (1984) has pointed out, there are a lot of developmental changes in children which seem surprisingly independent of the way in which parents treat their children: the literature on the development

of inhibitory controls over impulsiveness, for example, provides few unam-
biguous indications regarding any particular kind of input from adults that
is related to such development. Likewise with other psychological functions:
the correlations that have been obtained with parental characteristics and
rearing patterns tend to be low and by no means consistent from study to
study (Maccoby and Martin, 1983). It could be, of course, that parental
influences can be found under only certain quite specific conditions: Buss
and Plomin (1984), for instance, have suggested that parents are more likely
to influence their infants in the middle range of temperament, whereas at the
extremes of the temperamental range, infants influence parents. However,
this remains to be demonstrated.

In any case, we are still confronted by the familiar problem of going
beyond correlations to cause-and-effect statements in any attempt to investigate parental effects. I have recently reviewed the evidence on what may
be referred to as Joint Involvement Episodes (JIEs), i.e. those interactive
situations in which two individuals (for our purposes, an adult and a child)
pay joint attention to and jointly act upon some external object or event
(Schaffer, 1989; in press). There are suggestions that such episodes are the
key socialisation situations in the early years; according to Burton White's
observations of preschool children at home, they may occur dozens of times
a day, are usually initiated by the child rather than by the mother, and though
they last perhaps not more than half a minute at a time they give the mother
the opportunity to get an enormous amount of teaching in 'on the fly' (White
and Watts, 1973). Given the current interest in Vygotsky it is not surprising
to find that a lot of attempts are being made to investigate what goes on in
JIEs, with particular reference to the way in which adult and child intertwine
their behaviour and the consequences this may have for the child's cognitive
socialisation. Much of this work is based on two propositions (derived
largely from Vygotsky):

- First, that children's behaviour is richer, more complex and
  developmentally more advanced in JIEs than in any other setting;
- Secondly, that the long-term development of psychological
  functions is crucially dependent on involvement in JIEs, and that
  the more the child experiences such encounters, the more its
  developmental progress will be furthered.

To cut a long story short, there is plenty of evidence for the first of these
propositions but very little for the second. Performance level at the time is
indeed raised by suitable action on the part of the adult, and this has now
been demonstrated for level of play, attention span, verbal competence and
a whole range of problem-solving skills. However, showing that the consequences are internalised by the child and carried forward beyond the imme-

diate situation has proved difficult indeed. This does not mean, let us emphasise, that such episodes do *not* have long-term implications; it is rather a matter of the methodological difficulties we have always encountered when attempting to demonstrate cause-and-effect sequences with respect to parental treatment and children's development. Strictly speaking, we are still perforce operating largely on the basis of faith that parents *do* play some part in their children's psychological development.

Until the methodological problems in social influence research have been resolved we are confronted mainly by correlational data. Such data do, of course, have their uses. Take the finding that the children of depressed mothers are themselves at risk for developing some form of psychopathology by a factor of two or three in comparison with other children (Dodge, 1990). Such an association may not enable one to make cause-and-effect statements, but at least one is thereby enabled to define a vulnerable group and take appropriate action, and at least one can then begin the search for the mechanisms behind this association. However, as Dodge (1990) makes clear, such mechanisms can take many different forms: genetic transmission, imitation, disruptive parenting (which in itself refers to a great many different aspects), intermediate factors such as loss of social contact or unemployment on the part of the parent, marital discord, prolonged absence of the parent through hospitalisation, failure to expose the child to particular experiences, isolation of the child from favourable social settings such as peer groups or suitable schooling, and so forth. In addition one must consider child effects, for by no means all children succumb and one therefore has to take various vulnerability factors into account. Trying to isolate the relevant mechanism behind this and any other form of parent-child association is thus a very considerable task that for the most part remains to be dealt with by future research.

Viewing development in the context of concurrent and temporal events

It has become very apparent that single-factor explanations are inappropriate in attempts to understand the vast majority of developmental phenomena. Events impinging on children take place in the context of many other concurrent events; they also take place in a temporal context where they form but one link in a whole sequence of influences.

As an example of the influence of concurrent events, take the effects on children of maternal employment. Research in this area began with the 'common sense' expectation that clear-cut answers of the good/bad kind would be found. In fact the history of work on this, as on so many other such problems, has been one of locating a seemingly ever increasing number of variables that exercise some sort of moderating effect on the outcome – variables such as the child's age; the child's sex; the child's temperament; the child's previous history of out-of-home care; the mother's reasons for work-ing; her pattern of working (full-time or part-time); her ability to cope with role division (worker and housewife); the father's agreement with her deci-sion to work and the extent of his participation in child care and household activities; the support (psychological and practical) the mother receives from other members of her social network; the arrangements made for the child's substitute care in terms of type, quality and consistency, the cultural norms prevailing in society with regard to maternal employment; and so forth. Evidence is now available with regard to each of these variables that it plays some part in shaping the outcome as far as effects on children are concerned (Hoffman, 1989). And for that matter, thinking has now moved well beyond the point where psychologists conceived of maternal employment as a simple input variable that is somehow responsible for producing output in the form of behavioural changes in children. Instead it is seen as an experi-ence that is incorporated in a system of interacting family processes, where it both affects and is affected by ongoing relationships within the family (Gottfried and Gottfried, 1988).

As to the temporal context in which particular events are embedded, let us take the effects of parental divorce. Here too research began simplistically, treating divorce as a single event about which one could make generalisa-tions in terms of good/bad consequences. However, the work of Hethering-ton (1988), Wallerstein (1983) and others has shown very clearly that the impact of divorce can only be understood in the context of a longitudinal and multi-factorial research design which does justice to the constantly changing life situation of particular children – changes that may be linked to the divorce experience but which depend on a large number of dynamically interrelated variables referring to the nature of the child and of the family situation in which the child finds itself. Parental divorce cannot therefore be seen as a single event happening at some particular point of time; it is part of a long drawn-out process which may well produce marked effects on children (primarily through family conflict) long before the parents actually separate (Block et al., 1986), and which may or may not continue to reverb-erate in later years, depending on such subsequent links in the chain as the custodial parent's psychological and economic state, the amount and kind of access to the non-custodial parent, the need to move home and change school, the parent's remarriage and the kind of relationship established with the step-parent, and so forth. Viewed over time it becomes evident that the nature and severity of consequences will vary depending on the cumulative effects not only of the divorce itself but also of the events that preceded it and the events which flowed from it. Under these circumstances, ascribing any long-term consequences to some particular link in the chain would be hazardous indeed.

The same conclusion has emerged from research on the impact of other life events on young children, such as separation, parental death, natural disasters and other traumatic experiences (Schaffer, 1990). Any drastic and sudden change may be extremely upsetting at the time; in and by itself, however, it is unlikely to lead to lasting psychopathology. Children's resilience in the face of isolated stresses and their ability to recuperate subsequently, *given the right conditions*, has been underestimated in the past and is only now receiving the required attention. The 'super-environmentalism' (as the Clarkes, 1976, put it) with which the first few years of life have been regarded is indeed no longer tenable; any experience must be seen in the context of both the child's total life experience and the particular characteristics which the child brings to that event.

Summary

The notion that children's individuality is to be explained primarily by the rearing practices of parents, particularly during the early and so-called formative years, dominated the thinking of developmental psychologists for a long time. However, an increasing body of research has shown that such a conception is simplistic and in need of drastic revision. For one thing, there is a far greater diversity of individuals and agencies potentially available as socializing agents; for another, these agents do not influence the child in a simple additive fashion but impinge jointly in complex interactions; and finally, it is essential that one also takes into account influences stemming from the child's own individuality. A far more complex view of the socialization process must therefore be adopted: developmental change is not simply a function of parental input, nor is it necessarily shaped decisively by the earliest experiences encountered by the child. The idea that specific experiences, occurring at specific points of time and in specific contexts and associated solely with certain specific individuals, can in themselves have long-term consequences must be rejected in favour of a much more complicated, multi-determined and continuing process.

References

Belsky, J. (1979) Mother-father-infant interaction: a naturalistic observational study. *Developmental Psychology*, 15, 601–607.

Block, J. H., Block, J. and Gjerde, P. F. (1986) The personality of children prior to divorce: A prospective study. *Child Development*, 57, 827–840.

Block, J. H., Block, J. and Morrison, A. (1981) Parental agreement-disagreement on child rearing orientation and gender-related personality correlates in children. *Child Development*, 52, 965–974.

Bolger, N., Caspi, A., Downey, G. and Moorehouse, M. (1988) Development in context: research perspectives. In N. Bolger (ed.), *Persons in Context: Developmental Processes*. Cambridge: Cambridge University Press.

Bowlby, J. (1969) *Attachment and Loss. Vol. l: Attachment*. London: Hogarth Press.

Buss, A. H. and Plomin, R. (1984) *Temperament: Early Developing Personality Traits*. Hillsdale, NJ: Erlbaum.

Clarke, A. M. and Clarke, A. D. B. (1976) *Early Experience: Myth and Evidence*. London: Open Books.

Cohen, L. J. and Campos, J. J. (1974) Father, mother and stranger as elicitors of attachment behaviors in infancy. *Developmental Psychology*, 10, 146–154.

Crittenden, P. M. (1985) Social networks, quality of child rearing, and child development. *Child Development*, 56, 1299–1313.

Dodge, K. A (1990) Developmental psychopathology in children of depressed mothers. *Developmental Psychology*, 26, 3–6.

Dunn, J. and Kendrick, C. (1982) *Siblings: Love, Envy and Understanding*. Cambridge, Mass.: Harvard University Press.

Field, T. (1978) Interaction behaviors of primary versus secondary caretaker fathers. *Developmental Psychology*, 14, 183–184.

Frodi, A. M., Lamb, M. E., Leavitt, L. A. and Donovan, W. L. (1978) Fathers' and mothers' responses to infant smiles and cries. *Infant Behavior and Development*, l, 187–198.

Gottfried, A. E. and Gottfried, A. W. (Eds.) (1988) *Maternal employment and children's development*. New York: Plenum.

Hartup, W. W. (1983) Peer relations. In E. M. Hetherington (ed.), *Handbook of Child Psychology, Vol. IV: Socialization, Personality and Social Interaction*. New York: Wiley.

Hess, R. D., Price, G. C., Dickson, W. P. and Conroy, M. (1980) Different roles for mothers and teachers: contrasting styles of child care. In S. Kilmer (ed.), *Advances in Early Education and Day Care*. Greenwich, Conn.: JAI Press.

Hetherington, E. M. (1988) Parents, children and siblings: six years after divorce. In R. A. Hinde and J. Stevenson-Hinde (eds.), *Relationships within families: Mutual influences*. Oxford: Clarendon Press.

Hoffman, L. W. (1989) Effects of maternal employment in the two-parent family. *American Psychologist*, 44, 283–292.

Howes, C., Rodning, C., Galuzzo, D. and Myers, L. (1988) Attachment and childcare: Relationships with mother and caregiver. *Early Childhood Research Quarterly*, 3, 403–416.

Lamb, M. E. (1977) The development of mother-infant and father-infant attachment in the second year of life. *Developmental Psychology*, 13, 637–648.

Lamb, M. E. (1978) Qualitative aspects of mother- and father-infant attachments. *Infant Behavior and Development*, l, 265–275.

Liddell, C. and Kruger, P. (1987) Activity and social behavior in a South African township nursery: some effects of crowding. *Merrill-Palmer Quarterly*, 33, 195–211.

Liddell, C. and Kruger, P. (1989) Activity and social behavior in a crowded South African township nursery: a follow-up study on the effects of crowding at home. *Merrill-Palmer Quarterly*, 35, 209–226.

Long, F. and Gardyne, L. (1987) Continuity between home and family day care: caregivers' and mothers' perceptions and children's social experiences. In Peters, D. L. and Kontos, S. (1987) (eds.), *Continuity and Discontinuity of Experiences in Child Care*. Norwood, NJ: Ablex.

Maccoby, E. E. (1984) Socialization and developmental change. *Child Development*, 55, 317–328.

Maccoby, E. E. and Martin, J. A. (1983) Socialization in the context of the family: parent-child interaction. In E. M. Hetherington (ed.), *Handbook of Child Psychology, Vol. IV: Socialization, Personality and Social Interaction*. New York: Wiley.

Parke, R. D. (1981) *Fathering*. London: Fontana.

Peters, D. and Kontos, S. (eds.) (1987) *Continuity and Discontinuity of Experience in Childcare*. Norwood, NJ: Ablex.

Plomin, R. and Bergeman, C. S. (in press) The nature of nurture: genetic influence on 'environmental' measures. *Behavioral and Brain Sciences*.

Plomin, R., Corley, R. DeFries, J. C. and Fulker, D. W. (in press). Individual differences in television viewing in early childhood: Nature as well as nurture. *Psychological Science*.

Plomin, R., Loehlin, J. C. and DeFries, J. C. (1985) Genetic and environmental components of 'environmental' influences. *Developmental Psychology*, 21, 391–402.

Powell, D. R. (1980) Toward a socioecological perspective of relations between parents and child care programs. In S. Kilmer (ed.), *Advances in Early Education and Daycare*, Vol. l. Greenwich, Conn.: JAI Press.

Rutter, M., Maughan, B., Mortimore, P. and Ouston, J. (1984) *Fifteen Thousand Hours: secondary schools and their effects on children*. London: Open Books.

Scarr, S. (1988) How genotypes and environments combine. In N. Bolger (ed.), *Persons in Contexts: Developmental Processes*. Cambridge: Cambridge University Press.

Scarr, S. and Kidd, K. K. (1983) Developmental behavior genetics. In P. H. Mussen (ed.), *Handbook of Child Psychology, (Vol. 2), Infancy and Developmental Psychobiology*. New York: Wiley.

Schaffer, H. R. (1984) *The Child's Entry Into a Social World*. London: Academic Press.

Schaffer, H. R. (1989) Language development in context. In von Tetzchner, S., Siegel, L. S. and Smith L. (eds.), *The Social and Cognitive Aspects of Normal and Atypical Language Development*. New York: Springer-Verlag.

Schaffer, H. R. (1990) *Making Decisions About Children: Psychological Questions and Answers*. Oxford: Blackwell.

Schaffer, H. R. (in press) Joint involvement episodes as contexts for cognitive development. In McGurk, H. (ed) *Childhood Social Development: Contemporary Perspectives*. Hove and London: Erlbaum.

Schaffer, H. R. and Emerson, P. E. (1964) The development of social attachments in infancy. *Monographs of the Society for Research in Child Development*, 29, no. 3 (whole no. 94).

Sears, R. R., Maccoby, E. E. and Levin, H. (1957) *Patterns of Child Rearing*. Evanston, Ill.: Row, Peterson.

Singer, J. L. and Singer, D. G. Psychologists look at television: cognitive, developmental, personality and social policy implications. *American Psychologist*, 38, 826–834.

Tinsley, B. J. and Parke, R. D. (1984) Grandparents as support and socialization agents. In M. Lewis (ed.), *Beyond the Dyad*. New York: Plenum.

Tomasello, M., Mannle, S. and Kruger, A. C. (1986) Linguistic environment of 1– to 2–year-old twins. *Developmental Psychology*, 22, 169–196.

Wallerstein, J. S. (1983) Children of divorce: stress and developmental tasks. In N. Garmezy and M. Rutter (eds.), *Stress, Coping and Development in Children*. New York: McGraw Hill.

Watson, J. B. (1928) *Psychological Care of Infant and Child*. New York: Norton.

White, B. L. and Watts, J. C. (1973) *Experience and Environment: Major Influences on the Development of the Young Child*. Englewood Cliffs, NJ: Prentice-Hall.

Whiting, B. (1980) Culture and Social Behavior: a model for the development of social behavior. *Ethos*, 8, 95–116.

Part 2

Longitudinal Studies of Vulnerability and Resilience

Chapter 3

Assets and deficits in the behaviour of people with Down's syndrome – a longitudinal study

Janet Carr

People with Down's syndrome are characterised primarily by learning difficulties which, although a wide range of abilities may be represented, are severe in the large majority after infancy. Parents are understandably concerned about their child's ability level and about how well he or she will develop, and this is likely to be important in determining to some extent the kind of interactions they can expect to have with him or her. Nevertheless developmental level is only one aspect of the child and other aspects, such as personality and behaviour, also play a crucial part in family functioning. To many mothers this was an area of uncertainty, one where they felt they needed advice which they did not get. 'I would have liked advice on how best to train her. Nobody told me anything, I just had to fish around by myself.' The present study was seen as an opportunity to look at both child behaviours and parental handling over time and to see whether any particular parental practices could be related to particular outcomes for the child.

Background

The study described is a longitudinal, single cohort study of people with Down's syndrome. It was aimed at examining the development of the children from infancy, at how this was affected by environmental factors, and at how the families were affected by having these children in the family. It was essentially a non-interventionist study.

The population consisted of all the children with Down's syndrome who were born in one year (December 1963 to November 1964) in one area of south east England.

Table 1: The study population

	Referred to study	By 15 months	Still in study		
			By 4 years	By 11 years	By 21 years
	N	N	N	N	N
Total	54	47	45	44	41
Males	25	22	23	23	22
Females	29	25	22	21	19
Home reared	45	40	39	38	35
Boarded out	9	7	6	6	6

Fifty-four babies were referred, just over half of them girls, and the full range of social class was represented. Of those lost to the study, all were lost through death, except for two whose families emigrated while the children were infants and one young man whose mother refused contact at 21 because of her anxiety about the confidentiality of computer records. Forty-five of the children were brought up in their own homes, and nine, whose families felt unable to bring them up, in various foster homes and institutions at least for the first few years.

Each home-reared child was matched with a non-handicapped baby for sex, age and social class, and these control children were studied in the same way as were those with Down's syndrome.

The children or adults were visited in their homes or foster homes at varying intervals from six weeks to 21 years and were given psychological tests. Details of the testing may be found in Carr (1988), but a summary of the results may be seen in Figure 1, showing that mean ratio IQ fell from 79 at six months to 37 at 11 years and then rose to a mean of 42 at 21 years.

At ages 15 months, 4, 11 and 21, the mothers were interviewed using a semi-structured interview schedule. The data from the 15 months and four year interviews have already been reported (Carr 1975), so what follows here is a description of personality and behaviour, as seen by the mothers, at 11 and 21 years. The 15 months and four year data will be included as far as possible in the later section where longitudinal aspects of the data are discussed.

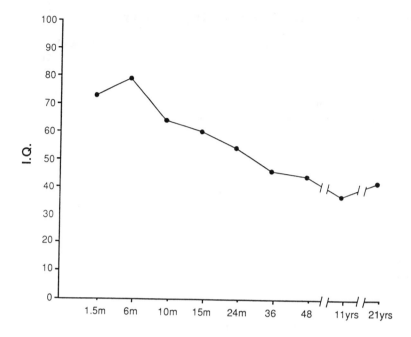

Figure 1: Ratio IQs from six weeks to 21 years old

Characteristics at 11 and 21

At 11 and 21 years old the mothers of both Down's syndrome people and controls were asked to rate their child's personality, cooperativeness and manageability.

Most parents of both groups and at both ages saw their children as having happy, easygoing personalities, although for between a third and three fifths this was tempered by some criticisms as well. No more than 10% of the Down's syndrome people, and slightly more of the controls, were described in only negative terms.

The number of children and young people who were seen as cooperative and easy to manage was again quite similar between the two groups, with a general tendency towards the young people becoming more agreeable and easier to deal with as they got older. A somewhat higher proportion of the controls was said to be not easy to manage. Understandably, the management problems seen by the two groups of mothers were different; for the controls, these were mainly connected with being self-opinionated, moody or rebellious (although in some cases these traits were seen as having a positive side). The four Down's syndrome children who at 11 years were not easy to manage were boys with low levels of ability; they were destructive,

Table 2: Personality and amenability

	Down's Syndrome		Control	
Age	11	21	11	21
	%	%	%	%
Personality				
Happy, no adverse comment	56	32	39	50
Happy, some adverse comment	39	58	47	37
Only adverse comment	5	10	14	13
Co-operativeness				
Usually agrees with requests	37	56	41	57
Varies	49	39	43	23
Usually objects	14	5	16	20
Manageability				
Easy to manage	56	76	62	70
Fairly easy	35	17	16	17
Not easy	9	7	22	13

Table 3: Behaviour Problems at 11 and 21 years (Down's Syndrome)

Age	11	21
	%	%
Aggressive	21	19
Rebellious	51(10)	68(5)
Pesters for attention	35(2)	27(10)
Temper tantrums	27	25(5)
Problem behaviour in public	39(10)	22(2)
Self-injurious behaviour	14	15(5)

Figures in brackets denote the proportion in whom the problem was more than occasional or minor. These are included in the main percentage figures.

difficult in company, unpredictable, demanding and stubborn. For the adults, problems were concentrated in the group with profound handicaps who continued stubborn and resistant and were more difficult to manage now they were bigger and stronger.

Behaviour problems – Down's syndrome group

Little change can be seen in the incidence of behaviour problems in the group as a whole from one age to the next. At each age about one fifth of the Down's syndrome group were thought to be aggressive (as were also 20% of these children at four years old). Around one third pestered, had tantrums and were difficult to take out in public at 11 years, and these proportions had declined somewhat by 21 years. Rebelliousness ('stubbornness'), however, increased from just half at 11 to over two thirds of the group at 21. Self-injury was seen in less than one sixth of the Down's syndrome group at each age. At 11, two children, both profoundly handicapped, banged their heads with an object or their hands, and five children, including one who also banged, picked at their feet, fingers or bottom. None of this self-injury, including the head banging, amounted to a serious problem. At 21, the two who had banged their heads now injured themselves severely and frequently, but the injury now consisted of self-scratching. One young man now banged his head occasionally and three others occasionally picked at faces, fingers or toes. Two more, not identified at 11, were said to have been minor headbangers in the past.

The longitudinal study

The consistency of the children's behaviours over time was explored. Two of the nine children rated as aggressive at four years old were similarly rated at 11 and 21 years; the remaining seven were not thought to be aggressive at either of the later ages. Of the eight children said to be aggressive at 11, half the survivors were still said to be so at 21, although now only occasionally. Two-thirds (65%) of those rebellious at 11 were found to be the same at 21 and only four of the rebellious children (20%) were never rebellious as adults. Nearly half (45%) continued to have tantrums. Half of those 47% who had pestered for attention continued to do so and constituted two-thirds (7/11) of those pestering at 21. Only three of the sixteen (19%) showing difficult behaviours in public at 11 were still doing so, at 21. Of the five said ever to have banged their heads, this behaviour persisted to a minor degree in one, led on to severe alternative self-injury in two more, minor alternative self-injury in the fourth and had disappeared in the fifth. Of the 11 (one quarter of the total) who had at any time showed any self-injury, some form of the behaviour persisted to some degree in six (14%) and had disappeared in the remaining five.

So, nearly half the children having temper tantrums at 11 continued to do so as 21–year-olds, and half continued to be aggressive to some extent, although an equal number of those not showing these behaviors at the earlier age had developed them later. A minority of those showing difficult behaviours in public at 11 still did so at 21, and very few children who neither pestered nor were aggressive or difficult in public at 11 showed these behaviours at 21 years. Self-injurious behaviour in this population was infrequent, affecting less than one sixth at any one time, and was generally minor. However, the behaviour persisted in about half of those ever showing it, and in the case of two profoundly handicapped young men became relatively severe.

Parental management

Simultaneously with asking the mothers about their children's personality and behaviours data were collected on how they handled their children and how they dealt with behaviour problems. Questions were asked about disciplinary methods – smacking, by mother and by father; sending to bed early or out of the room; depriving of sweets, TV or pocket money; the use of rewards or threats, and of supervision; and about the parents' attitudes to discipline – agreement, consistency, strictness, belief in smacking and so on. Also included were the mothers' ratings of their own health, since an ill or exhausted mother might have had greater difficulty in exercising discipline. In addition, the mothers' responses to questions about the children's and young people's behaviour were rated, usually on three point scales. Data on disciplinary methods and the times at which they were collected were: smacking by mother (15 months, four and 11) and by father (11); sending the child to bed early or out of the room (four and 11); using threats or rewards (11); and supervision (15 months, four and 11). Data on parental attitudes to discipline and the times at which they were collected were: mother believed in smacking, that smacking does good, used little smacking for any of her children, and mother's permissiveness score (four); parents consistent on discipline, father stricter, mother stricter (11); and parents agree on discipline and mother happy about her handling of the children (four and 11). Data on the mother's health, that is, whether she was depressed or depressed and run down, were collected at 11 and 21; and data on the child factors and the times at which they were collected were: amenability (15 months); tantrums (15 months and four); and getting into mischief (four and 11).

These ratings were individually related to cooperativeness and manageability at 11 and 21 and to frequency of behaviour problems at 21. Manageability, which was rated at four, 11 and 21 years, was also correlated across ages. The expectation was that there would be a significant relationship between the disciplinary approaches used by the mothers and outcome in terms of cooperativeness, manageability and presence or absence of behaviour problems in their children.

The first analyses concerned the relationships between child characteristics at one age and the dependent variables at later ages. The results showed that the controls tended to be easier to manage at 11 if they had had few tantrums at four ($p = .053$), and the Down's syndrome young people were easier to manage at 21 if they had had few tantrums at 15 months ($p = .019$). The young people were found more cooperative at 21 if in the Down's syndrome group they had been easy to manage at four (p = .004) and if at 11 they had kept out of mischief (p = .043) and been cooperative (p = .048). Tantrums at 15 months showed the same trend, of greater cooperativeness where tantrums were fewer, but did not quite reach significance (p = .075). The controls were seen as more cooperative at 21 if they had had few tantrums at four (p = .043) and kept out of mischief at 11 (p = .047), whilst being found easy to manage at four, although not quite significant, showed the same trend (p = .060).

Overall, then, there was a tendency for those who were cooperative and easily managed, who kept out of mischief and were not subject to tantrums, to be more cooperative and easy to manage at later stages of their lives. Some consistency and some regularity was shown in the behaviour of these young people as seen by their mothers.

Next to be considered were the relationships between the ratings of manageability and cooperativeness at 11 and 21, and of behaviour problems at 21, with the earlier ratings of parents' usage of and attitudes to discipline. Only three significant results were obtained. The controls were easier to manage at 11 if, at four, the mother had believed in smacking (p = .044), and more cooperative at 21 if, at 11, the mother had been the stricter parent (p = .034). In the Down's syndrome group there were fewer behaviour problems at 21 if, at four, there had been little smacking for any child in the family (p = .050). No other factor – smacking by mother or father, sending the child to bed early or out of the room, using rewards, whether the mother believed smacking did good or had confidence in her child rearing methods, agreement between the parents on the child's upbringing nor mother's health – could be shown to have any relationship with later behaviour. Since individual disciplinary methods had not been shown to affect behaviour, they were combined into discipline scales. These comprised, at 15 months, how the parents dealt with sleep disturbance, tantrums, naughtiness and destructiveness; at four, how tantrums were dealt with and the use of smacking and or other disciplinary approaches (sending the child to bed early or out of the room, depriving of sweets, TV etc); and, at 11, how habits were dealt with, and the use of other disciplinary approaches (as above) and of rewards and threats.

Scores on the scales were then related to cooperativeness, manageability and behaviour problems at 21. None of the relationships was significant.

The failure to find evidence of systematic relationships between parental handling and later behaviour was unexpected and puzzling. In seeking an explanation, an earlier study by Caldwell (1964) seemed perhaps relevant. Caldwell had studied, among other things, the methods of toilet training experienced by a group of young normal children, and had attempted to relate the use of these methods to the children's later psychological developmental. She was unable to demonstrate the connections between these factors that have been commonly held to exist (for example between a rigid toilet training regime and later obsessionality). The absence of such effects, Caldwell believed, must be due to other intervening factors, and she pointed to the potential importance of the 'inter-personal context' in which such training was carried out. It seemed reasonable to suppose that something similar could be playing a part in the present case. Although the questionnaire in the present study had not been designed with this in view there was one item, intended to bridge the transition from the enquiry about basic living skills to that of behaviour and management, which asked, 'How would you describe N as a person now?' This was an open-ended question and the mother's replies were recorded verbatim. Later the replies were divided into three groups: those in which the mother had made only positive comments, those in which the mother had made positive but also negative comments, and those whose comments were only negative. Because there were so few of the latter they were combined with the comments containing both positive and negative aspects, and this bipolar factor (labelled 'Mother's Attitude') at 11 and 21 years was related to measures of cooperation at each age. Results for both the Down's syndrome and control group are given in Table 4.

Table 4: Relationships between mother's attitude and child cooperativeness: ages 11 and 21, Down's Syndrome and controls

		M.att.,11	Co-op 11	Co-op 21
Down's Syndrome				
	M.att.,11		p = .005	p = .007
	M.att.,21	n.s	n.s	n.s
Controls				
	M.att.,11		n.s	p = .055
	M.att.,21	p = .021	n.s	p = .0013

The tests used were Chi-square or Fisher's Exact Test, as appropriate.

In the Down's syndrome group, mother's attitude at 11 is related to cooperativeness not only at 11 but also at 21. The mother's attitude at 11 is not, however, related to her attitude at 21; neither is her attitude at 21 related to cooperativeness at 21; nor is cooperativeness at 11 related to the mother's attitude at 21 (suggesting that it is not the child's cooperativeness at 11 that results in a positive attitude in the mother at 21). So, although not related to her attitude at 21, mother's attitude at 11 is related to cooperativeness in the young person at 21. In addition, while cooperativeness at 21 is associated with cooperativeness at 11 (p = .048), the association with mother's attitude at 11 is the stronger one. Although the findings can only be regarded as tentative, they suggest that a positive attitude on the part of the mother of a Down's syndrome child may have a role in facilitating his later cooperativeness.

In the controls the position is somewhat different. Mother's attitude at 11 is not significantly related to cooperation at either 11 or 21 but is significantly related to her attitude at 21 (p = .021), which in turn is related to cooperation at that time.

Discussion

The data from the present study indicate some consistency in the ratings of the behaviours of this group of children with Down's syndrome from one age to another. In general, those who rarely had tantrums, were easy to manage, kept out of mischief and were cooperative at one age, were found easier to manage and more cooperative at subsequent ages. Where parental discipline was concerned, however, of all the numerous possible associations tested, only two were significant for the controls and only one – that of fewer behavioural problems at 21 if there had been little smacking in the family at four – for the young people with Down's Syndrome. There is, then, little evidence from this study that disciplinary methods had a noticeable effect on subsequent behaviour, although a positive attitude on the part of the mothers, especially those of the Down's syndrome children, appeared to be linked to a positive later outcome.

These findings, on the effects of discipline on later behaviour, run counter to straightforward expectation. Families, and in particular parents, expect that they will be able to influence their children's behaviour: that praise or reward will result in the child becoming more 'good'; more commonly, that punishment will result in the child becoming less 'bad'. 'All parents have in common that they intend to be effective in whatever means they use to instil "goodness" in their children' (Newson and Newson, 1989, p.21). Professionals, too, have similar expectations and are prepared, when they see parental methods failing, to advise the parents to adopt others, possibly more subtle, but still based on very similar principles to those underpinning the methods adopted by the parents. Both groups expect to be able to channel the child towards behaviours which are seen as both positive for him or herself and acceptable to society at large. This states the case simplistically, and both parents and professionals recognise that other factors will have a bearing on what the child does and how he behaves at any one time: nevertheless, they broadly believe that their efforts will make a significant contribution to the enhancement of their child's social and moral development.

So, how are we to explain the present findings which appear to support few of the expectations described above? Some cautions regarding the status of the present study will be put forward later, but first it may be relevant to explore how far these findings are in line with those of other studies. Since longitudinal studies in the area of learning difficulties are thin on the ground, studies of non-handicapped children will be discussed first; and, in particular, two major studies – those carried out in New York (Thomas and Chess 1977, Chess and Thomas 1984) and in Nottingham (Newson and Newson 1963, 1968, 1989). Both are longitudinal studies, from infancy to adulthood, based on substantial populations (133 and over 700 respectively). Both have included the exploration of the relationships to be seen between parental practices and, later, child character, temperament and behaviour. The studies differ from each other not only in the geographical but also in the social class background of their populations; the families in the New York study were almost exclusively professional and predominantly Jewish, and the children's mean IQs over 120 (Chess and Thomas 1984, page 51). The Nottingham sample was composed of families from a spread of social class that was reasonably representative of the area, and the children's IQs represented a wide range with a mean of just under 100. (Newson and Newson, 1977).

In the New York study, using a variety of measures and of statistical approaches, some temperamental continuities, from child-to adulthood, emerged. Temperament scores ('difficult-easy') at three were significantly related to adult temperament scores even when three year adjustment and parent attitude scores were controlled for, and were related also to adult adjustment. 'Adjustment' at three was also almost invariably related to adult adjustment.

On the other hand 'maternal attitudes' at three years were even more highly related to adult adjustment. 'Maternal attitudes' consisted of a set of eight cluster variables including strictness, inter-parental conflict and standards of living, of which interparental conflict emerged as especially important. The authors conclude: 'Outstanding in the high risk factors in childhood for a relatively poor overall adjustment in early adult life were difficult temperament, parental conflict, the presence of a behaviour disorder and the global adjustment score at age three years'. (Chess and Thomas 1984, p.99).

In this study, then, measurements of temperament and adjustment in childhood were good predictors of the same factors in adult life, and the data from the present study are in agreement with this conclusion. In addition, however, is the finding of the effect of parental attitudes and practices, although the major influence here seems to lie more with the parents' relationship with each other than with the parent's disciplinary approaches to their children (although the children's *response* to disciplinary measures, a factor labelled 'discipline', also features in some of the analyses).

In the Nottingham study, children who were rated as difficult at 11 years were more likely to be described as troublesome at 16, and more likely to go on to acquire a criminal record within four years (both significant at .001), than were those not difficult at 11 (Newson and Newson 1989). Here again there is some consistency in at least one kind of behaviour from one age to another. The more interesting of the Newsons' findings, however, relate to those concerned with the relationship between earlier parental disciplinary methods and later behaviour. Children who at 11 years were physically punished on a regular basis (once a week or more), where one parent at least used an implement to punish, and especially where these two factors were combined with the mother's reliance on corporal punishment, were more likely to be seen as troublesome at 16 and more likely eventually to acquire a criminal record than children not subjected to these regimes. This association held even where sex, family size and social class were controlled for. The extent to which parents were prepared to deceive the child (including the use of idle threats in order to exert discipline), a factor entitled by the Newsons 'bamboozlement', was also associated with poorer outcomes. The Newsons are careful not to draw the conclusion that punishment and deception *cause* troublesomeness and delinquency in the children, but they point to the fallacy of the dictum, 'Spare the rod and spoil the child'; their data do not show smacking and beating to be effective ways to teach children to behave better.

In the Nottingham study, then, there are some clear associations between the type of discipline exerted by the parents and later behavioural outcome, even if this is not the outcome expected or intended by the parents.

In the Down's syndrome study, the criterion of smacking used by the Newsons (distinguishing children who were smacked once a week or more from those who were smacked less) was considered. In the controls, 13% were smacked once a week or more at 11 years, compared with 18% in the Newsons' sample, but no relationship could be seen with how cooperative or easy to manage they were at 21. In the Down's syndrome group, 21% were smacked once a week or more at 11 years; at 21 years, all the relationships – with uncooperativeness, being difficult to manage, and showing two or more behaviour problems – showed, like the Nottingham study, more problems in those smacked more frequently, but the figures do not reach significance.

Besides these two studies of non-handicapped children, there are two longitudinal studies of children with learning difficulties which present data relevant to the present enquiry. The first is that of Richardson and his colleagues, on children with mild learning difficulties in Scotland; and the second that of Cunningham, Sloper, Byrne and associates, of Down's syndrome children in Manchester. Richardson et al (1985) report on a population sample of children with mild learning difficulties, studied during childhood and followed up at 16 and 22 years old. Each child with mild learning difficulties was individually matched for age, sex, area of residence and social class with a child without learning difficulties. Behaviour disturbance in the child and the stability of his or her upbringing were each rated on five-point scales. There was significantly more behaviour disturbance in the children with mild learning difficulties than in the comparison group, and in both groups behaviour disturbance increased as stability of upbringing decreased. When stability of upbringing was controlled for there was no significant difference in behaviour disturbance between the groups, nor did the presence of central nervous system involvement in the learning difficulties group contribute towards behaviour disturbance. Finally, the authors conclude that the greater degree of instability in the families of the children with mild learning difficulties was not due to the presence of these children but was more likely to result from other factors, such as low income, large family and 'various forms of social pathology' (Richardson et al 1985, page 7). Thus, from this study, the main conclusion is that the behaviour disturbance exhibited by this group of young people is probably not due to their intellectual disability but to the stressful conditions they experienced as they grew up.

The Manchester Down's syndrome study (Byrne et al 1988) has of course direct lines of comparison with the present one, and has the advantage of larger numbers (although the children reported on were younger, not yet having reached adolescence). Again some consistency of behaviour over time was noted: 75% of mothers who had been concerned about their Down's syndrome child's behaviour at ages ranging from two to ten years were still concerned about behaviour two to three years later. Factors which were related to behaviour problems included unemployment in the father, a poor relationship between mother and child, and low developmental status of the child. Despite one of the avowed aims of this study being to examine the factors that affected later development, efforts to relate disciplinary methods to later outcome were largely unproductive; the only associations found were of less problem behaviour where the mother had felt happy about how she handled the child ($r = 0.23$, $p = < 0.005$) and more problems where she had threatened to send the child away ($r = 0.22$, $p = < 0.05$, Sloper, personal communication).

Once again, child behaviour shows some uniformity from one age to another, and the disciplinary methods exerted by the mother are not shown to have had a pronounced effect on the future behaviour of the child.

Limitations of the present study

Before attempting to sum up the evidence from the studies discussed it is necessary to register some caution regarding the present study and the data derived from it. First, the numbers in the study are very small, which restricts the scope of statistical analysis which can be applied. If numbers had been larger it may have been possible to do more fine grained analyses – to look, for example, at the effectiveness of specific forms of punishment or reward, or more particularly, to look at the interaction of effects, which process may result in richer and more informative data than it has been possible to provide here. Second, the research instrument used (the questionnaire schedule) may not have been sufficiently sensitive to allow differences in parental approaches or in behaviour to emerge. The schedule was, however, similar to those used in other studies (Newson and Newson 1963, 1964, Hewett 1970) and it is difficult to see what alterations to it would have produced better results. Third, since all the data are derived from the mother's reports – due to resource constraints on the 21 year study no other agency was approached, neither had any of the young people in the study acquired a criminal record – any continuities seen could be construed as continuities of the mother's perceptions, and not necessarily of their off-springs' behaviour. Finally, there may yet be further analyses of the data to be done that would yield positive results, although it is believed that the major ones have already been carried out.

Nevertheless, despite these very considerable limitations the study has yielded a small number of results and the conclusions from them and from the other studies described above will now be discussed.

Conclusions

A major aim of the present study was to provide pointers to the most effective ways of handling the young child with Down's syndrome, to enable him or her to grow up into a happy, well adjusted individual who would be welcomed in his or her social setting. This aim was especially seen as important because so many mothers had expressed uncertainty as to how they should deal with children who were in some respects different from the children with whom they were familiar.

This aim has been largely unachieved. Our data cannot be translated into much in the way of confident recommendations as to how the young child with Down's syndrome should be dealt with. (It may be worth mentioning here that the study does not offer adequate information on the use and value of behavioural approaches. Only two mothers, of very difficult 11–year-old boys, received psychological advice on managing their sons. Both young men were rated as cooperative at 21, one as easy to manage and the other as not easy and showing a number of behaviour problems still). Nevertheless, although the specific aim of providing guidance for parents of Down's syndrome children has not been realised, looking at the five studies discussed a number of pointers are discernible. First, there are indications from the New York, the Manchester and the present studies that a certain degree of consistency of behaviour can be seen in the child from one age to another. Normal or handicapped, pleasant easygoing little children tend to be pleasant easygoing people as they grow older, and those with behavioural difficulties at one age are likely to demonstrate difficulties later on (although this is far from inevitable). Second, instability of upbringing, including factors such as poor care, absence of one or both parents, and parental discord are likely to be associated with a poor behavioural outcome in the child. Third, the use of physical punishment has not been shown in any of the studies discussed to result in better behaviour in the child in the future. On the contrary, its use on a regular basis and as the main form of discipline is followed in the Nottingham study by significantly worse levels of behaviour, and the trends in the present and, to some extent, in the Manchester studies are consistent with this.

This finding, although negative, could be cogent: many mothers of learning disabled children who use smacking say they do so because 'it's the only thing he understands'. This is a persuasive argument, and the association between a short sharp slap and here-and-now deterrence seems clear and straightforward. But many mothers are concerned not only with the here-and-now but also with the child's future behaviour. If they were aware that, far from having a reformative effect on him, frequent smacking appears to be linked with greater behaviour difficulties in the future, it might make them more hesitant about using corporal punishment. As one mother said, apropos of the effect of smacking on her four-year-old with Down's syndrome; 'It works at the time, but it doesn't really alter his behaviour'. This mother recognised that smacking was not a good long term approach to the management of her child's behaviour but found it difficult to come up with anything better. Perhaps she could have been helped to look more carefully at his behaviour, at the circumstances of and the spin-offs from it; and then helped to ensure that the consequences of any of his acceptable behaviours were more to his liking than were the consequences of his unacceptable behaviours. I say 'perhaps', for the functional analysis and reinforcement strategies outlined above have never been the subject of large scale longitudinal study. Although they look promising, we are not in a position to know whether they would perform any better than the other disciplinary methods that have come under such research scrutiny.

Similarly there may be a range of other ways in which mothers could be helped, from holidays and respite care to home helps and, especially, childcare – the largest single category of help that mothers of four-year-olds with Down's syndrome said they wished they had had (Carr 1975, p.99). What effect this kind of help to mothers would have on the later behaviour of their children is as yet unknown.

Finally, there is some evidence that the atmosphere in the home, i.e. the mother's relationship with and attitude to the child (possibly also the father's), or what Caldwell described as the 'interpersonal context' of child rearing, may have some influence on the child's later adjustment. If this is so, then as well as trying to help parents of difficult children to develop more effective ways of handling them in the short term we should perhaps also be looking for ways of enabling the parents to see and enjoy the positive aspects of their children's personalities and behaviours. In the long term, this might pay off.

References

Byrne, E. A., Cunningham, C. C., and Sloper, P. (1988) *Families and their children with Down's sydrome: one feature in common*. London: Routledge.

Caldwell, B. M. (1964) The effects of infant care. In Hoffman, M. L. and Hoffman, L. W. (eds). *Review of Child Development Research* Vol. 1. New York: Russell Sage Foundation.

Carr, J. (1975) *Young children with Down's syndrome*. London: Butterworths.

Carr, J. (1988) Six weeks to twenty one years old: a longitudinal study of children with Down's syndrome and their families. *Journal of Child Psychology and Psychiatry*, 29, 4., 407–431.

Chess, S. and Thomas, A. (1984) *Origins and evolution of behaviour disorders: from infancy to adult life*. New York: Brunner-Mazel.

Hewett, S. (1970) *The family and the handicapped child*. London: Allen and Unwin.

Newson, J. and Newson, E. (1963) *Infant Care in an Urban Community*. London: Allen and Unwin.

Newson, J. and Newson, E. (1964) *Four Years Old in an Urban Community*. London: Allen and Unwin.

Newson, J. and Newson, E. (1977) *Perspectives on School at Seven Years*. London: Allen and Unwin.

Newson, J. and Newson, E. (1989) *The extent of parental physical punishment in the UK*. London: APPROACH (Association for the Protection of All Children).

Richardson, S. A., Koller, H. and Katz, M. (1985) Relationship of upbringing to later behavior disturbance of mildly mentally retarded young people. *American Journal of Mental Deficiency* 90 (1) 1–8.

Thomas, A. and Chess, S. (1977) *Temperament and development*. New York. Brunner-Mazel.

Chapter 4

Interactions between offspring and parents in development

Stella Chess and Alexander Thomas

The topic of this book has been elaborated by the Clarkes in their classic and seminal publication *Early Experience, Myth and Evidence*. 'The whole of development is important, not merely the early years. There is as yet no indication that a given stage is clearly more formative than others; in the long-term all may be important' (Clarke and Clarke, 1976, p.272). The Clarkes then emphasize that even if the influence of infancy and early childhood is by *itself* very limited for long-term roles, it would be most unfortunate if this were mistranslated into 'it doesn't matter what happens early in life.' 'Children do suffer from undesirable environmental influences – bad institutions, "problem families", ghetto life, prejudice, etc.' (p.272).

We can pay our respects to the theses prepared by the Clarkes by reporting the findings documented by the New York Longitudinal Study (NYLS) and our other research projects.

The New York Longitudinal Study (NYLS) is our most extensive and intensive developmental study, comprising a native born middle-class American sample of 133 subjects followed from early infancy into the middle and late twenties. Our major goal was to identify the specific characteristics of temperament and its functional significance for healthy and disturbed psychological development (Thomas, Chess and Birch, 1968; Chess and Thomas, 1984; and Chess and Thomas, 1990).

We have conceptualized temperament as having a constitutional biological basis that influences the style or *how* of behaviour. Behaviour is also manifested by the abilities, or *what* of behaviour, and motivations, the *why* of behaviour. We have characterized nine categories of temperament – activity level, rhythmicity, approach or withdrawal, adaptability, threshold of responsiveness, intensity of reaction, quality of mood, distractibility, and attention span and persistence; and three constellations: (1) easy temperament (regularity of approach, high adaptability to change, and mild or moderate mood intensity, which is preponderantly positive); (2) difficult temperament (the opposite spectrum) and (3) slow-to-warm-up temperament (withdrawal, slow adaptability, and mild to moderate mood intensity) (Chess and Thomas, 1984). The majority of temperament researchers have followed our temperament definitions, but some others have offered several other formulations (Goldsmith, et al., 1987).

In our various publications, as cited above, we have formulated the concept of 'goodness of fit', which provides a model for the interaction of offspring and parents.

Briefly defined, goodness of fit exists when the demands and expectations of the parents and other people important to the child's life are compatible with the child's temperament, abilities, and other characteristics. With such a fit, healthy development and resiliency can be expected. Poorness of fit, on the other hand, exists when demands and expectations are excessive and not compatible with the child's temperament, abilities, and other characteristics. With such a fit, the child is likely to experience excessive stress and vulnerability, and healthy development is jeopardized. A similar concept of goodness of fit, or the term 'match or mismatch', has been utilized by a number of developmental psychologists (Gordon, 1981; Greenspan, 1981; Harkness and Super, in press; Lerner, 1984; Murphy, 1981).

The vulnerable child

The child may be vulnerable for a number of reasons. Amongst these are severe psychosocial pathology in the child's family or mental or physical handicaps. Our chapter is focused on the effects on vulnerability which result from poorness of fit in the parent-offspring interaction. First, we will generalize various factors in the parent-child interaction, which apply to the goodness of fit model.

Middle-class parents expect the growing child at sequential age-periods to master new levels of socialization activities and behaviour. The infant is expected to achieve regular sleep and feeding schedules, and to cooperate with bathing, dressing and toilet training. In the preschool years, the child is expected to learn safety precautions, adapt to the specific routines and rules of the individual family structure, begin to participate in organized play activity with peers, and to adapt to the activities and roles of play groups, day care centres and nursery schools. In the middle childhood years, parents begin to expect the youngster to master more complicated behaviours –

academic and social school functioning, responsibilities toward some of the family's needs, and the adaptation of the community's standards and values.

This process of the child's socialization is a two-way street. Parents and families differ in their child-care practices and attitudes. Some parents are permissive with regard to manners and social niceties; others have strict standards in this regard. Some parents may express affection openly; others are reserved. One type spends a great deal of time with their children in activities of joint interest; others are less involved. Some parents and children confide easily in each other on intimate personal issues; others do little of this kind of communication. There are parents who lay stress on the child's early socialization of various functions; others are less strict and demanding with respect to these achievements.

Fathers can play a very active role in their babies' daily care and concentrate upon specific activities as their children grow older. Children may be brought up in a tight nuclear family – father, mother and at most one brother or sister, while there are those who live in an extended family, with several sibs, and perhaps grandparents and other relatives close by.

Variants of the family structure have developed in increasing numbers in recent years. A high proportion of mothers now work outside the home; recent years have seen the emergence of a group of mature, self-supporting single mothers or fathers. The high divorce rate also makes for differing arrangements for children; custody with mother or father, or joint custody, for example.

Children are also different. Whether younger or older, children have individual differences in their talents and abilities, in their motivational interests and goals, and in their behavioural style or temperament.

It is this phenomenon of individual differences in children and in parents that can produce a goodness or poorness of fit. For example, one might find a professional family who expect their perfectly normal child with average intellectual endowment to achieve superior academic performance. Excessive stress and poorness of fit results in deleterious results on the child's development.

Another type of poorness of fit may result from a child's recreational goals. For example, a boy may develop passionate interests in natural phenomena – plants, flowers, exploring caves, etc., but have little interest or ability in athletics. The father may assume that a natural boy must be actively involved in sports, and may interpret his boy's disinterest in active physical games as abnormal. Maybe, the father worries, the boy is headed for disastrous homosexual development. The father pressures the boy continuously to turn off his interests and become successful at baseball or another similar activity, and the youngster increasingly becomes intimidated, anxious and insecure. (This illustration is an actual clinical case.) The poorness of fit is destined to a pathological developmental course.

Temperament and goodness or poorness of fit

The interaction between the child's individual temperamental characteristics and the parents' child care practices are further significant potential sources of poorness of fit. This happens because the many demands during the growing child's sequential age-periods, for more sophisticated socialization activities and behaviour, can be consonant or dissonant with the influence of the child's temperament upon the manner of response to the parents' expectations. If the child's socialization activities are deviant from the parents' expectations, they may respond negatively. Typically, parental explanations include 'this is an abnormal child', 'this is our fault, in some way or other', or they feel that the child is intimidating and victimizing them. A poorness of fit is then inevitable through interactional process: the child cannot favourably master the parents' expectations in view of his or her temperament; the parents then respond unfavourably to the child's behaviour; the parents then demand forcefully that the child change; this demand intensifies or increases the disapproved child behaviour; the parents react more negatively, and the poorness of fit fulfills the potential of the child's behaviour problem development, leaving the parents with feelings of helplessness, guilt, resentment or necessity to punish.

There are innumerable examples of the vicious cycle of a poor fit of parent-child interaction that produces a vulnerable child with a behaviour disorder (Thomas, Chess and Birch, 1968; Chess and Thomas, 1984; and Chess and Thomas, 1987). Basically, no temperament pattern confers an immunity to behaviour disorder development, nor is any fated to create psychopathology.

Cultural factors and goodness of fit

As indicated above, middle-class parents expect their growing children to master cultural expectations at sequential age-periods of socialization, task activities, and other maturational demands. In some cases, however, certain parents have idiosyncratic norms that may reflect different standards. The parents who have such special demands may achieve a goodness of fit, especially with the temperamentally easy child, who has approach responses, easy adaptability and positive mood and mild intensity of expression. Parents may shape such a child, who then develops the idiosyncratic behaviour pattern expected by the parents' unusual expectation. However, when the child subsequently begins to socialize with the peer group, the goodness of fit changes to a poorness of fit. As one example, one set of parents had trained their four-year-old boy, Harold, to acquire formal manners and meticulous politeness. These 'mid-Victorian' standards had been accepted thoroughly by their temperamentally easy son. But Harold then began to participate in play and social activities with the community peer group. Rather than receiving approval for his parents' demands of behaviour, his peer companions evaluated Harold as 'queer' and worthy of being a scape-goat. He became a bewildered youngster, and the butt of the tricks and mockery of his age-period companions. The parents consulted one of us when they became aware of Harold's helpless and anxious behaviour. In a playroom session the boy indeed acted as 'a stuffed shirt', a caricature of his parents' formalities, and it became clear why he had become the peer group's scapegoat.

Fortunately, the parents were able to understand Harold's problem and accepted the advice to permit the child to adopt peer standards outside of the home while within the family he could conform to the parents' idiosyn-cratic standards. With the parents' acceptance of this schedule of specific practices and attitudes, Harold changed his behaviour appropriately and achieved a goodness of fit with his community social group.

Another example illuminated the influence of cultural norms in the NYLS. Forty-two parents with concerns about their children's possible be-havioural disturbances consulted one of us (S.C.). The author's standard clinical evaluation in each case provided a diagnostic judgement and the dynamics of the psychopathy were found in most of these instances to be structured by a poorness of fit. Parent guidance was deemed to be the optimum intervention, aimed at achieving the parents' understanding of the parent-child dissonance. Specific changes in the parents' attitudes and beha-viour were recommended to rectify the child's behaviour disorder. Only a few guidance sessions were required to bring about positive results in 50% of the parents who responded to the consultant's advice. The favourable outcome occurred with a variety of types of parent personalities and a range of children's temperamental characteristics.

But parent guidance was a clear failure in all of the disturbed children with the distractible and nonpersistent temperamental characteristics. These parents attached great importance to educational achievement for both sexes and especially to success in professional or business courses for their male children. For both of these goals persistence, discipline and concentration were considered to be vital for successful careers. If, by contrast, there was a distractible and non-persistent child, the parent, especially of a boy, would consistently label the child as 'lacking in character' and 'lazy'. The parents of children with difficult temperament characteristics, which included slow adaptability and negative intense mood, could more easily accept and respond to guidance. The negative consequence of these characteristics could be ameliorated by patience and flexibility and parents could believe that children with such characteristics would eventually function with persistence and intensity, characteristics judged as desirable within the norms of their culture. But the parents of individuals with distractibility and nonpersistence could not understand that they could function successfully and sometimes exhibit exceptional and talented abilities. The parents rejected guidance suggestions such as encouraging short periods of work and relaxation breaks to enhance achievement. They could not accept the thought that their children would maintain distractible and nonpersistent styles of learning, no matter how well mastery was finally achieved in this manner. So, all the parents of these four children were failures in parent guidance and it was no surprise that all these children were boys (Thomas, Chess and Birch, 1968).

We also compared the NYLS sample with a group having different socio-cultural values, using children of stable working-class Puerto Rican families (Korn and Gannon, 1982). The behavioural adjustment of the children at five years was analyzed statistically. A significant correlation was found between symptomatology and a difficult temperament rating in the NYLS youngsters, but not in the Puerto Rican group. The most likely explanation for this finding appeared to be differences in parental child-care practices in the two samples. The NYLS parents made many more demands than the other group for the early acquisition of regular sleep and feeding schedules, for the establishment of early self-feeding and self-dressing, as well as for quick adaptation to new situations and for relating to new people – demands which are especially stressful for children with difficult temperament.

There is one especially dramatic study which highlights the importance of cultural influence in parent-child interaction. DeVries studied children of a semi-nomadic tribe in Kenya, living in the sub-Sahara region (deVries, 1984). He obtained temperament ratings on 47 infants, age two to four months, using a translation of the Carey questionnaire, at a time when a severe drought was just beginning. With these ratings, he identified the 10 infants with the most easy temperament, and the ten with the most difficult temperament. He returned to this tribal area five months later, by which time the drought had killed off 97 percent of the cattle herd. He was able to locate seven of the easy babies and six of the difficult ones. The other families had moved in an attempt to escape the drought. Of the seven 'easy' babies, five had died, whereas all of the six 'difficult' infants had survived. Thus, the adaptive fit of easy versus difficult temperament is indeed a matter of the goodness or poorness of fit with specific characteristics of the child's environment. This was a tribe with a warrior tradition. It can be postulated that the 'difficult' children's survival as a group may have been influenced either or both by their more intense indication of hunger and also because their vigour was prized as an expression of the fierce warrior tradition of the culture.

The resilient child

As emphasized at the outset of this chapter, the Clarkes have challenged the usual prediction that in early childhood stressful experience is fated to lead to a vulnerable and unfavourable life course (Clarke and Clarke, 1976). Their thesis has been confirmed in the dramatic finding in Werner and Smith's large scale longitudinal study in Kauai, Hawaii. 'In this cohort of 698, 204 children developed severe behaviour or learning problems at *some time* during the first two decades of their lives . . . Yet there were others, also *vulnerable* – exposed to poverty, biological risks, and family instability, and reared by parents with little education or serious mental health problems – who remained *invincible* and developed into competent and autonomous young adults who "worked well, played well, loved well and expected well"' (Werner and Smith, 1982, pp.2–3).

A major challenge to developmental psychology and psychiatry is to be found in serious studies such as this on the sources of resiliency to such stress-resistant, high-risk children. As Garmezy points out (Garmezy, 1981, p.215), this is 'an area in which there exists neither a substantial body of empirical data nor a formal conceptualization'. However, a number of empirical studies and pilot projects have demonstrated the possibilities of positive mastery and resiliency in disadvantaged and deprived children.

Parent-child interactions and resiliency

In the present chapter, we have identified in our NYLS a number of parent-child interactions which have led to sequential outcomes for resiliency. While the quantitative NYLS data has suggested directions for exploration of this issue of resiliency, the identification of effective mechanisms in individuals brings us into clear agreement with Michael Rutter's suggestion of an idiographic approach. 'It is difficult to make valid, broad, sweeping generalizations about human behaviour. Attention must be paid to the specification of person-situation interactions . . . it may be suggested that it is preferable to take an idiographic approach, which explicitly focuses on the individuality of human beings – not just in the degree to which they show particular traits, or even in terms of the traits which are relevant to them, but more generally in terms of the idiosyncrasies which make each person uniquely different from all others' (Rutter, 1980, p.3).

We have used our idiosyncratic analysis of the outcomes of resilient children subjected to stress of marked degree compared with duration of severity and/or various characteristics of stress. This approach has found the concept of goodness or poorness of fit, as we have formulated it earlier in this chapter, to be highly useful in tracing the specific dynamic sequences in parent-child intervention in the development of success or failure in resiliency in individual children.

Brief case vignettes will illustrate this generalization.

Goodness of fit and resiliency

Bernice showed an easy temperament from infancy into later childhood and early adult life. Her psychometric tests and school functioning have always displayed superior intelligence. Both parents were permissive and flexible and agreed upon their child care practices and attitudes. The child experienced no special problems or demands in the early child-parents relationship, and her successive age-stage socialization periods were mastered smoothly. Bernice then had to cope with the separation and divorce of the parents in her early school years. Each parent remarried and Bernice, with her sibs, lived with mother and stepfather. She adapted quickly to both stepparents, who were amicable people, and showed a minimum of stress reactions in her relationship with both sets of parents as her years went on. Now, as a young adult, Bernice has demonstrated her positive functioning throughout her academic life, her social life and notably in her self-confidence. She has an excellent marriage; husband and wife have adopted a Korean orphan with whom they have a close bond, and subsequently had a 'home-grown' young baby. Bernice had no unusual psychological stress through a demanding academic curriculum and has now launched her professional career.

By contrast, Carl had one of the most extreme difficult temperament scores of the NYLS subjects in his early years. Any one of Carl's new experiences, whether the first bath or first solid foods in infancy, the beginning of nursery school and elementary school, first birthday parties or the first shopping trips, evoked stormy responses, with loud crying and struggling to get away. Fortunately, his father responded positively to the young boy's behaviour. The father, himself a quiet and mild-mannered person, looked on his son's shrieking and turmoil as a sign of 'lustiness'. His father learned to anticipate Carl's reactions, and quickly learned that when he was patient, despite intense negative reactions, Carl would finally adapt positively. By contrast his mother condemned herself as a 'bad mother' who had created Carl's difficult behaviour. The mother was so overwhelmed by guilt that she required psychotherapy. With this professional help, her husband's supportive reassurance that Carl was a normal child, and with the boy's gradual positive behavioural functioning, the mother finally resolved her guilt and self-blame with the passage of time.

With this goodness of fit, Carl's school and social adaptation became easier and successful as he matured, and did not develop into a behaviour problem. Also, in his later childhood and high school years, Carl met very few radical new situations. He lived in the same community and went through the neighborhood school with the same schoolmates and friends. Academic progress was gradual and new situations were not introduced abruptly. He became enthusiastically involved with a number of activities and developed an appropriate, positive and confident self-image.

The story suddenly changed when Carl went off to college, away from home. He was simultaneously confronted with a whole series of new situations – strange living surroundings, an entirely new peer group, new types of faculty approaches, school schedules and curriculum, and a complex relationship with a girl student with whom he began to live. Several months after he started at college, Carl requested a consultation with one of us (S.C.). He felt depressed, unable to cope with the academic and social situation at college, had made virtually no friends and found studying difficult. He was bewildered at what was happening, explaining 'This just isn't me!' I agreed 'it isn't me', but explained to him the significance of temperament. Again, as when he had been faced with the many new adaptive demands in early childhood, his temperamental responses of withdrawal and intense negative reactions were now expressed. I explored all the other possibilities for his difficulties, but no evidence of any of these were elucidated. It was clear that a new poorness of fit led to his symptoms, in contrast to his benign previous years of a goodness of fit.

Only one discussion was necessary with Carl to clarify for him his temperamental pattern and the techniques he could use to achieve adaptation. He took a number of steps to force himself to discipline himself with regard to his various new situations and new demands, no matter how uncomfortable he felt. By the end of the academic year Carl reported that his difficulties had disappeared and his subsequent functioning had been on the previous positive level. I cautioned Carl that similar negative reactions to new experiences might occur in the future. His response was 'That's all right. I know how to handle them now.' And Carl was right. Once he had gained his insight he had achieved mastery over any potential temperamental vulnerability. By now, in his late twenties, his life course has been of successful achievement of his chosen professional career, with a good capacity for intimate personal relationship and friendships.

Two illustrations, Bernice and Carl, emphasize how the growth of resiliency during childhood and adulthood can be achieved by goodness of fit, with different temperaments, differing parent-child relationships, and diverging pathways to the mastery of stresses.

Poorness of fit and resiliency

As discussed earlier in the chapter, poorness of fit develops if or when, due to the child's temperament or other characteristics, he or she cannot fulfill the expectations and standards that the parents have for the child's socialization and behaviour. Such dissonance of the parent-child interaction produces excessive stress in the child and, consequently, lack of resiliency with behaviour disorder development.

Fortunately, a number of possible interventions can reduce such excessive stress with resiliency and improvement or recovery from the behaviour disorder. Amelioration of the poorness of fit may succeed by use of parent guidance or unpredictable adventitious influences. Alternatively, the child may learn to cope with the parents' excessive demands.

Parent guidance is described in the section 'Cultural Factors and Goodness of Fit' in which the case vignette, Harold, is illustrated. To repeat, the clinical evaluation of a child's behaviour disorder focused on the identification of the dynamics of a poorness of fit of the parent-child interaction. Once the specific pattern is identified, a program can then be formulated which will relieve the excessive stress that the child is experiencing. This program can be spelled out with the parents, and their understanding and implementation of the changes to be made in their actions can be monitored in the follow-up sessions.

The strategy of parent guidance rests on the commitment to the *individualization* of the treatment strategy for any child and set of parents, and the specific guidance advice may vary qualitatively from one child to another. By contrast, counselling in general global terms is inadequate and even counterproductive. [Our parent guidance program is detailed in Chess and Thomas, 1984, Chapter 20].

Parent guidance was evaluated by qualitative clinical judgment as moderately or highly successful in approximately 50 percent of the forty two NYLS childhood behaviour disorder cases. This rating was estimated both by the indication of parental change in the desired direction and by improvement in the behaviour disorder, two factors which went hand in hand in a reciprocal relationship. In the other 50 percent of cases, however, parent guidance was judged to be unsuccessful.

Unpredictable adventitious influences. The interplay of parent and child is so variable and complex that unpredictable adventitious influences can sometimes dramatically change a goodness to a poorness of fit or vice versa. Two case vignettes will illustrate this point.

In her early years Beth was temperamentally active, approaching and intense. This temperamental combination led her to a pattern of impulsivity which gave her occasional behavioural difficulties. But these childhood problems disappeared with quiet, firm, and consistent limit setting by her parents. With this goodness of fit, Beth's development through childhood was essentially positive and favourable. When she was 13, her behavioural difficulties again appeared in relationship to increased academic demands, the onset of puberty, and the complexities of adolescent peer interactions. Shortly thereafter, her father, who had always been a stabilizing authoritative (but not authoritarian) figure in the family, died suddenly and unexpectedly. The same advice for quiet, consistent limit setting had again been recommended, but this time the mother could not follow this regime. Bereft of her husband and his influence, stretched to her limits physically by having to fulfill a full-time, demanding and difficult job, while attending to the needs of her three other young daughters, she was unable to cope with Beth's crises and outbursts. Beth's problems escalated, her interaction with her mother and sisters became increasingly hostile and disruptive, and she developed a severe sociopathic behaviour disorder. It appears that if her father had lived, he and her mother, working together as they had in Beth's earlier years, would probably have been able to cope with this highly unfavourable adolescent development. The adventitious event, the father's death, had transformed a good fit to a poor fit.

Nancy, in her early years, was temperamentally difficult. Her father demanded quick positive adaptation which this temperamentally difficult child could not possibly achieve. The father responded with rigid, punitive criticisms, creating excessive stress for Nancy, and a severe poorness of fit. By the time she was six years old, she had marked symptoms of explosive anger outbursts, fear of the dark, hair-pulling, and poor peer group relations. Parent guidance was a complete failure. The mother was intimidated by both the father and the child.

In spite of all explanations of Nancy's intrinsic positive potential, the father could only evaluate her, in his terms, as 'a rotten kid'. Then, unexpectedly, when in the fourth and fifth grades, she showed evidence of musical and dramatic talent. This now brought increasingly favourable attention and praise from other parents and classmates. Fortunately for Nancy, these talents also ranked high in her parents' own hierarchy of desirable attributes. Her father now began to see his daughter's intense and explosive personality, not as 'a rotten kid' but as evidence of a budding artist. Nancy was now a child he could be proud of, and he easily accepted her behavioural pattern as evidence of her 'artistic temperament'. Both parents began to relax and relate to Nancy, and in the next few years behaviour problems literally melted away. When we interviewed her in our routine follow-up at age 17, she was bright, alert and lively, and showed no symptoms of psychological malfunctioning. Her self-description as 'hot-headed' was confirmed in a separate interview with her parents, but neither she nor her parents considered this to be a problem. We have now followed her until her late twenties and she has consistently maintained a positive life-course. Thus, an adventitious unpredictable modest talent had transformed a negative to a positive fit. It is of interest that in our interviews with her in her twenties, she has recalled her childhood as a happy one, remembers a mutuality of interests with her father, and had no recollection of his hypercritical and punitive attitudes and behaviour toward her in early childhood.

Emotional distancing. Several youngsters in the NYLS clinical problem group have spontaneously developed a coping mechanism for avoiding the excessive stress generated by a severe poorness of fit in the parent-child relationship. Instead of continuing to struggle actively but helplessly and unable to achieve the parent's unrealistically persistent expectations, the youngsters separated from the intense pathogenic emotional entanglements with their parents. One youngster remained as aloof as possible from the parent's nagging anger by remaining away from home as much as possible. He made friends, involved himself in special activities after school, found part-time jobs, found parent surrogates. Once such a child grew older and reached adolescence, he or she became progressively able to achieve disentanglement from the parents. We label this mechanism for coping with the excessive stress of an unhealthy parent-offspring interaction *emotional distancing*. Two case vignettes can illustrate this coping mechanism.

Roy was in constant conflict with a compulsive, pressuring and controlling mother. His father was a passive figure who dealt with his wife's battles with their son by avoidance. The boy's conflict with his mother did not derive from a difficult temperament pattern, but rather from his high distractibility. This led typically to 'forgetting' various tasks or failing to meet time deadlines. To the mother, Roy's failure to carry through a number of her requests and demands only meant that he was challenging and opposing her.

With this severe conflict with his mother, Roy developed a number of tics and adjustment difficulties in his first school years. A number of our parent guidance discussions with the mother failed to alter in the least her subjective judgments of her son's behaviour, or to alter her intrusive, controlling demands. However, as he grew older, first in middle childhood and then in adolescence, Roy learned on his own to limit his conflicts with her. This he did primarily by not communicating his plans and activities to her, and in effect progressively freezing her out of his life. With this effective decrease of the stress and tension in his life, Roy's symptoms gradually improved until they had disappeared in adolescence, and his peer relationships and school activities became competent and sources of positive feedback. When interviewed at age 22, Roy's functioning was positive in the important areas of his life and there was no evidence of significant psychopathology. Of interest, though his emotional detachment from his mother was pronounced, he was now able to be more objective about her, realizing that she had psychological problems of her own, which were unrelated to him, and perhaps they could get to accept each other. At his most recent follow-up, Roy, now 30 years of age, had continued a positive development in his life course. With his mother he was now 'closer than it has ever been', though this closer relationship has not basically changed their emotional distancing. He keeps his visits to her brief and makes many engagements that dilute the time spent together.

Olga was a temperamentally difficult child. By her middle childhood, her parents had developed negative and critical judgments and expectations of her, and she became the family 'scapegoat'. She exhibited symptoms of explosive anger outbursts, insomnia and overeating and by age 13 these had become severe enough to warrant the diagnosis of conduct disorder. By age 16, Olga was a drug abuser, mainly of barbiturates, and severe depressive symptoms had developed. Clinical evaluation at that time evoked the diagnosis of severe depressive neurosis.

However, a most unpredictable and dramatic change occurred within the year. She went through a sudden religious conversion experience with no apparent precipitating event or influences. Following this, progressive improvement in symptoms and functioning developed, and when interviewed at age 20 only mild residual symptoms remained. Follow-up inquiry two years later confirmed the continuation of positive functioning. Her new religious commitment was maintained but the ritual observances were quite superficial. At her most recent follow-up, then at 27 years of age, Olga's positive life-course has continued. Her religious conversion has now changed and she has begun to regain her family's religious heritage. She also now speaks in positive terms, even emotionally, of her present relationship with both parents.

In reviewing her life course, it appears that Olga coped with the excessive stress of her parent-child poorness of fit by emotional distancing through her religious conversion. Her separateness from her parents' religious beliefs enabled her to neutralize the previous excessive stress in her intensive entanglement with them.

Several other NYLS subjects, like Roy and Olga, demonstrated resiliency, becoming able to cope with a pathogenic poorness of fit by emotional distancing from the parents. However, others of our behaviourally disturbed youngsters did not achieve effective emotional distance from a vulnerable destructive interaction with a parent. We can only speculate as to possible explanations for the achievement of this coping mechanism, but we have not, as yet, found any answers. Hopefully, further NYLS data analyses in progress will shed light on this intriguing issue.

Self Insight: Parents and others can, in many ways, help their children's self-insight grow over the developmental years. Such insight is a highly important asset in the youngster's learning how to master environmental demands and challenges effectively and appropriately.

To give one example, Elaine had a markedly difficult temperament pattern from early childhood and onward. Her parents were bewildered by her frequent and loud outbursts of anger, could not find any reason for this behaviour, and reacted, as so many other parents do with a child with difficult temperament, with guilt and anger themselves. This only made matters worse in such an escalating poorness of fit, and Elaine finally developed symptoms of a behaviour disorder. The parents sought our help, and a clinical evaluation clearly identified the pathogenic parent-child interaction. The parents were thoughtful and realistic adults, listened carefully to our analysis and understood the nature of their girl's problem. They changed their attitudes and behaviour according to our parent guidance approach and it took only a short time for Elaine's symptoms to disappear and for her to develop a progressively close relationship to both her parents.

Over Elaine's childhood and adolescent years, she struggled with her stressful, intense negative reactions to various new situations – new schools, new peer groups, new work demands, etc. At such points her parents would reassure her, explain that her turmoil was a normal reaction due to her temperamental characteristics, and reassure her that she would cope with this stress, and gradually adapt successfully. And indeed, this sequence occurred with each new demanding situation, ending with mastery. Now, in her most recent follow-up, this 29–year old young woman, mature and poised, had a happy personal life and is launched on a successful professional career. She thinks her self-confidence is increasing. 'I've come a long way'. With new situations 'Each new stage of life brings on a little anxiety for me. I was always that way.' She clearly remembered that her parents understood her anxiety from consultation with us, encouraged her that she would be O.K. and 'pointed out to me all the new things I had done'.

In this recent interview, when asked how often she gets angry she smiled and said 'hardly ever'. Elaine explained that she had the tendency to violent outbursts if she got angry, just as she did in her earlier years. But she has learned, especially from her parents, that such outbursts would boomerang on her. At the same time, she explained, she did not want to avoid issues and confrontation, when they were necessary, so she had taught herself various strategies to deal with such issues effectively, but in a way so that she did not have to become angry.

No one approach in life can be a panacea. Not all cases in our study have ended up as well from childhood to early adult life as this young woman has done. But we have been impressed in so many cases at how this kind of insight into one's own temperament can be a positive force for healthy psychological development and functioning.

Conclusion

In this chapter we have documented a number of our own research findings that have confirmed the Clarkes' fundamental thesis, 'The whole of development is important, not merely the early years. There is as yet no indication that a given stage is clearly more formative than others; in the long-term all may be important' (Clarke and Clarke, 1976, p.272).

This chapter can be concluded by the illuminating vision of the great novelist, Gabriel Garcia Marquez: 'he allowed himself to be swayed by his conviction that human beings are not born once and for all on the day their mothers give birth to them but that life obliges them over and over again to give birth to themselves' (Garcia Marquez, 1988, p.165).

References

Chess, S. and Thomas, A. (1984). *Origins and Evolution of Behaviour Disorders*: From Infancy to Early Adult Life. New York: Brunner/Mazel.

Chess, S. and Thomas, A. (1987). *Know Your Child*. New York: Basic Books.

Chess, S. and Thomas, A. (1990). The New York Longitudinal Study (NYLS): The Young Adult Periods. *Canadian Journal of Psychiatry*, 35: 557–561.

Clarke, A. M. and Clarke, A. D. B. (1976). *Early Experience: Myth and Evidence*. London: Open Books.

deVries, M. W. (1984). Temperament and Infant Mortality among the Masai of East Africa. *American Journal of Psychiatry*, 141: 1189–1194.

Garcia, Marquez, G. (1988). *Love in the Time of Cholera*, translated from the Spanish by Edith Grossman. New York: Penguin.

Garmezy, N. (1981). Children under Stress. Perspectives in antecedents and correlates of vulnerability and resistance to psychopathology. In Rubin, A., Aronoff, J., Barclay, A. M. and Zucker, R. A. (Eds.) *Further Exploration in Personality*. New York: Wiley and Sons.

Goldsmith, H. H., Buss, A. H., Plomin, R., Rothbart, M. K., Thomas, A., and Chess, S., Hinde, R. A. and McCall, R. B. (1987). Roundtable What is temperament? Four approaches. *Child Development*, 58: 505–529.

Gordon, B. N. (1981). Child temperament and adult behaviour: An Exploration of 'goodness of fit'. *Child Psychiatry and Human Development*, 11: 167–178.

Greenspan, S. I. (1981). *Psychopathology and Adaptation in Infancy and Early Childhood*, New York: International Universities Press, pp. 63, 204.

Harkness, S. and Super, C. M. (in press). Culture and psychopathology. In Lewis, M. and Miller, S. (Eds.) *Handbook of Developmental Psychopathology*, New York: Plenum, in press.

Korn, S. J. and Gannon, S. (1983). Temperament, Cultural Variation, and Behaviour Disorder in Preschool Children. *Child Psychiatry and Human Development*, 13, 203–212.

Lerner, J. V. (1984). The Role of Temperament in Psychosocial Adaptation in Early Adolescence: A test of a 'goodness of fit' model. *Journal of Genetic Psychology*, 143: 149–157.

Murphy, L. B. (1981). Explorations in Child Personality. In Rubin, A. I., Aronoff, J., Barclay, A. M. and Zucker, R. A. (Eds.) *Further Explorations in Personality*, New York: Wiley and Sons, p. 168.

Rutter, M. (1980). Introduction. In Rutter, M. (Ed.) *Scientific Foundations of Developmental Psychiatry*. London: Heinemann, pp. 1–7.

Thomas, A. and Chess, S. (1977). *Temperament and Development*. New York: Brunner/Mazel.

Thomas, A., Chess, S. and Birch, H. G. (1968). *Temperament and Behaviour Disorders in Childhood*. New York: New York University Press, pp. 63, 204.

Werner, E. E. and Smith, R. S. (1982). *Vulnerable but Invincible*. New York: McGraw-Hill.

Chapter 5

Escaping from a bad start

Doria Pilling

The individual's potential for development

To me, the work of the Clarkes is synonymous with optimism, but it is an optimism not simply based on a humanitarian attitude. It is a somewhat cautious optimism, always firmly grounded in research evidence that has been painstakingly examined, its methodological strengths and weaknesses meticulously weighed up and taken into account. Above all their work has been intertwined with the theme that there is always the possibility of an individual changing, improving in intellectual abilities and personality characteristics.

In 1960 the Clarkes pointed out that a depriving environment, apart from the most extreme, does not act in a mechanically similar way on all children and that next to nothing was known of the reasons for this, and of the factors determining differences in vulnerability. They made a few suggestions: 'inherited predisposition, experiences preceding and circumstances surrounding the deprivation, and the child's personality *in toto*, in addition to the deprivation itself'.

By the mid-1980s, when they were reviewing 30 years of child psychology (Clarke and Clarke 1986), there had been several important studies specifically concerned with the factors related to vulnerability and resilience (e.g. Elder et al 1984; Garmezy and Tellegen 1984; Werner and Smith 1982). These certainly suggested that vulnerability was related to external forces and not just those within the child. Nevertheless there was still a dearth of studies concerned with differences in recovery from adverse circumstances.

Social disadvantage and development in the National Child Development Study

This brings me to the point where I was fortunate enough to become personally acquainted with Alan Clarke, having already been familiar with the writings of both the Clarkes for many years. I started work in 1983 on a study at the National Children's Bureau investigating the factors associated with 'escape' from disadvantage. It was decided to set up a small Advisory Group, which Alan Clarke very generously agreed to join.

The study drew on, and was in the tradition of, previous work carried out at the National Children's Bureau, on children from a disadvantaged background, in the National Child Development study (NCDS). One of the three longitudinal studies in Britain, this has followed up at the ages of seven, 11, 16 and 23 all the children, approximately 16,000, born in England, Scotland and Wales in the week March 3rd to 9th 1958. Those born abroad in this week, but living in Britain at the time of one of the first three follow-ups, were added to the sample, it being possible to identify them through the schools. But there was no similar means by which those entering the country after this could be identified and added to the sample at the time of the 23–year follow-up.

The clearest findings from the NCDS have been the association between various social circumstances and school attainment and behaviour (e.g. Davie et al 1972; Fogelman 1975). If single 'disadvantaging' factors were independently linked with poorer attainment and behaviour, how would children who were multiply disadvantaged fare? This question led to the study of multiply disadvantaged children in the NCDS.

Children in the NCDS were selected as being multiply disadvantaged if they had experienced disadvantages in three areas – income, housing and family situation (large family or one parent). These were all circumstances that research evidence had shown to be independently linked with poorer development, with the possible exception of the one-parent family. Here the link was probably for the most part with the accompanying material adversities, rather than the parental situation itself, but as these were the result of there being only one adult in the family it was seen as reasonable to regard this as a disadvantaging social factor (Essen and Wedge 1982).

The first study of multiply disadvantaged children in the NCDS (Wedge and Prosser 1973) was of those who had experienced disadvantages in the three areas by the age of 11 (i.e. taking into account their circumstances at the time of the seven- and 11–year follow-ups). On tests used at the 11–year NCDS follow-up, about five times as many of the non-disadvantaged children as the multiply disadvantaged had 'good' reading ability (scores in approximately the top third of the range) and four times as many had 'good' maths ability. A second study of multiply disadvantaged children (Essen and Wedge 1982) had similar results, with just over five times as many of those non-disadvantaged as multiply disadvantaged children at 16 scoring in the top third on each test at the 16–year follow-up. This study was also able to show that the attainment and adjustment of the multiply disadvantaged children was as would be expected from their combination of disadvantaging circumstances, although it was no worse.

The criteria of disadvantage were the same in the second study of multiple disadvantage (Essen and Wedge 1982) as the first (Wedge and Prosser 1973), but the definition of multiple disadvantage was slightly different, in that children had to have experienced disadvantages in all three areas – income, housing and family situation – at the same point in time to be included. The sample for the study consisted of those identified as multiply disadvantaged at the time of the 11– or 16–year follow-ups, or at both times. The main reason for adopting this particular definition of disadvantage in the second study was that one of its main features was the exploration of the extent to which disadvantage during childhood is transitory or persistent.

The Essen and Wedge (1982) study of multiply disadvantaged children in the NCDS was part of the 'transmitted deprivation' research programme, arising out of the famous speech by Sir Keith Joseph in 1972, then Secretary of State at the DHSS. He asked why deprivation persisted in relatively affluent post-war Britain, and why it appeared to be concentrated in particular families in successive generations, and speculated whether it would be possible to break the cycle by discovering the mechanisms through which it occurred.

In their exploration of the continuity of disadvantage, Essen and Wedge (1982) were not able to investigate whether children in the NCDS who came from multiply disadvantaged families would suffer the same kinds of deprivations as their parents in adulthood; the latest information available on the cohort at that time was at the age of 16. But they were able to show that the children had characteristics, in terms of poorer school attainments and social adjustment, that made it likely that they would be multiply disadvantaged later in life.

There was actually found to be a considerable discontinuity of disadvantage during childhood – at least in the sense of having simultaneous disadvantages in the three criteria areas of income, housing and family situation. Of all those identified as multiply disadvantaged at 11 or 16 (6% of the total cohort), only a quarter were multiply disadvantaged at both ages, a half at 11 and a quarter at 16. The amount of discontinuity suggested that the children were not an extreme group with long-term disadvantages, set apart from other children. It suggested that those identified as multiply disadvantaged at any one age are likely to be part of a much larger group experiencing this combination of disadvantages at some stage in childhood.

Children who were multiply disadvantaged at either follow-up generally had many more difficulties in their lives – apart from those included in the criteria of disadvantage – than the non-disadvantaged. In the main, those not yet or no longer disadvantaged suffered these additional problems – such as, mothers with chronic ill-health, poor preventive health care, greater likelihood of having been 'in care' – almost to the same extent as those who were disadvantaged at the time. For example, at the time of the 11–year follow-up, both those multiply disadvantaged at this age and those not yet disadvantaged (the disadvantaged at 16 only), were ten times as likely to have been 'in care' as the non-disadvantaged children. For many, their adversities were by no means transitory. On the whole, those multiply disadvantaged at both ages tended to experience more additional difficulties than those multiply disadvantaged at 11 or 16 only.

Very disappointingly, children who had been multiply disadvantaged at 11 but were no longer so – in study terms – at 16, had attainment and adjustment scores that were only very slightly better than those of the children who were multiply disadvantaged at 16. This was so even after allowances had been made for other adverse circumstances that might affect attainment or behaviour.

The picture looked gloomy for the multiply disadvantaged children, but there was a brighter side. Not all of them did badly on the attainment tests. At 16, 21% had reading test scores and 14% maths test scores that were above average for the cohort as a whole. Even here there seemed to be factors holding these children back, for they had entered for fewer public examinations than non-disadvantaged children of similar attainment, although when they did enter they were almost as likely to pass.

How did those with above average scores on the reading or maths test, the 'higher achievers', differ from the rest of the multiply disadvantaged? The main difference was in behaviour and attitudes. They were much better behaved than the rest of the disadvantaged, being at least as well-behaved as the non-disadvantaged children. They were more highly motivated towards school work, being similar in this to the non-disadvantaged. Both their aspirations for further education and those of their parents for them were considerably higher than those of the rest of the disadvantaged, although they were well short of those for the cohort as a whole. They were also more likely to be boys than the rest of the disadvantaged (62% and 52% respectively), to no longer be disadvantaged at 16, and to go to schools where there was a higher proportion of children with fathers in non-manual jobs. These findings set the scene for the study of 'escape' from disadvantage, reported in this chapter and in detail elsewhere (Pilling 1990).

The study of 'escape' from disadvantage

There was little firm evidence at the start of the study about the extent of the continuity of multiple disadvantages. Single disadvantages have been found in other research to show continuity across generations, but the strength of the association varies with the type of adversity and there is a considerable amount of discontinuity as well (Brown and Madge 1982). Multiple disadvantages might be expected to be more difficult to break out from, and the earlier Essen and Wedge (1982) findings seemed to support this.

By the time the study took place, findings from the 23–year NCDS follow-up were available. It was still not possible, of course, to determine whether the multiply disadvantaged, defined in terms of the criteria used in the previous studies, would experience similar disadvantages to their parents at the same stage in their life-histories. But the 23–year findings did confirm a continuity of disadvantage. Those who had been multiply disadvantaged at 11 and/or 16 were doing less well than the total cohort in terms of educational qualifications, employment, social class, earnings per hour and home ownership.

Given that Essen and Wedge (1982) had found that even the multiply disadvantaged with good attainment scores seemed to be hindered in their public examination achievements, we were somewhat apprehensive about whether we would be able to find a group who were doing well; who could be said to be on the way, at least, to 'escaping' from disadvantage. But our fears turned out to be unjustified. Almost a fifth had 'above average' attainments (i.e. above the median for the total cohort), this time measured by a scale of educational and vocational qualifications. The scale was devised for the 23–year study and had a similar hierarchical ordering of qualifications to that used in the 1981 General Household Survey. Nor were all the multiply disadvantaged doing badly in terms of employment, earnings and housing compared with the total cohort, including some who did not have 'above average' qualifications.

The study was considered as exploratory. It was to consist of a comparison of 'achievers' with other members of the multiply disadvantaged sample using both previously collected NCDS data and data from an interview carried out specifically for the study, with selected groups, when the study members were aged 26 or 27. The interview was to be semi-structured, and was to ask for the individual's own views of their current situation, of their 'success', of their childhood experiences and how these had affected them. It also included more specific questions about areas, such as activities with parents in childhood and parental ambitions for them, that the literature suggested might be related to 'escaping' from disadvantage. As well as quantitative comparisons, case histories would be constructed and compared. A massive amount of data were available on the study members from previous follow-ups; from parents, teachers, doctors, the study members themselves (since the age of 11), attainment tests (constructed for the study by the NFER) and public examination results.

It was decided to retain the same definition of multiple disadvantage as in the Essen and Wedge (1982) study. The sample consisted, as in its predecessor, of those with disadvantages in all three of the criteria areas – income, housing and family situation – at the time of the 11–year or the 16–year follow-ups, or at both times. It was considered, though, that it would be more appropriate to define 'achievement' in terms of 23–year criteria, rather than in terms of attainment test scores at the age of 16.

After much debate, those with 'above average' qualifications (five or more 'O' levels or the equivalent, such as City and Guilds Craft or above) were taken as the 'achievers', who were likely to 'escape' disadvantage as adults. One of the main reasons for this was the significance of educational achievement as an indication that disadvantages had been overcome, the sample having been specifically selected on criteria known to be associated with poorer attainment. Another was the relative stability of educational and vocational qualifications, compared with possible criteria such as earnings, housing or even occupation, which may have a very different significance at 23 from that later in adult life. Those with this level of qualifications were also generally better off than the rest of the multiply disadvantaged in their material circumstances, although not exclusively so.

There was a marked sex difference among the educational achievers, the proportion of men to women being roughly four to one. Whether different cut-off points for educational achievement should be taken for the sexes was again a matter that was much discussed, the decision against this mainly being taken on the grounds that it was preferable to provide a 'realistic' view of the actual situation.

To confine the sample of those likely to 'escape' to the educational achievers seemed to be too narrow a view. Those among the rest of the multiply disadvantaged in childhood who were doing very well in material terms in comparison with the total NCDS cohort at 23 (on at least two counts in terms of earnings, income, social class, home ownership) were included as a separate group of 'alternative' achievers.

The groups selected for interview from the multiply disadvantaged sample consisted of the 'alternative' achievers (13), a random sample of the educational achievers (41 out of 66) and a comparison group (36 out of 86), matched with the educational achievers on the age at which they were multiply disadvantaged: 11, 16 or both. The comparison group were selected so as to provide a clear-cut contrast with the educational achievers, but were not an extreme group. Those with no educational or vocational qualifications, who were below the median for the total NCDS cohort on the 'alternative' criteria, formed the comparison group.

The highest qualifications of the educational achievers interviewed are shown in table 1.

Table 1. Highest qualifications of the educational achievers interviewed

	Male		Female		Total	
	n	%	n	%	n	%
Degree	2	(6)	-		2	(5)
Non-graduate teacher	1	(3)	-		1	(2)
Non-CNAA diploma	-		1	(11)	1	(2)
HNC/HND;HTEC/BTEC	2	(6)	-		2	(5)
Nursing	1	(3)	1	(11)	2	(5)
City and Guilds Adv; ONC/OND	10	(31)	1	(11)	11	(27)
City and Guilds Craft	14	(44)	1	(11)	15	(37)
5+ 'O'levels	2	(6)	5	(56)	7	(17)
Totals	32	(100)	9	(100)	41	(100)

The interview confirmed that at around the age of 27 the educational achievers were faring much better in material terms than the comparison group members. This was true for unemployment, occupational status, gross earnings per hour and family equivalent income (total family income adjusted to take into account family composition). For example, only eight per cent of the educational achievers were unemployed, compared with 26 per cent of the comparison group, unemployment being 40 per cent among the male comparison group members. Over a quarter of the educational achievers but none of the comparison group were in social class II, while more than two-thirds of the comparison group had semi- or unskilled manual occupations, compared with ten per cent of the educational achievers. For the most part the educational achievers were doing better materially than the 'alternative' achievers, who were specifically selected on the basis of material success at the time of the 23–year follow-up.

'Escaping' from disadvantage

It is not intended to discuss all the findings of *Escape from Disadvantage* here. Rather, a few themes will be picked out, and the interplay illustrated of various factors: material circumstances, family stress, parental values and attitudes towards education, the school attended, the individual's personal characteristics, and the opportunities in the area, all of which appear to influence the likelihood of 'escaping' (Pilling, 1990).

The educational achievers overlapped considerably with, but were by no means identical to, the 'higher' achievers in the Essen and Wedge study (1982) (those with above average scores on the maths and/or reading tests carried out for the study at the 16–year follow-up). At 16, 70% had a reading or maths score above the median for the total NCDS cohort, while none of the comparison group had a score above the median at this age. At seven there were already distinct differences between the groups, but they were nowhere near as great. At this age 15% of the comparison group were 'above average' on both tests compared to a quarter of the educational achievers. The general picture is of a movement upwards for the educational achievers between seven and 16, and a dramatic movement downwards for the comparison group, mainly between seven and 11. This suggests that a change in circumstances had occurred.

The point of matching the educational achievers and comparison group members interviewed was to obtain two groups with roughly the same experience of childhood disadvantage: we did not want our main finding simply to be that it is the less disadvantaged who manage to 'escape'. At the interview undertaken for the study, when the study members were aged 26 or 27, they were asked about their experiences in childhood of the identifying disadvantages – low income, poor housing, atypical family situation, and whether the family had ever experienced 'hard times'. Their descriptions gave a definite impression of 'harder times' for the comparison group members.

Further examination of the duration and degree of disadvantage experienced by the disadvantaged groups, using the NCDS data collected in earlier follow-ups, and extending the analyses back to the age of seven (necessitating the use of some different indicators of the disadvantages) confirmed that this was so. This was despite the educational achievers and comparison groups interviewed having been matched for the age at which they were multiply disadvantaged. The differences between the educational achievers and comparison group in the multiply disadvantaged sample as a whole were more distinct. Few in any group were multiply disadvantaged over the entire period, but the educational achievers were somewhat more likely to have experienced only short-term disadvantages. There was a considerably higher proportion of disadvantage at the age of seven among the comparison group, 48% compared with 18% among the educational achievers, taking the matched interview groups (table 2).

So, the findings forced us, almost of their own accord, to emphasise that 'escape' is easier for those who are less rather than more disadvantaged. But it is also important to emphasise that the majority of the educational achievers were substantially disadvantaged. Do the findings also suggest that earlier experience of disadvantage is, after all, more important than later?

Table 2. Disadvantages at the time of the 7, 11 and 16-year NCDS follow-ups.
Educational achievers and comparison group compared.

	Educational achievers		Comparison group	
	All	Interview sample	All	Interview sample
	%	%	%	%
Disadvantaged in 3 criteria areas (income, housing, family situation) at:				
3 follow-ups- 7, 11 and 16	5	7	17	11
2 follow ups- 7 and 16	-	-	5	4
7 and 11	10	11	24	33
11 and 16	18	21	14	7
1 follow-up- 11 or 16 + 2 disadvantages at 1+ other follow-up	42	46	32	33
11 or 16 +0/1 disadvantage at other follow-ups	25	14	8	11
Total	100	100	100	100
n	(40)	(28)	(59)	(27)

Perhaps, but this is mainly because early experience sets up 'chains of consequences' as the Clarkes (Clarke and Clarke 1984) have put it, influencing not only the kinds of environment and opportunities likely to follow, but how they are met by the individual.

Again it was the interviews that focused our attention on the greater amount of family stress – broken families and families with relationship problems – among the comparison group. It was possible to substantiate this, using 'objective' data from previous NCDS follow-ups provided by others than the study members themselves. When a number of problems additional to the criteria of disadvantage (chronic parental illness, father's long-term unemployment, atypical family situation other than one-parent family) were added up, over three-quarters of the comparison group were found to experience at least one problem, compared with less than half of the educational achievers. Living with a parent alone, although one of the criteria for disadvantage, was found from the case histories to 'symbolize' (among the disadvantaged group) a host of material and relationship problems. When this was added to the problems counted, a quarter of the comparison group compared with only seven percent of the educational achievers had two or more family problems.

Taking all available evidence, including that from the 26/27–year interviews, over a quarter of the comparison group had a period in their lives when they had no supportive relationship from either parent. Several described their feelings of isolation after the family broke up, the parent with whom they remained having ill-health or being too depressed with his or her own worries to give support. One study member told of her distress after her parents separated; of how she moved from relative to relative, unable to settle. The findings are in line with Rutter's (1979) on the potentiating effect of multiple stresses and the protective function of one good relationship with a parent.

The third main area in which there were differences between the families of the educational achievers and comparison group members is in the 'cultural environment of the home'. Both the qualitative accounts from the interviews and the quantitative comparisons using NCDS data from the seven- and 11–year follow-ups suggested that there was a good deal of overlap between the groups in parents' involvement in activities with their children, though there were differences at the extremes. For the most part, the main difference was that both parents (mostly fathers) were less often involved among the comparison group, and sometimes activities were cut off by family break-up or poor relationships. Relationships were by no means always affectionate between parents and children of the educational achievers, but some involvement in activities with at least one parent was maintained.

Differences were somewhat more distinct on literacy measures, particularly in belonging to a library. It is, though, in the levels of interest in their child's education as reported by teachers, and aspirations for the child's further education, that the differences were striking. They also widened considerably between the seven- and 16–year follow-ups. When the study members were 16, 56% of the parents of the educational achievers interviewed wanted their children to stay on at school beyond the minimum level, compared with 11% of parents of the comparison group members.

The proportion of parents of educational achievers wanting their children to stay on at school is very similar to that of parents of children with a maths and/or reading test score above the median at 16 (52%). This is so, although nearly a third of the educational achievers did not have either a maths or reading test score above the median at 16. Other research evidence suggests that parental interest in their children's education and aspirations for them to some extent is a reflection of the children's school performance, but not entirely so, since characteristics such as social class also have an influence

(Pilling and Pringle, 1978). Social class differences were small between the educational achievers and comparison group, but there were indications that parental value systems might sustain aspirations for their children among some of the educational achievers (Pilling, 1990).

Only a minority (10 out of 41) of the educational achievers interviewed obtained the qualifications that brought them into this category through the school (or school plus higher education). In the majority of these cases (seven out of 10), the pattern was of a large family, suffering from over-crowding and being in receipt of free school-meals. 'There was only enough money for basics, not hardship', was how more than one study member put it. Parent-child relationships were reasonably good, and all but one of the parents said they wanted the child to stay on at school beyond the minimum age at the time of the 16–year follow-up. Only two attended the neighbourhood secondary school, either because they went to the grammar school (or the school where 'O' levels were taken), or the parents selected a different school on religious grounds. All were encouraged to obtain qualifications by the school because this was 'expected', or because one or more of the teachers took a special interest in the study member. One who was more disadvantaged than most, his father having been unable to work for a long time through illness, said he would never have thought of taking 'O' levels without the encouragement of teachers in the local school. He was able to do so because his older brothers and sisters were working and his mother told him to take the chance. He took CSEs at school and obtained two Grade 1s; he went on to technical college to do 'A' levels (there was no 6th form) and then went to university.

All those educational achievers who obtained their qualifications through school (sometimes plus higher education) received encouragement in some form through both the school and home. Almost all the other educational achievers experienced more difficulties with their home backgrounds. Often there were negative as well as positive influences on educational achievement. Although there was some interest in the study members' education, and ambition for them, there were also pressures to help at home, particularly for girls, and often financial worries, even in families no longer defined as disadvantaged. Parents who placed a high value on education were also often very firmly set on their sons gaining a skill through an apprenticeship. There were other pressures against staying on at school: attitudes in the neighbourhood; dislike of having free school meals; the feeling that school was an alien culture. Half of the educational achievers obtained their 'above average' qualifications through apprenticeships, including several who became the most materially successful, setting up their own businesses.

Apprenticeships provided an opportunity for male educational achievers that they were ready to take. Sometimes they were an opportunity that the study members themselves put a great deal of effort into obtaining. One, for example, said he went through the Yellow Pages trying every firm until one agreed to take him on. Some were spurred on by dislike of the situation in which their parents had found themselves. This included several whose NCDS attainment scores at 16 were below the median in both maths and reading. But as well as the opportunity, there was generally some encouragement from home; fathers, for example, would go along with sons to the interview.

Six educational achievers gained their 'above average' qualifications through vocational training, such as nursing or day release sponsored by an employer. Five (in addition to the educational achiever who went to university afterwards) reached this level through studying at a college of further education. The two men who took this route did apprenticeships afterwards but the three women had their careers interrupted by marriage and children.

There were also several comparison group members who were very determined not to repeat their childhood circumstances, but with low school attainments, little family encouragement and living in areas with poor employment prospects, their motivation in itself was not enough. Some other comparison group members (10 out of the 36) did have the opportunity to take some kind of training course, but failed to complete them in eight cases, for a variety of reasons: poor wages, lack of interest in qualifications, fears about ability to cope. Most regretted this very much when interviewed.

Female study members for the most part lacked the kind of opportunity presented by apprenticeships. This was one of the reasons for the overrepresentation of males among the educational achievers, but it was not the only reason, there being more males than females among the 'higher' achievers in the Essen and Wedge (1982) study. More females than males did attain 'O' levels or CSEs but did not reach the 'above average' level of five or more 'O' levels or the equivalent, and it is quite likely that some will 'escape' at a later stage, through successful careers or marriage. All but one of the female 'alternative' achievers had 'O' levels or CSEs but it was only possible to find six women who met the 'alternative' achievement criteria at 23 (out of the total of 13 'alternative' achievers).

There have been suggestions in other studies (e.g. Werner and Smith, 1982) that males are particularly susceptible to social disadvantage in earlier childhood, and females susceptible during adolescence. There was some support for this in that those no longer multiply disadvantaged at 16 were overrepresented among the female – but not the male – educational achievers. Also there was only an overrepresentation of females among those disadvantaged at 16 in the comparison group (15 to seven), not to any marked degree in the group as a whole (46 to 40). Case histories in *Escape from Disadvantage* suggest that the difference in role expectations for the sexes in adolescence acts against achievement for females, both in their having to take family responsibilities, and in attempts to 'escape' through teenage pregnancy and marriage, particularly where there were severe strains in family relationships. There were several female comparison group members in whom a decline in school performance could be traced following acute stresses in family relationship and/or long-term and continuing severe material problems. These circumstances seemed to outweigh teachers' encouragement, parental interest in their education and even, on occasion, parental aspirations for further education. When interviewed at 27, some seemed trapped, but for several new possibilities of 'escape' were developing. For example, one had attained a 'good' job with self-taught secretarial skills and was buying her own house.

There were other hopeful findings. Those interviewed were asked about their ambitions for their children. More of the comparison group (63%) than of the educational achievers (52%) had educationally or career-oriented aspirations for their children. It could be contended that most parents are ambitious for their children when they are young, but the aspirations of the parents of the comparison group members were already very much lower than those of educational achievers at the time of the seven-year follow-up. Many of the comparison group members talked about how their aspirations for their children differed from those they had had for themselves.

Discontinuities in disadvantage

The message of *Escape from Disadvantage* is of an unexpected degree of resilience if circumstances change. Essen and Wedge suggested that an adaptational theory of social disadvantage (Gans 1968) might explain their findings that 16–year-olds who were no longer disadvantaged – in study terms – had attainment and adjustment scores little better than those who were still disadvantaged. Families adapt their behaviour to cope with disadvantaged circumstances, and when these change they are unable to change their aspirations quickly in response. There was some evidence in support of this in the 'escape' study; comparison group members were not always able to take opportunities even when they were offered. This may also have applied to some of the educational achievers, who could probably have stayed on at school rather than leave to take apprenticeships. Nevertheless, although attitudes may not change immediately, the 'escape' study would suggest that they do change in time with a changing situation. Many of the educational achievers had become very career-minded, including some in skilled manual jobs. Among the comparison group there was not only often a resurgence of hope on family formation, but several seemed to have better job prospects at 27 than 23. Overall, possibilities for 'escape' looked more promising at 27 than they had at 16.

However, it would be unwise to be too optimistic. For many of the comparison group, whether or not their hopes are maintained will depend more on the country's economic circumstances than their individual actions. Nor have all of the educational achievers necessarily escaped permanently from disadvantage. Some of the skilled workers in declining industries may not have been able to transfer their skills or acquire new ones.

The study findings, like the Clarkes' work, emphasises human potential for development beyond the early years, probably well into adulthood. There are opportunities for some to break the environmental chain, but until a society is created in which no family has to suffer an accumulation of adversities, much potential for development will never be realised. Changing society in this way is a formidable task, as the Clarkes have often stressed.

References

Brown, M. and Madge, N. (1982) *Despite the welfare state*. London: Heinemann.

Clarke, A. D. B. and Clarke, A. M. (1960) 'Some recent advances in the study of early deprivation'. *Child Psychology and Psychiatry*. 1, 26–36.

Clarke, A. D. B. and Clarke, A. M. (1984) 'Constancy and change in the growth of human characteristics'. *Journal of Child Psychology and Psychiatry*. 25(2), 191–210.

Clarke, A. M. and Clarke, A. D. B. (1986) 'Thirty years of child psychology: a selective review'. *Journal of Child Psychology and Psychiatry*. 27(6), 719–59.

Davie, R., Butler, N., and Goldstein, H. (1972) *From birth to seven*. The second report of the National Child Development Study. London: Longman in association with the National Children's Bureau.

Elder, G. H. Jnr., Liker, J. K. and Cross, C. E. (1984) 'Parent-child behaviour in the great depression: life-course and intergenerational influences', in Baltes, P. B. and Brim, O. G. (eds), *Life-span development and behaviour*. Vol. 6. London: Academic Press.

Essen, J. and Wedge, P. (1982) *Continuities in childhood disadvantage*. London: Heinemann.

Fogelman, K. (1975) 'Developmental correlates of family size'. *British Journal of Social Work*. 5(1), 43–57.

Gans, H. J. (1968) 'Culture and class in the study of poverty: an approach to anti-poverty research', in Moynihan, D. P. (ed), *On understanding poverty*. New York: Basic Books.

Garmezy, N. and Tellegen, A. (1984) 'Studies of stress resistant children: methods, variables and preliminary findings', in Morrison, F., Lord, C. and Keating. D. (eds), *Advances in applied developmental psychology*, Vol. I. New York: Academic Press.

Pilling, D. (1990) *Escape from disadvantage*. London: The Falmer Press.

Pilling, D. and Pringle, M. K.(1978) *Controversial issues in child development*. London: Elek.

Rutter, M. (1979) 'Protective factors in children's response to stress and disadvantage', in Kent, M. W. and Rolfe, J. E. (eds), *Primary prevention of psychopathology*, Vol. III, Social competence in children. Hanover: University Press of New England.

Wedge, P. and Prosser, H. (1973) *Born to fail?* London: Arrow Books.

Werner, E. E. and Smith, R. S. (1982) *Vulnerable but invincible. A study of resilient children*. New York: McGraw-Hill.

Chapter 6

Vulnerability and resilience of adults who were classified as mildly mentally handicapped in childhood

Stephen A. Richardson and Helene Koller

Children with mild mental handicap may reasonably be regarded as meeting the definition of vulnerable. Vulnerable comes from the Latin *vulnus*, wound, and its definition includes defenceless against injury, open to attack or damage, inviting ridicule, and offering an opening to criticism. All children with mild mental handicap have intellectual impairment and in some cases other developmental disabilities. They come to the attention of educational authorities in countries with compulsory education, because of their failure to meet minimal standards expected for school performance. Unless mainstreamed, they are placed in special classes to provide them with a teaching program appropriate to their capabilities. This avoids the negative effects of frequent failure in school work in regular classes, and provides shelter from the pressures and stigma resulting from displaying incompetence in regular classes, but it has other consequences. The labelling of the child as mentally handicapped by the school authorities carries with it the risk of being exposed to derogatory behaviour and rejection outside the special class.

After leaving school, the uniform standards set by society for school performance no longer hold, and different, and, in some cases, more flexible, standards for adult role functioning obtain. There is the general expectation that, after leaving school, young people seek and obtain jobs, remain fairly stable in their employment, and do not have an undue amount of time unemployed. The job market, unlike the schools, provides more flexibility in the levels of skills and performance required, and a wide variety of jobs exist. The shift in role from school child to employee is abrupt. Other shifts in societal expectations are more gradual. They include the emancipation from parental supervision and sheltering, the development of economic independence, and the assumption of responsibility for personal affairs. There is the expectation that continues from childhood of having interpersonal relationships with peers. For some there will be the assumption of marital, parental and housewife roles, with attending obligations and responsibilities.

At school leaving, some young people with mild mental handicap will be judged unable to function adequately in some adult roles, and will continue to be sheltered and supervised in adult mental handicap services. For others, entry into these services occurs only after the young person has unsuccessfully attempted to obtain and hold a job and function with some independence. These young people continue to fit the definition of vulnerable. There are other young people who, after leaving special classes or schools, disappear from further services for the mentally handicapped. This chapter will focus on what happens to them and whether they continue to fit the definition of vulnerable, or whether they appear to be resilient. We concur with a definition of resilience given by Rutter (1983): 'Young people who "do well" in some sense in spite of having experienced a form of stress which in the population as a whole is known to carry a substantial risk of an adverse outcome (p. 2).'

Previous research. Some idea of the proportion of all children with mental handicap who disappear from special services after leaving school was provided many years ago by Gruenberg (1964). In a review of epidemiological studies, he consistently found that the prevalence of mental handicap rose during the school years and then dropped by approximately one half in the immediate post-school years. These studies included those with severe mental handicap, almost all of whom continued to receive special services. This suggests that a majority of those with mild mental handicap disappear from services. Subsequent studies of children administratively classified as mentally handicapped and placed in special schools have yielded similar findings (Richardson and Koller, 1985). For those who disappear from mental handicap services after leaving school, Gruenberg (1964) suggested alternative outcomes that fit the definitions of vulnerable and resilient.

> 'Either these individuals are continuing to be extremely handicapped in later life and are unknown because the services they need are unavailable to them . . . or they have stopped being retarded in any real sense at all and do not need any special protection, help or services . . . (p. 274).'

Earlier in this century there were numerous studies that followed up children who had been administratively classified as mentally handicapped after leaving school. In a review of these studies, Tizard (1965) concluded, 'It is apparent . . . that even during the depression years substantial numbers of mentally subnormal children were able, upon leaving school, to find jobs for themselves and live as self-supporting, socially competent members of society' (p. 506). Kushlick and Blunden (1974) reviewed the epidemiology of mental subnormality and concluded, 'Mild subnormality appears to be a temporary incapacity characterized mainly by educational difficulties experienced at school (p.42)'. A different conclusion was reached by Edgerton (1984), based on anthropological studies of young adults with mild mental retardation. These studies reported that young adults with mild mental retardation were not accepted by members of non-retarded peer groups.

> '. . . They are set apart from their peers, principally by the same academic limitations that troubled them in school – reading, writing and numerical calculations. They are seen as handicapped by their parents and other non-retarded persons and they themselves feel limited, often painfully so . . . In general, women have their primary ties with other mentally retarded persons, and the sources of social support most often and reliably come from their families (pp. 5–6).'

The findings of Edgerton suggest continued vulnerability of individuals with mild mental handicap after leaving school, while the conclusions of the two reviewers quoted suggest resilience. This may be the consequence of selection bias: Edgerton studying individuals at the lower end of the range of mild mental handicap, and the studies reviewed were based on subjects from the upper end of the range. From the information given, there is no way of determining how representative were the subjects of all adults who had been classified as mildly mentally handicapped in childhood.

In order to obtain a representative study population, all children of specific ages with mild mental handicap living in a defined geographic area have to be identified and then followed into adulthood. Even when this is attempted, there will be some subjects who cannot be traced, and of those traced some will not participate in the study, or will only give partial information. Unless these losses are taken into account, even the results of representative studies may be biased.

In all the quotations given, the expectations or conclusions are posed in dichotomous terms. Study subjects were generally described as functioning adequately, or inadequately, with the inference that they all functioned in a similar manner. With a representative population of children with mild mental handicap followed into adulthood, it might be expected that there would be a wide distribution in how well the young adults functioned. Further, there is no basis for assuming that all subjects would be uniform in their level of functioning across a number of different roles. Rather, one might expect that, while some would function adequately across various functional roles and others inadequately, there would be some who show different levels of functioning in the various roles and do better in some than others.

For each functional role in adulthood, we need to distinguish adequate from inadequate functioning. For some types of functioning, this judgment may be based on general knowledge of the society. For example, conduct that violates the law and psychiatric illness constitute inadequate functioning. For other aspects of adult functioning, however, the degree of adequacy can only be judged comparatively. For example, unemployment histories of individuals with mild mental handicap need to be understood in relation to the unemployment histories of peers in the same community and from similar social backgrounds who are not mentally handicapped. It is necessary to take into account the particular conditions of the job market and work force at the time and place of the study.

The follow-up study of children with mental handicap in Aberdeen, Scotland

In the follow-up study that we carried out, we were fortunate in being able to base it on an epidemiological study of a well defined population of all children with mental handicap in Aberdeen, Scotland. This provided us with a carefully selected representative population (Birch et al 1970).

A concern of the epidemiological study was to determine whether the children administratively classified as mentally handicapped by the local authorities would also have been considered as mentally handicapped in other Western industrialized countries. A team of American psychologists independently evaluated every child and concluded that they would also have classified the children as mentally handicapped. The study provided a description of the population, and the social and economic conditions of the community, so that persons who might wish to use the findings as estimates for another community could determine how similar were the circumstances and conditions of the two communities. The epidemiological study included all children born in the years 1952–54 who were residents in the city in 1962. They were aged 8–10 at the time of the study. One of the authors (SAR) of this chapter was a co-investigator in this study. In 1970, he began a follow-up study of these children when they reached age 22, enlarging the number of subjects to include the birth years of 1951 and 1955.

Subjects with mental handicap

From the total population born in the years 1951 through 1955 and resident in Aberdeen in 1962 (n = 13,842), all children with mental handicap were identified, defined as those who, at any time up to age 16, had been placed in any special mental handicap facility (special school, training centre, day care, or residential facility). One hundred and twenty one males and 100 females met this definition. One hundred and seventy five of these children had mild mental handicap (IQs of 50 and above), and they will be the focus of this chapter.

Comparison subjects without mental handicap

For each child with mild mental handicap, a non-retarded peer was selected from a 20% random sample from the population of 13,842 at risk. None of the children in the sample had been classified as mentally handicapped by the local authorities and all had IQs of 75 and above, as measured by at least one of the two group intelligence tests given to the total population of children in the city at ages seven and nine. From this sample, children with mental handicap were matched with a child of the same age, sex and social class.

We obtained the data needed for the study by separately interviewing the young adults and their parents. An observational protocol was used by the interviewer after completion of each interview that included various aspects of the informant's appearance and behaviour. Data were also obtained from a number of documentary sources. These included health, school, social work and court records. These data were particularly valuable because they were not retrospective; they provided cross-checks on the interview data, or they gave information that informants were unable to give, e.g. medical test results.

Measures of adequacy of functioning as young adults

1. *Long term services for adults with mental handicap.* Everyone who continued to receive special services met the definition of being vulnerable, having been judged inadequate to play at least one of the salient adult functional roles expected by society.

2. *Suicide.* Perhaps most clearly, those who commit suicide may be considered to have been vulnerable.

For the remaining study population with mild mental handicap who were not receiving adult services, we selected four functional roles based on general societal expectations for adjustment in young adulthood. For each of these roles, we developed a measure and defined a cutting point on the scale of the measure which differentiated adequate from inadequate functioning. The measures and cutting points are as follows:

3. *Social interaction.* This measure was a factor score derived from descriptions given by the young adults of their leisure time activities.

It was based on three variables: (1) The amount of time spent in activities where social interaction is an important component; (2) Time spent visiting or being visited; (3) Amount of leisure time spent alone. The first two variables were negatively correlated with the third variable (Richardson et al, unpublished report). No distinction was made about whether the persons interacted with were family or non-family, or with the same or a different generation. The factor was derived from the combined population of the young adults with mild mental handicap who had disappeared from services and their non-retarded peer comparisons. To make a distinction between adequate and inadequate social interaction, we used the 90th percentile of the range of standardized factor scores for the non-retarded comparisons, based on an assumption that the poorest 10% of the non-retarded comparisons would represent inadequate functioning in social interaction.

4. *Peer relationships*. In the interview, the young adults were asked several questions about friends and socializing in various settings, which included neighborhood, workplace, and clubs attended. A score was assigned to each study subject based on all friendship questions throughout the interview. From this, the following three categories of peer relationships were defined (Koller et al, 1988).

   (a) *Frequent*. Socializing at least once a month with two or more peers, i.e. friends who were close in age and were not relatives.

   (b) *Seldom*. Socializing with two or more peers less than once a month, or with one peer, no matter how frequently.

   (c) *None*. Total or near total absence of socializing with peers.

We defined frequent and seldom as adequate and none as inadequate.

5. *Behaviour disturbance*. All evidence of behaviour disturbance for each study subject uncovered in the interview and various record sources for the age period 15–22 years of age was rated as to severity on a five point scale from mild to severe. Severity ratings were based on (1) the amount of time and the degree to which the problem impaired the individuals ability to function in the activities expected of him or her; (2) evidence of concern about the behaviour by the person himself, his family, or some authority. Adequate behaviour was defined as no or slight behaviour disturbance, and inadequate as moderate to severe disturbance. For a full description, see Koller et al. (1983).

6. *Job histories*. Three measures of job history were selected (Richardson et al, 1988).

(1) *Percentage of time out of the labour force.* The number of months not employed or seeking employment, divided by the number of months between school leaving and age 22 years three months. Time spent as housewife or in full time education were not counted as time out of the labour force because they were both productive alternatives. Time out of the labour force was time not working or seeking employment for a variety of reasons.

(2) *Percentage of time unemployed while in the labour force.* The number of months unemployed divided by the total of the number of months employed plus unemployed and seeking work.

(3) *Job turnover.* The number of jobs held per year while in the labour force.

To determine what was adequate and inadequate for each of these three job measures we used the performance of some of the non-mentally handicapped comparisons. In Aberdeen, students in their last year of regular secondary school took national examinations that, if passed, gave qualifications that were prerequisites for entry into further education and training and for certain skilled jobs. None of the young people with mental handicap had these educational qualifications. For these reasons, we based the cutting point for the three measures only on those comparisons who left school without any educational qualifications. We determined separately for males and females for each of the three job history measures, the 90th percentile on the distribution of scores for comparisons without qualifications.

This was based on the assumption that 10% of the comparisons would function inadequately on each measure. To provide an overall measure of job history we defined as adequate those who were adequate on all three job measures.

Summary measures of four functional roles

There are 16 possible combinations of adequate-inadequate on the four measures of functioning we have described. Each young adult was characterized by the particular combination of functioning across the four measures.

None of the measures so far described provides an indicator of the skills of the young people. It might be expected that those who are adequate in functioning are more likely to have better skills. To measure this, we used level of job skill. Of those employed at age 22, 36% of the young adults with mild mental handicap held semiskilled manual jobs. The rest were in un-skilled manual jobs.

Childhood measures. We wished to learn whether childhood characteristics of those who disappeared from services would predict the various combinations of adult functioning. We chose two cognitive measures and a biological measure: IQ in childhood, return to regular classes, and the presence of brain dysfunction.

'*Brain dysfunction*' was an assessment of the relative contribution of factors suggesting possible biologic etiology of mental handicap. Factors were ranked according to probability of etiologic significance: High probability (rated 3) included 14 known genetic syndromes (e.g. Down syndrome), cerebral malformations, post-natal and on-going injuries, cerebral palsy, and macrocephaly. Medium probability (rated 2) included uncomplicated epilepsy and macrocephaly. Low probability (rated 1) included autism and small size for gestational age (Goulden et al, 1988). There was some probability of brain dysfunction in 24% of those who disappeared from services.

IQ. Scores were obtained from tests administered when the children were in the age range of seven-12 years. Scores were based on the WISC for the birth cohorts 1952–4. For the 1951 and 1955 cohorts, Terman Merrill Test scores were converted to WISC scores based on the relation between the two test scores found among Aberdeen children.

Return to regular classes. Some of the children who met the definition of mild mental handicap, after spending a period of time in special classes, made such progress in their school performance that the educational authorities returned them to regular classes for the remainder of their school career. Returning to regular classes was a second measure of cognitive ability.

Family stability. We wished to examine the influence of a child's environment on his or her adequacy of functioning as a young adult. To examine the family environment of the child, we chose a measure of Family Stability. This measure was based on data from the interview and social work records dealing with the parents' presence in the home; their work and health histories; their dealings with the courts, the police and the social work department; and any changes in the caretaking situation and reasons for these changes. This information was then evaluated and assigned to one of five categories. The upper end of the scale was defined as follows:

1. Stable Family Environment, in which child lived throughout with both parents, who were in at least moderately good health; father was employed with reasonable steadiness; mother may or may not have worked outside the home, no aberrant or disturbed behaviour was noted in parents, and there was no evidence that child was not well cared for.

The lowest end of the scale was defined as:

5. Markedly Unstable Environment, in which child was abused, neglected or abandoned. Family disorganization, disruptions and discord were present. Parents were incompetent or had disturbed behaviour, necessitating intervention by authorities. Upbringing marked by instability and uncertainty and often included a series of different caretakers. (See Richardson et al 1985a and 1985b for a full description of this measure.)

Results

For the total population of children with mild mental handicap followed to age 22, 30 (20%) were in long term adult services and 2 (1%) were known or suspected suicides. According to our definition, they were all vulnerable.

The remaining 79% of the mildly mentally handicapped population were not in services for adults with mental handicap. For these 138 subjects, we had complete data for 90, partial data for 31 and minimal information for 17. The following analysis will deal with the 90 subjects with full data. The information we have on the 47 subjects with partial data will then be used to estimate whether the results from the 90 subjects may be biased.

Two roles that have important consequences for the daily lives of young adults, and may be related to how they function on the four measures we have selected, are sex and marital status. Neither sex nor marital status, however, was found to be related to adequacy of functioning on the four measures, so all subjects, males and females, single and married are combined in Table 1. The subjects are grouped according to the number of measures on which they met our definitions of adequacy. All combinations of adequate-inadequate on the four measures are represented among the 90 subjects for whom full data were available. Of those who disappeared from services, 27% functioned adequately on all four measures. These may reasonably be considered as resilient since leaving school. At the other end of the scale, 15% functioned adequately on none or one of the four measures. They may be considered as continuing to be vulnerable in the post-school years. The remaining 58% are adequate in two or three of the four functions and inadequate in the remainder. For these young adults, it is difficult to assess their degree of resilience.

We might expect that those who were in jobs with higher levels of skills would be found more often among those who showed adequate functioning on several measures than among those who showed adequate functioning on few or none of the measures. There is some support for this expectation, with those functioning adequately on 3–4 of the measures more often holding semi-skilled manual jobs than those with adequacy on 0–2 of the measures

Table 1. Functioning on four measures for young adults not in adult MH services for whom full data were available (n = 90)

				N	Total	Percentage
Adequate in all four measures				24	24	27
Adequate in three measures						
S				9		
	F			2		
		B		4		
			J	6		
					21	23
Adequate in two measures						
S	F			5		
	F	B		1		
		B	J	8		
S		B		5		
	F		J	3		
S			J	9		
					31	34
Adequate in one measure						
S	F	B		4		
	F	B	J	3		
S	F		J	2		
S		B	J	1		
					10	11
Adequate on none of the four measures				4	4	4

S = inadequate on social interaction
F = inadequate on peer friends
B = inadequate on behaviour
J = inadequate on job history

(Table 2). It is of interest that there is no significant difference between the percentage of those who hold more skillful jobs and those who are and are not adequate in the job measure, which does not include level of skill. If more skilled job performance is added to adequacy of functioning on all four measures, 7/90 or 8% of those who disappeared from service meet this more stringent requirement of resilience.

The relation between childhood measures and functioning as young adults

Return to regular classes. The educational authorities monitored the progress of the children in special classes and returned children to regular classes if this seemed warranted by their progress. Because, from the teachers' perspective, these were the most able children, it might be expected that they

Table 2. Proportion of young adults with level of job skill higher than unskilled manual in different combinations of functioning (n = 90)

				Proportions with semi-skilled manual jobs*	Percentage
Adequate in all four functions				7/24	29
Adequate in three functions					
S				2/9	
	F			1/2	
		B		2/4	
			J	3/6	
			Total	8/21	38
Adequate in two functions					
S	F			1/5	
	F	B		0/1	
		B	J	1/8	
S		B		1/5	
	F		J	0/3	
S			J	2/9	
			Total	5/31	16
Adequate in one function					
S	F	B		1/4	
	F	B	J	0/3	
S	F		J	0/2	
S		B	J	0/1	
			Total	1/10	10
Adequate in one of four functions				0/4	0

*One male held a skilled manual job.
S = inadequate on social interaction
F = inadequate on peer friends
B = inadequate on behavior
J = inadequate on job history

would generally be more adequate in their adult functioning than those who remained in special classes until they left school. Half of the children who were returned to regular classes were adequate on all four functions, compared to a quarter of those who remained in special classes. All those who returned to regular classes were adequate on at least two functions. We will not pursue this measure further because we are unable to describe the basis upon which it was decided to return some children to regular classes.

We wished to determine how well the two childhood characteristics of IQ and brain dysfunction and the environmental measure of family stability, each in the context of the other, would predict the patterns of adult function-ing on the four measures. To examine this, we carried out a multiple regres-sion analysis of the childhood measures to predict the number of functional measures on which the young adults were adequate. The model was weak but significant, accounting for 13% of the variance. Family stability and brain dysfunction each made a significant contribution, but not IQ. Family stability made the stronger contribution (Family stability B = .35; brain dysfunction B = .21).

Possible bias in the results reported

The 90 subjects on whom the results were based represent 65% of all those in the total population who received no services. We compared the 90 for whom we had data on all four functional measures with those for whom we did not have the functional measures, using what data we had available. The only differences found were that those with minimum data had a higher proportion of females and a greater probability of brain dysfunction than those with full data. Because, throughout the analyses, we found no sex differences, the sex difference here does not suggest any bias in the results reported. The greater probability of brain dysfunction suggests a possible bias in slightly overstating the adequacy of functioning for the population in the results.

Discussion

In this chapter we have attempted to answer the question posed by Gruen-berg (1964) about children with mental handicap who, after leaving school, disappeared from further mental handicap services. He asked whether they continue to be handicapped (vulnerable), or whether '. . . they have stopped being regarded as retarded in any real sense at all and do not need any special protection, help or services . . . (resilient)' (p. 274).

Apart from anthropological case studies, previous follow-up studies have presented fragmented pictures of persons with mild mental handicap, with no comprehensive view of their functioning across roles. As a consequence, it is not possible to determine whether each individual was functioning uniformly well or poorly, or whether he or she functioned well in some roles and poorly in others. As a step toward a more comprehensive view, we selected four functional roles and presented the results so that performance across the four roles could be examined. The results show wide variation in both the number and kinds of functional roles in which individual perfor-mance was adequate. For a quarter of those who disappeared from services, there is reasonable evidence that they are resilient. For 15%, we consider they were vulnerable. For the remaining, who form a majority of cases, we cannot answer the question as posed by Gruenberg of two alternatives. Rather, we find a mixed pattern in which resilience is shown in some roles and vulnerability in others.

The four functional measures we have used give a limited view of the overall lives of those in our study. For those who functioned adequately on all four measures, we still cannot be confident that they have shown resilience in their lives since leaving school. As a rough check, we identified the seven cases who were adequate on all four measures and in addition held jobs at age 22 which were above the lowest level of unskilled manual labour. For these cases, we reviewed their entire histories based on all our sources of data. What follows are some impressions from these readings.

One young man, whom we will call John, came from a small middle class family.[1] After leaving school, John's father found him an apprenticeship in the glass company where he was a Director. John was still in the same job at age 22. He was allowed to continue doing the same work after the normal period of apprenticeship, even though he was unable to pass the qualifying written exams to become a journeyman. He had developed skills on the job, but his foreman was fearful of letting him use some of these skills in case he made costly mistakes. He was still often given jobs assigned normally to younger people, such as cleaning up and going on messages for the older men. According to his mother, the company felt his work was not up to standard. Two nights a week he went to evening classes in preparation for the journeyman's exam, which he still hoped to pass. He had accumulated savings from his pay. He was single and lived with his parents. Although not now manifest, he had had epilepsy and behaviour problems as a young child, and his mother joined and was still active in an organization for parents of handicapped persons. The parents initially had high expectations for their son. Since leaving school they felt he had blossomed in many ways. John was tall, good looking, and fashionably dressed. He felt shy with other people, especially with women. His best friends were young men he knew from the special class where he went to school. He has had difficulty in making new friends. He had few interests beside television, visiting pubs and drinking beer and sometimes going dancing. In the interview he showed good comprehension, was attentive and friendly and had fairly good verbal ability. He had some nervous habits and said he worried a lot.

A young woman, whom we will call Susan, came from a large family with many closely spaced siblings. Her father had stopped working for the past fifteen years because of chronic bronchitis. Her mother had always been a housewife. They lived in an undesirable neighbourhood where the mother was afraid to hang out laundry for fear of its being stolen. Living conditions in their home were crowded. Like all her siblings who had left school, Susan worked in the fish processing industry. She had worked continuously since

leaving school and had acquired, on the job, filleting skills, which can provide
a good income. At the special school, it was noted that Susan's backwardness
might have been due to speech and vision problems. At age 22, speech
problems were no longer evident, but her vision was still poor and she
complained of eye strain. Except for being overweight, her appearance was
unremarkable. She was engaged to be married and spent most of her spare
time with her fiancé, going places in his car and sharing activities with her
married siblings. She looked after her own money. We gained the impression
that she was indistinguishable from the peers with whom she associated and
was not seen as different from other people by her parents.

These two young adults provide an interesting contrast. John received
continuing help and sheltering from his middle class parents, but it was
difficult for him to live up to the standards that might have been expected
from such a family background. Susan, in the context of her poorly functioning lower class family, was doing well as an adult and appeared indistinguishable from her siblings.

These brief histories exemplify the ways that standards of expectations
vary, depending on the family environment in which the young people were
raised. It is more difficult for someone from an upper class and aspiring
family to meet their parents' and their own expectations than for someone
from a lower class family where the parents have had poor work histories
and had limited aspirations for their children. It seems resilience needs to be
considered not only in terms of general societal standards, but also in the
context of the subculture and family background of the young adult. It
should be noted also that the family stability measure was highly correlated
with social class.

We chose to use relatively objective measures of functioning. The question
of vulnerability end resilience may also be examined by asking how vulnerable or resilient the young adults feel in their daily lives. Edgerton (1984)
touches on this in his conclusion '. . . they themselves feel limited, often
painfully so.' We are presently working on a measure of self-esteem, and it
will be interesting to see if Susan's self-esteem is higher than John's.

Because we found a diversity of functioning of the mildly mentally
handicapped who disappeared from services, we examined some childhood
factors as a step toward understanding which antecedent factors may account for differences in the functioning of the young adults. Although the
three factors of brain dysfunction, IQ and the history of family stability
produced a rather weak predictive model (they accounted for 13% of the
variance in a multiple regression analysis), it is of interest that family stability
made the larger significant contribution to the prediction and brain dysfunction the smaller contribution, while IQ made no contribution. The salience
of the family background measure may be due to our limiting the analysis

to the group that received no post-school services, which does not include as many young adults with low IQ and evidence of brain dysfunction as are included in the group receiving services for adults with mental handicap. Thus, the variability on these measures is less, and the personal characteristics of the child are less likely to mask the influence of family background. To examine this, we used a discriminant analysis to determine how well the three childhood factors would distinguish between the adult service and no service groups. In a significant model, brain dysfunction contributed most and IQ made a smaller significant contribution. Family background was not significant. We looked at the family background of those receiving services and found that family stability was strongly related to type of adult service. Those in residential care came far more frequently from unstable family backgrounds whereas those attending day services came largely from stable family backgrounds.

It has long been held that the family upbringing constitutes the primary socializing influence of a child. The measure of family stability we have used in this chapter is relatively simple, but we have found it to have some relationship to young adult functioning (Richardson et al, 1985a; Richardson et al. 1990). We have developed a more comprehensive measure of family upbringing using a large number of measures in cluster analysis (Koller, et al., in press). This yielded clusters of families who are similar to each other across all the measures. The families of children with mental handicap were combined in the cluster analysis with families of the non-mentally handicapped comparisons in order to see how many clusters include families from both groups and how many clusters are made up of families from only one group. To go beyond the four measures of young adult functioning described in this chapter, we are also applying the cluster analysis technique to a large number of measures of the characteristics and functioning of the study subjects in order to gain a more comprehensive picture of the young adults. The results from these two cluster analyses will enable us to examine the kinds of young adults that come from various kinds of families.

We considered the relevance of our results for those children who are presently classified as mentally handicapped. Our study was carried out at a time when the classification and segregation of children with mild mental handicap and the use of IQ testing throughout the school system were accepted practice. Further, the special classes were of good quality and facilities were large enough to include all children needing special education.

Policies and values relating to the administrative classification of children as mentally handicapped have changed since the 1950s and 1960s, when the children in our study were classified. Concepts of normalization (Nirje, 1976) and mainstreaming have become influential. There is recognition that labelling children as mentally handicapped and segregating them for educational purposes may have stigmatizing consequences. This has led to reluctance to classify children as mentally handicapped. The widespread use of IQ testing in many places has become unacceptable for fear of its stigmatizing consequences, so it becomes very difficult to determine which children may be defined as mentally handicapped on psychometric grounds. A consequence of this is that fewer children are being identified as mentally handicapped. (Children with severe handicap are not affected by these changes.) These shifts have led to the reporting of lower prevalence rates in many recent epidemiological studies. Our study of mild mental handicap gave a prevalence rate of 12.5 per thousand. Recent studies in Sweden give the lowest prevalence rates, ranging from 3 to 6.3 per thousand (Kebbon, 1987). It is possible that this reflects some true drop in prevalence. It is also likely that there are now more children not classified as mentally handicapped and in regular classes who would have been classified at earlier times. There has been an emphasis in research to confirm the damaging consequences of stigmatizing children by labelling them as mentally handicapped. There is need to balance these studies by identifying children who might previously have been classified as mentally handicapped and now are not. It is important to find out what happens to them during their childhood and on into adulthood. Our study suggests that such children may have unidentified problems and needs as adults that are not now being recognized.

In the earlier studies referred to, distinctions were often not made between children with mild mental handicap who, after leaving school, did and did not continue to receive mental handicap services. To compare our study with the earlier studies, we will look at the vulnerability and resilience of all mentally handicapped children in the study population who had an IQ of 50 and above ($n = 175$). Of the 175 we had full data on 127 cases. For these cases, 19% could reasonably be considered resilient (adequate on all four functional measures), 40% showed mixed patterns of functioning (adequate on two or three functions), and 41% were vulnerable (adequate on 0 or one function, in adult mental handicap services, suicides). These results are for 73% of the total population. Our examination of possible bias introduced by missing cases showed there was little reason to believe that there was bias in the above results. Any bias would be in the direction of slightly less favourable outcomes. The results show a far less optimistic picture than indicated by Tizard (1965) and Kushlik and Blunden (1974) and are more like Edgerton's conclusion (1984), which was quoted earlier.

Acknowledgement

This study was supported by the Foundation for Child Development, the William T. Grant Foundation, the National Institute of Child Health and

Human Development Grant No. HD07907, Bowen and Jan McCoy and Tom and Mary Alice O'Malley. The authors wish to thank Raymond Illsley and the late Gordon Horobin of the British Medical Research Council for their help with the study and Janice McLaren who played an important role in gathering the data for the study.

Footnote

1. We have made some changes in these descriptions to protect the anonymity of the young adults and their families. The alterations do not change the essential aspects of their lives.

References

Birch, H., Richardson, S. A., Baird, D., Horobin, G., and Illsley, R. (1970), *Mental Subnormality in the Community: A Clinical and Epidemiological Study*. Baltimore: The Williams and Wilkins Co.

Edgerton, R. B. (1984). Introduction, in Edgerton, R. B. (Ed.) *Lives in Process: Mildly Retarded Adults in a Large City*. Washington, DC: AAMD.

Goulden, K. J., Richardson, S. A., and Shinnar, S. (1988). Factors suggesting biologic etiology of mental retardation from the Aberdeen cohort. *Developmental Medicine of Child Neurology* Volume 30, Supplement 52, p. 36.

Gruenberg, E. M. (1964). Epidemiology, in: Stevens, H. A. and Heber, R. (Eds.) *Mental Retardation*. Chicago and London: University of Chicago Press.

Kebbon, L. (1987). Relation between criteria: Case-finding method and prevalence. *Uppsala Journal of Medical Sciences*, Supplement 44:19–23.

Koller, H., Richardson, S. A., and Katz, M. (in press). Families of children with mental retardation: A comprehensive view from an epidemiologic perspective. *American Journal on Mental Retardation*.

Koller, H., Richardson, S. A, and Katz, M. (1988). Peer relationships of mildly retarded young adults living in the community. *Journal of Mental Deficiency Research*, 32:321–331.

Koller, H., Richardson, S. A., Katz, M., and McLaren, J. (1983). Behaviour disturbance since childhood in a five-year birth cohort of all mentally retarded young adults in a city. *American Journal of Mental Deficiency*, 87, 4:386–395.

Kushlick, A., and Blunden, R. (1974). The epidemiology of mental subnormality, in Clarke, A. M. and Clarke, A. D. B. (Eds.), *Mental Deficiency, the Changing Outlook*. London: Methuen.

Nirje, B., (1976). The normalization principle, in Kugel, R. B. and Shearer, A. (Eds.), *Changing Patterns in Residential Services for the Mentally Retarded*. Washington, DC: President's Committee on Mental Retardation.

Richardson, S. A., Katz, M., and Koller, H., (1990), *Leisure Activities of Mentally Retarded Adults Who Disappeared from MR Services After Leaving School*. (Unpublished report)

Richardson, S. A, and Koller, H. (1985). Epidemiology, in Clarke, A. M., Clarke, A. D. B. and Berg, J. (Eds.), *Mental Deficiency: The Changing Outlook*. 4th Edition, London: Methuen.

Richardson, S. A., Koller, H., and Katz, M. (1985a), Relationship of upbringing to later behaviour disturbance of mildly retarded young people. *American Journal of Mental Deficiency*, 90, 1:1–8.

Richardson, S. A., Koller, H., and Katz, M. (1985b), Continuities and change in behaviour disturbance, a follow-up study of mildly retarded young people. *American Journal of Orthopsychiatry*, 55:2, 220–229.

Richardson, S. A., Koller, H., and Katz, M. (1988), Job Histories in Open Employment of a Mentally Retarded Population of Young Adults – I, *American Journal on Mental Retardation,* volume 92, no. 6, 483–491.

Richardson, S. A., Goulden, K. J., Koller, H, and Katz, M. (1990), the Long Term Influence of the Family of Upbringing on Young Adults with Mild Mental Retardation, in Fraser, W. I. (Ed.), *Key Issues in Mental Retardation Research,* pp. 190–202, Routledge: London.

Rutter, M. (1983), Stress, Coping and Development: Some issues and some questions, in Garmezy, N. and Rutter, M. (Eds.), *Stress, Coping, and Development in Children,* New York: McGraw-Hill.

Tizard, J., (1965), Longitudinal and follow-up studies, in Clarke, A. M. and Clarke, A. D. B. (Eds.), *Mental Deficiency: The Changing Outlook.* London: Methuen.

Part 3

Vulnerability, resilience, and rehabilitation from biological and psycho-social stress

Chapter 7

Reducing mental and related handicaps:
a biomedical perspective

J. M. Berg

Introduction

Though often demonstrating remarkable resilience, the human organism is vulnerable to a vast array of adverse influences of both genetic and environmental origin that can lead to mental retardation, frequently associated with other dysfunctions and morphological changes that may be recognizable as distinct syndromes. Readers interested in these syndromes will find, among other current and informative sources, descriptions and pictorial depictions of many of them in the recent update (Jones, 1988) of Smith's excellent volume on human malformations. The ideal of primary prevention of the disorders mentioned by eliminating or avoiding their causes can be achieved to some extent, but is often not yet possible or even within reach in the immediately foreseeable future. Nevertheless, when the latter is the case, other measures of a biomedical, psychosocial and educational kind can frequently reduce the deleterious consequences of the causal influences referred to above.

In this chapter, the focus is predominantly on organic (physical), in contrast to psychological, determinants of mental handicap, and biomedical means for counteracting these determinants or minimizing their harmful effects. The considerations involved have ramifications that extend beyond the areas of biology and medicine into such realms as public policy and ethics, to which some attention is also given in the context of the technical data presented.

Aetiological considerations

The ability to prevent mental retardation is essentially dependent on an understanding of its aetiology. Prospects for amelioration of this and related disabilities and disorders are also enhanced if aetiological factors can be elucidated, although beneficial symptomatic treatment can frequently be undertaken despite obscure causation.

It has been traditional for a long time to subdivide the multiple biomedical aetiologies of mental deficit into genetic and environmental categories. This remains useful provided that, in doing so, it is recognized that the two categories are not mutually exclusive and are closely intertwined in producing eventual clinical outcomes. Thus, the effects of adverse genetic factors can be modified by environmental circumstances and interventions, and the impact of environmental hazards can be influenced by an individual's genotype. Furthermore, a direct causal relationship between genetic and environmental events may be evident in the production of phenotypic abnormality, as exemplified by reference to genetically determined maternal hyperphenylalaninaemia in untreated phenylketonuric mothers constituting an environmental risk to the fetus (Levy and Waisbren, 1983), or the possibility of ionizing radiation prior to conception producing gene mutations that result in mental and physical defects in offspring (Thompson and Thompson, 1986).

Bearing these considerations in mind, distinct genetic varieties of mental retardation fall into two main groups – that is, specific gene defects usually transmitted in an autosomal recessive, autosomal dominant or X-linked recessive manner, and morphologically recognizable numerical and structural chromosomal aberrations involving excess or deficiency of cytogenetic material. As for types of mental retardation primarily due to physical determinants of environmental origin, these are most suitably grouped in accordance with the time of direct exposure to the extrinsic hazard – that is, pre-, peri- and postnatally.

From a biomedical perspective, all these circumstances generally result in central nervous system pathology, which is the basis for clinically manifesting mental deficit and associated abnormalities such as motor disorders and epilepsy. Though nearly all persons with severe mental retardation (say IQ below 50) have such neuropathology recognizable during life or at autopsy, the aetiological factors that underlie it can be detected at present in only about half the cases, in some of which the precise process or mechanisms culminating in the pathology remains essentially unclear. Many of these aetiological factors can also result in less severe, or even imperceptible, mental retardation. However, relatively mild or marginal mental deficit is frequently not associated with recognizable cerebral pathology either because it is absent or because it cannot be detected by current investigative procedures. In these instances, it is often thought that the aetiological basis for the mental retardation is multifactorial – that is, a combination of the effects of multiple genes (polygenic) and environmental influences (physical and/or psychosocial) of various kinds, in contrast to the retardation being essentially due to a specific causal factor such as a harmful gene or a teratogen. Continuing advances in biology and increasing understanding of the impact of environmental circumstances are contributing to further eluci-dation of currently aetiologically obscure varieties of both severe and mild mental deficit and of related manifestations. In the context of this brief background, existing and prospective biomedical preventive and ameliora-tive interventions in this field are considered below.

Prevention

Cure (i.e., restoration to complete normality) of mental retardation, as op-posed to amelioration, by biomedical means is virtually non-existent in the present state of knowledge. The objective of prevention of this disability, preferable of course even if curative measures were available, thus becomes a matter of especially great concern. As outlined below, the biomedical approaches to, and prospects for, achieving this objective differ in accordance with the different genetic and environmental aetiologies involved.

Genetic aspects

With a few gratifying exceptions, though not necessarily with entirely suc-cessful outcomes – for example, prompt dietary management of phenylketo-nuria (Fishler, Azen, Friedman and Koch, 1989) and galactosaemia (Hayes, Bowling, Fraser, Krimmer, Marrinan and Clague, 1988) by, respectively, restriction of phenylalanine and avoidance of galactose (contained in milk and milk products) – mental retardation is essentially not preventable once the underlying causal genetic defect is operative. At a basic level, the possi-bility of early treatment before cerebral damage occurs, such as by means of gene therapy (Anderson, 1989; Weatherall, 1991), is an exciting prospect, though not yet a practical reality. Preventive approaches therefore currently occur mainly within the framework of genetic counselling and, as an expan-ding and increasingly utilized offshoot of that, prenatal diagnosis.

GENETIC COUNSELLING

It has become increasingly possible to provide well-founded information about the chances of mental retardation occurring or recurring in prospective offspring. Usually such counselling is sought when there is a history of an affected family member or members, most often among children or siblings (i.e., first-degree relatives) of those seeking information. When that is the case, an aetiological diagnosis in the affected person(s) is of crucial value in providing accurate statistical odds. Thus, for specific gene disorders with a Mendelian pattern of transmission (McKusick, 1990), recurrence risk percentages can be exact – for example a 25% chance of an autosomal recessive disorder recurring in a sibling of an affected individual; or a 50% chance, irrespective of gender, of recurrence in a child of an autosomal dominant condition transmitted by a parental carrier of the gene concerned, the same chance applying only to male offspring of heterozygous, clinically unaffected females when the disorder is X-linked recessive. Recurrence risks of chromosomal aberrations are usually less precise because, in most instances, they can be based only on empirical data; these risks generally happen to be well below the percentages mentioned above for specific gene defects, for example of the order of 1% for recurrence of standard (regular) trisomy 21 Down syndrome in the large majority of sibships. Empirically derived recurrence percentages can be provided as well for various disorders or syndromes of uncertain aetiology but with a very probable genetic component; a neural tube defect, some types of which are associated with mental retardation, is an example, with the chances of recurrence in a first-degree relative of a single affected family member in the neighbourhood of 4%. Evidence has been reported of a marked decrease in recurrences following maternal vitamin supplementation periconceptionally and early in pregnancy (Smithells, 1986), but there have been inconsistent findings (Mills and his co-investigators, 1989) in that regard.

Genetic counselling is also advised or sought in various circumstances before any children with developmental or other disabilities have been conceived or born. Consanguinity, relatively advanced maternal age, and ethnic background that may be associated with a raised risk of a particular disorder are three such circumstances. Consanguineous unions can increase chances of autosomal recessive disorders occurring in offspring and, with advancing age of the mother, the odds of having children with chromosomal aberrations due to non-disjunction (most notably standard trisomy 21 Down syndrome) also rise. An example of the third circumstance mentioned is the relatively high frequency of the gene for Tay-Sachs disease in persons of Ashkenazi Jewish background, so that preconceptual biochemical screening for heterozygous carriers of clinically normal potential parents with that background can be useful (Kaback, 1981).

Genetic counselling, in the context of the kind of situations exemplified above, can have preventive consequences concerning mental retardation and related conditions before conception occurs. Depending to some extent on their concerns about the size of the risk involved and on their perceptions of the seriousness of the disorder in question, some couples at increased risk may, for example, decide to avoid natural further pregnancies or an initial one; or instead to opt for such procedures as artificial insemination with donor sperm or *in vitro* fertilization of a donor ovum, if relevant to their circumstances; or to adopt the relatively simple expedient, even if inconvenient, of pregnancy at younger rather than older maternal age in order to decrease the chances of having children with chromosome abnormalities. Though such choices, particularly those involving use of germ cells from someone other than the spouse, can be emotionally stressful or ethically troublesome, some couples will find them less so than a possible alternative option of pregnancy termination following prenatal diagnosis of an affected fetus.

PRENATAL DIAGNOSIS

The rapidly growing scope for prenatal detection of fetal abnormality has been among the most remarkable biomedical developments of the last few decades. Techniques for this purpose commonly include ultrasonography for increasingly precise visualization of morphological appearances of the fetus, and the more invasive (and hence not entirely safe) procedures of amniocentesis, chorionic villus sampling and cordocentesis that provide material for determining chromosomal, biochemical and molecular biological components of fetal status (Weaver, 1989). A large proportion of the deviations from normal thus recognizable would be associated with mental deficit of greater or lesser degree in postnatal life. Effective treatment *in utero* would, of course, constitute a highly desirable benefit of prenatal diagnosis and some progress in that regard is being made (Schulman, 1990). However, for the present, the ability to diagnose fetal defects greatly exceeds the capacity for preventive therapeutic interventions. Hence, at this point in time, the option of pregnancy termination should 'incurable' fetal aberrations be found is a significant reason why many potential parents at increased risk of having an abnormal child opt to have prenatal diagnostic investigations like those mentioned. This consideration raises sensitive ethical questions that are the subject of extensive and often emotional debate.

There are widely varying outlooks in different societies and among individuals as to the moral legitimacy or otherwise of abortion and as to what circumstances, if any, would make it acceptable; demonstrated, for instance, by the series of papers on the subject in the book, *Biomedical Ethics* (Mappes and Zembatty, 1986). Between the extremes of abortion being considered reprehensible whatever the grounds for undertaking it and the view that it should be available when desired by prospective parents for virtually any reason, variables such as the perceived seriousness of detected fetal defects and the temporal stage of a pregnancy influence public policy positions and statutory regulations concerning pregnancy termination in different countries.

Whatever may be the prevailing attitudes and legal requirements in these respects, in any country, it needs to be added that prenatal diagnostic undertakings of the kinds referred to have significant life-creating and life-preserving facets as well. Thus, some couples at increased risk of having a child with fetal abnormality that would be associated with mental and related disabilities postnatally would avoid pregnancy but for the availability of prenatal diagnostic testing. Furthermore, as the tests much more often than not yield normal results, some pregnancies which prospective parents might have chosen to terminate without such investigations continue to term with the birth of a healthy child.

In essence, increasing diagnostic accessibility to the fetus has had both comforting and troublesome ramifications. In the latter respect, considerations of safety and reliability of the procedures involved can raise concerns in some instances, but perhaps the most uncomfortable overall problem has resulted from the contrast between the extensive capacity to detect fetal genetic defects and disorders (many connected with eventual mental deficit) and the current inability to treat most of them effectively. This has led to the reality of pregnancy termination as the only 'prevention' option in many cases. The ethical dilemmas and emotional stresses of numerous couples in these circumstances are a significant burden (Black, 1990), but, it can be anticipated, one that will diminish with prospective biomedical advances that narrow the gap between diagnostic scope and therapeutic possibilities.

Environmental aspects

Physical factors of environmental origin that can result in mental deficit and associated abnormalities are ubiquitous. The following are but some of many examples. Prenatally, particularly during the early stages of pregnancy, infections (e.g., the spirochaete of syphilis; the virus of rubella; the protozoan parasite of toxoplasmosis), drugs (e.g., the anticonvulsant Hydantoin; the anticoagulant Warfarin; the acne medication Isotretinoin) and other hazards (e.g., irradiation; alcohol; methyl mercury) are among those that can cause death *in utero* or impair normal development of liveborn survivors. Effects can range from catastrophic to inapparent ones, depending on variables that include timing of exposure, its extent and fetal resistance, influenced to some degree by genetic constitution. Near or at the time of birth, adverse occurrences resulting in cerebral asphyxia/hypoxia or mechanical trauma can be the basis for subsequent mental defect. These considerations are particularly applicable to infants who are unduly small because of intra-uterine growth retardation or premature birth for whatever reason. During postnatal life, additional hazards include bacterial and viral infections causing meningitis and/or encephalitis, absorption of noxious chemicals like lead, and such accidents as head injury and near-drowning which may result in central nervous system damage. Space limitations do not permit a comprehensive review of these and other such aetiological determinants originating in the environment, but a number of their nuances require attention here.

Prevention of disability is a distinctly attainable goal in many of the kinds of circumstances mentioned by measures involving removal of the danger, protection from exposure to it or counteracting it before harmful consequences ensue. Doing so can be relatively simple in individual instances (e.g., avoidance of alcohol consumption during pregnancy, or the application of suitable restraints, such as seat belts and special infant seats, in motor vehicles), but is often dependent on socio-economic realities, public policy priorities and attitudes that determine the development, availability and use of relevant resources. All too often there are significant discrepancies between what can be achieved in preventive terms and what takes place in practice. A striking example concerns iodine deficiency which, amongst other undesirable consequences, can impair mental development. Hetzel (1986) has pointed out that iodized salt and iodized oil can greatly reduce the deficiency on a mass scale and at relatively modest cost. However, these measures appear not to have been comprehensively introduced in all jurisdictions in Asia, for instance, where approximately 400 million people have been estimated to be at risk.

More general dietary inadequacies, resulting in the widespread scourge of malnutrition and, in some circumstances, starvation, are also a matter of great concern, not only in underdeveloped and economically disadvantaged countries but in some communities within comparatively affluent industrialized societies as well. Because undernutrition involves deficiencies of different dietary ingredients in different situations, and because the phenomenon is usually linked with other environmental deprivations and psychosocial stresses, its pre- and post-natal effects on brain structure and function are difficult to pinpoint precisely in humans. Nevertheless, without casting any aspersions on many laudable undertakings to reduce malnourishment, the mental and physical health of much of the world's population would surely be greatly enhanced if national governments and international regulatory agencies would marshall more of their resources to counteract the problem and associated environmental determinants of disability; the latter include undue exposure to infections and chemical pollutants due to such factors as overcrowding, lack of hygiene and deficient or underutilized public health safeguards.

In addition, constant vigilance is necessary to avoid a resurgence of conditions the occurrence of which had been markedly reduced with the use of efficacious treatment. Syphilis is an illustration. There had been an over 50–fold decline in the incidence of reported cases of congenital syphilis in the United States in 1979 compared to 1941 (Budell, 1984). However, Dorfman and Glaser (1990) drew attention to a recent dramatic increase of the disease in that country, particularly in urban areas, associated with socio-economic adversity, widespread use of 'crack' cocaine and prostitution. It is an indication that the existence of effective screening and therapy (in this case, penicillin) is *per se* not necessarily a wholly preventive solution without concomitant improvements in living conditions and life styles.

It seems relevant to refer here as well to how changing circumstances during the perinatal period that illustrate significant progress can also create new dilemmas. There have been remarkable and well-documented (e.g., in many papers published in the journal *Seminars in Perinatology*, now in its fifteenth year) recent advances in obstetrics and neonatology in the recognition of factors that can damage the central nervous system near, at, or soon after birth, in the capacity to diagnose such damage, and in prevention and management strategies in these regards. One of the consequences of these developments is the markedly improved survival rate of very small babies, some weighing as little as 500–750g, who are particularly vulnerable to such occurrences as peri-/intra-ventricular haemorrhage and hyperbilirubinaemia, leading to subsequent mental and neurological impairments. This has raised sensitive issues concerning the appropriateness or otherwise of intensive neonatal care in at least some of these infants when the prognosis regarding their subsequent neuropsychological state appears to be bleak. As Young and Stevenson (1990) have pointed out, conflicting views derived from principles of beneficence, non-maleficence and distributive justice are made all the more difficult to reconcile because decision-making about type and intensity of neonatal interventions often has to take place in the context of prognostic uncertainty. Here too, further heed to adverse socio-economic and health care factors that apply to many actually or prospectively pregnant women could reduce the birth of very small infants, among others, at high risk for mental and physical defects.

Amelioration

Once mental retardation has occurred, whether primarily of genetic or environmental origin, amelioration generally becomes the predominant focus of attention. Psychosocial and educational undertakings of various kinds, beyond the scope of this chapter, are clearly of great value in making a wide-ranging contribution to improvement of function and adaptation of affected persons. As indicated below, what may broadly be termed as medical and medically related measures also have a substantial and significant ameliorative role to play, most notably with respect to the many abnormalities and disorders that frequently accompany mental deficit and exacerbate its effects.

Medication as a means of directly enhancing intellectual and cognitive functioning of mentally retarded persons as a whole has been essentially ineffective, although scientifically unsubstantiated claims to the contrary are periodically advanced. Thus, for example, Black, Kato and Walker (1966), in a methodologically sound study of sicca cell therapy, found no evidence of improved intellect or behaviour in retarded children of various types, despite enthusiastic advocacy in some quarters for this form of cellular treatment. Like observations can be made concerning some other medications (e.g., various combinations of chemical substances) that have been purported, on tenuous grounds, to reduce the mental deficit of retarded persons in general. As the basis for mental retardation differs widely in different individuals, it is unlikely, to say the least, that any particular medication would be universally beneficial in improving mental capacity. Rational specific ameliorative medical treatment for manifestations of particular mental retardation syndromes is a more realistic approach for improving function, and hence the quality of life, of affected individuals, though here also evidence of efficacy and safety under different conditions (e.g., age group, dose) needs to be established before routine clinical use of the treatment.

The last-mentioned approach can be illustrated by reference to two disorders involving chromosomal aberrations, namely the fragile-X and Klinefelter syndromes. Since folic acid had been found to decrease the proportion of fragile-X cells detectable in laboratory preparations, it was felt that treatment with folic acid could have ameliorative effects on disadvantageous mental features in the syndrome. However, the results emerging from a number of studies have been inconsistent, in terms of effects on both mental level and behaviour, as evidenced by a series of papers on the subject in a special issue of the *American Journal of Medical Genetics* (1986, Vol. 23, No. 1/2). In Klinefelter syndrome, inadequate testosterone production has led to treatment with this hormone, with reported considerable improvement in behaviour and adaptation to the environment in the majority of cases, even when therapy was commenced in adulthood (Nielsen, Pelsen and Srensen, 1988).

In addition, apart from established means for largely preventing mental and associated disability in a few biochemical disorders (exemplified in the prevention section of this chapter), medical amelioration of such manifestations in various other inborn errors of metabolism has been attempted with some evidence of good effect. Lesch-Nyhan syndrome is an example of such a disorder (in this case of purine metabolism) in which attempted specific medication for distinctive neuropsychiatric problems has been relatively ineffective, though not entirely without benefit in some instances. Occasionally, behaviour has improved to some extent with administration of 5–hydroxytryptophan combined with carbidopa (Nyhan, 1976). Bone marrow transplantation as a means of replacing a deficient enzyme is another therapeutic possibility, illustrated in a report by Hobbs and his colleagues (1981) of physical improvement and apparent arrest of developmental deterioration in a young child with Hurler's disease (a mucopolysaccharide disorder), who underwent such a transplant from his mother in an attempt to replace iduronidase.

Besides specific ameliorative medications geared to particular mental retardation syndromes, some medications are suitable for certain manifestations commonly associated with many types of mental handicap. Particularly notable among these associated manifestations are different varieties of psychiatric illness and other behavioural disturbances that occur among persons of all ages and all grades of mental retardation (Reid, 1982; Stark, Menolascino, Albarelli and Gray, 1988). For the present purpose, suffice it to say that delineation of the types and complex nature of these problems in people with concomitant mental deficit and the institution of well-founded treatment (including appropriate psychotropic drugs, psychotherapy and behaviour modification procedures within the framework of a supportive environmental milieu that reduces emotional stresses) is a significant component in facilitating the function of many mentally retarded individuals to the best of their potential. A comprehensive review of psychotropic medications and their use in persons with mental retardation is provided by Gadow and Poling (1988).

Epilepsy in its various forms is also a frequent occurrence in mentally retarded persons as a whole, particularly those with severe mental deficit, and may in some instances contribute to intellectual decline. A considerable array of anti-convulsant medications is now available that are effective in controlling seizures (Gadow and Poling, 1988). However, they need to be prescribed with caution and careful monitoring because of possible untoward side-effects that include behavioural and/or cognitive deterioration (Corbett and Pond, 1985). As with psychotropic medications, simultaneous use of several drugs, sometimes referred to as polypharmacy, should be avoided unless absolutely necessary.

The focus above has been almost exclusively on medications intended to improve the outlook for persons with mental retardation by ameliorating mental deficit *per se* or accompanying behavioural and physical disorders that add to the burdens of those affected. Surgery also has a substantial role to play in the treatment of certain types of actual or potential mental handicap. A major example is cerebrospinal fluid shunt operations, in children with forms of hydrocephaly suitable for such procedures, that have for several decades been undertaken with considerable success in improving mental and physical prognosis, and that more recently have been attempted also, with less encouraging initial results, on hydrocephalic fetuses *in utero* (Manning, Harrison and Rodeck, 1986).

Direct operations on the brain involving the severing or excision of cerebral tissue have also been performed for some time in retarded individuals, less with the objective of reducing mental deficit as such than of eliminating or diminishing associated handicaps, particularly intractable epilepsy and severe behavioural problems. Prefrontal leucotomy, somewhat in vogue at one stage as a treatment for some severely disturbed persons with mental retardation, appears to have been largely abandoned (Engler, 1948). Hemispherectomy is sometimes undertaken and can be beneficial in carefully selected cases; for instance, Hoffman, Hendrick, Dennis and Armstrong (1979), among others, have reported favourable outcomes, with regard to mental development, seizure occurrence and reduction of hemiparesis, following hemispherectomy in young children with Sturge-Weber syndrome (a form of haemangiomatosis). Temporal lobectomy (Hopkins and Klug, 1991) and extratemporal cortical resections of frontal, parietal, occipital and multilobular tissues (Adler, Erba, Winston, Welch and Lombrosco, 1991) have also been done with some success in controlling epilepsy unresponsive to anticonvulsant drugs, and also with apparent consequent improvements in behavioural and intellectual respects; these operations may occasionally be suitable in children with mental deficit.

In contrast to surgical extirpation of cerebral tissue, neural transplants derived from fetuses, already attempted as possible treatment in Parkinson's disease (Sladek and Gash, 1988), may in due course have a practical therapeutic application for some mental retardation syndromes. The transplantation of neural and other fetal tissues (e.g., liver, pancreas, thymus) has significant ethical ramifications concerning the circumstances in which such tissues might be obtained, including the possibility of conception and subsequent abortion being decided upon for the purpose of donating or selling the tissues (Council on Scientific Affairs and Council on Ethical and Judicial Affairs, 1990).

Some mental retardation entities involve craniofacial and other malformations (e.g., acrocephaly and related skeletal anomalies in Apert's syndrome) that are amenable to surgical correction with resultant functional and cosmetic benefits. In addition, the repair of internal organ defects, some of which are common in various syndromes (e.g. congenital cardiac abnormalities in Down syndrome) may be necessary to reduce morbidity or to save life. Refraining from such treatments has raised ethical concerns and been the subject of legal proceedings as well (Herr, 1984). More controversial in Down syndrome is facial plastic surgery, intended to 'improve' appearances and hence acceptance in the community, and/or to facilitate breathing, eating and development of speech (May, 1988). There is a paucity of data as to what extent the latter objectives are achieved; regarding the former one, changes in public attitudes seem more likely to be beneficial to affected individuals than changes in physiognomy.

Besides the disciplines of medicine and surgery and the specialties within them, other medically related specialists (e.g., physiotherapists, optometrists, audiologists, speech pathologists) also obviously have a valuable role in the amelioration of disorders connected with mental handicap. Many of the conditions that come within the orbit of such specialists (e.g., sensory and motor ones) are more prone to occur in those with mental retardation than in the population at large. It need hardly be said that mentally retarded persons are no less entitled to receive treatment in these respects than anyone else and that provision of such treatment contributes significantly to successful adaptation of these persons within the societies in which they live. The need to undertake the interventions mentioned can reasonably be considered to be more pressing at present than in earlier years, partly because more efficacious therapies now exist but perhaps even more importantly because of the trend in many countries to integrate those with mental handicap into the general population, as opposed to relative isolation in institutions.

Conclusion, with a personal note

Vulnerability and resilience, the title of this Festschrift volume, are certainly characteristics that manifest themselves in various ways with regard to mental retardation and related disabilities. From a biomedical perspective, in addition to vulnerability to the manifold and diverse factors that can result in these disabilities, resilience is partly evidenced by the remarkable variability in phenotypic outcome that can follow exposure to each of these factors. Persons carrying the tuberous sclerosis gene or fetuses confronted by the rubella virus early in pregnancy, to choose but two of very numerous specific examples, may emerge from these circumstances virtually unscathed, or relatively mildly affected, compared to others who become gravely incapacitated, both mentally and physically. Clearer understanding of the reasons for such divergent outcomes might contribute substantially to the currently available armamentarium of biomedical preventive and ameliorative measures briefly reviewed in this chapter.

These perspectives have been considered in detail by various authors, together with highly significant and interrelated psychosocial and educational considerations concerning causation, interventions and prospects, in *Mental Deficiency: The Changing Outlook* (Clarke, Clarke and Berg, 1985), among other relevant texts. Mention of that book leads me to add that it was a privilege to be associated with Ann and Alan Clarke in its production, both because of warm regard for them as friends of longstanding and because of admiration of their deservedly distinguished record as scholars and scientists in the best sense of these words. It is a particular pleasure therefore to join with other contributors to this present Festschrift in their honour.

References

Adler, J., Erba, G., Winston, K. R., Welch, K., and Lombrosco, C. T. (1991), 'Results of surgery for extratemporal partial epilepsy that began in childhood'. *Archives of Neurology* 48(2), 133–140.

Anderson, W. F. (1989) 'Gene therapy', in Evans, M. I., Dixler, A. O., Fletcher, J. C., and Schulman, J. D. (eds), *Fetal Diagnosis and Therapy: Science, Ethics and the Law*, chapter 15, section 4, pp. 421–430. Philadelphia: J. B. Lippincott Company.

Black, D. B., Kato, J. G., and Walker, G. W. R. (1966), 'A study of improvement in mentally retarded children accruing from siccacell tberapy'. *American Journal of Mental Deficiency* 70(4), 499–508.

Black, R. B. (1990), 'Prenatal diagnosis and fetal loss: Psychosocial consequences and professional responsibilities'. *American Journal of Medical Genetics* 35(4), 586–587.

Budell, J. W. (1984) 'Syphilis', in Kelley, V. C. (ed), *Practice of Pediatrics*, revised edn., vol. 3, chapter 103, pp. 1–18. Philadelphia: Harper and Row.

Clarke, A. M., Clarke, A. D. B., and Berg, J. M. (eds)(1985) *Mental Deficiency: The Changing Outlook*, 4th ed. London: Methuen and Co. Ltd.

Corbett, J., and Pond, D. (1985) 'The management of epilepsy', in Craft, M., Bicknell, J., and Hollins, S. (eds), *Mental Handicap: A Multidisciplinary Approach*, chapter 33, pp. 373–381. London: Baillière Tindall.

Council on Scientific Affairs and Council on Ethical and Judicial Affairs, American Medical Association (1990), 'Medical applications of fetal tissue transplantation'. *Journal of the American Medical Association* 263(4), 565–570.

Dorfman, D. H., and Glaser, J. H. (1990), 'Congenital syphilis presenting in infants after the newborn period'. *New England Journal of Medicine* 323(19), 1299–1302.

Engler, M. (1948), 'Prefrontal leucotomy in mental defectives'. *Journal of Mental Science* 94, 844–850.

Fishler, K., Azen, C. G., Friedman, E. G., and Koch, R. (1989), 'School achievement in treated PKU children'. *Journal of Mental Deficiency Research* 33(6), 493–498.

Gadow, K. D., and Poling, A. G. (1988) *Pharmacotherapy and Mental Retardation*. London: Taylor and Francis.

Hayes, A., Bowling, F. G., Fraser, D., Krimmer, H. L., Marrinan, A., and Clague, A. E. (1988), 'Neonatal screening and an intensive management programme for galactosaemia: early evidence of benefits'. *Medical Journal of Australia* 149, 21–25.

Herr, S. S. (1984), 'The Philip Becker case resolved: a chance for habilitation'. *Mental Retardation* 22(1), 30–35.

Hetzel, B. S. (1986) 'Mental defect due to iodine deficiency: A major international public health problem that can be eradicated', in Berg, J. M. (ed), *Science and Service in Mental Retardation*, pp. 297–306. London: Methuen and Co. Ltd.

Hobbs, J. R., Barrett, A. J., Chambers, D., James, D. C. O., Hugh-Jones, K., Byrom, M., Henry, K., Lucas, C. F., Rogers, T. R., Benson, P. F., Tansley, L. R., Patrick, A. D., Mossman, J., and Young,

E. P. (1981), 'Reversal of clinical features of Hurler's disease and biochemical improvement after treatment by bone-marrow transplantation'. *Lancet* 2(8249), 709–712.

Hoffman, H. J., Hendrick, E. B., Dennis, M., and Armstrong, D. (1979), 'Hemispherectomy for Sturge-Weber syndrome'. *Child's Brain* 5, 233–248.

Hopkins, I. J., and Klug, G. L. (1991), 'Temporal lobectomy for the treatment of intractable complex partial seizures of temporal lobe origin in early childhood'. *Developmental Medicine and Child Neurology* 33(1), 26–31.

Jones, K. L. (1988) *Smith's Recognizable Patterns of Human Malformation* 4th ed. Philadelphia: W. B. Saunders Company.

Kaback, M. M. (1981) 'Heterozygote screening and prenatal diagnosis in Tay-Sachs disease: A worldwide update', in Callahan, J. W., and Lowden, J. A. (eds), *Lysosomes and Lysosomal Storage Diseases*, pp. 331–342. New York: Raven Press.

Levy, H. L., and Waisbren, S. E. (1983), 'Effects of untreated maternal phenylketonuria and hyperphenylalaninemia on the fetus'. *New England Journal of Medicine* 309(21), 1269–1274.

Manning, F. A., Harrison, M. R., and Rodeck, C. H. (1986), 'Catheter shunts for fetal hydronephrosis and hydrocephalus. Report of the International Fetal Surgery Registry'. *New England Journal of Medicine* 315(5), 336–340.

Mappes, T. A., and Zembaty, J. S. (1986) Biomedical Ethics, 2nd ed., chapter 9, pp. 449–488. New York: McGraw-Hill Book Company.

May, D. C. (1988), 'Plastic surgery for children with Down syndrome: normalization or extremism?'. *Mental Retardation* 26(1), 17–19.

McKusick, V. A. (1990) *Mendelian Inheritance in Man: Catalogs of Autosomal Dominant, Autosomal Recessive, and X-linked Phenotypes*, 9th ed. Baltimore: The Johns Hopkins University Press.

Mills, J. L., Rhoads, G. G., Simpson, J. L., Cunningham, G. C., Conley, M. R., Lassman, M. R., Walden, M. E., Depp, O. R., Hoffman, H. J., and the National Institute of Child Health and Human Development Neural Tube Defects Study Group (1989), 'The absence of a relation between the periconceptional use of vitamins and neural-tube defects'. *New England Journal of Medicine* 321(7), 430–435.

Nielsen, J., Pelsen, B., and Srensen, K (1988), 'Follow-up of 30 Klinefelter males treated with testosterone'. *Clinical Genetics* 33(4), 262–269.

Nyhan, W. L. (1976), 'Behavior in the Lesch-Nyhan syndrome'. *Journal of Autism and Childhood Schizophrenia* 6(3), 235–252.

Reid, A. H. (1982) *The Psychiatry of Mental Handicap*. London: Blackwell Scientific Publications.

Schulman, J. D. (1990), 'Treatment of the embryo and the fetus in the first trimester: Current status and future prospects'. *American Journal of Medical Genetics* 35(2), 197–200.

Sladek, J. R., and Gash, D. M. (1988), 'Nerve-cell grafting in Parkinson's disease'. *Journal of Neurosurgery* 68(3), 337–351.

Smithells, R. W. (1986) 'Prevention of neural tube defects by vitamin supplements', in Berg, J. M. (ed), *Science and Service in Mental Retardation*, pp. 277–280. London: Methuen and Co. Ltd.

Stark, J. A., Menolascino, F. J., Albarelli, M. H., and Gray, V. C. (eds)(1988) *Mental Retardation and Mental Health: Classification, Diagnosis, Treatment, Services*. New York: Springer-Verlag.

Thompson, J. S., and Thompson, M. W. (1986) *Genetics in Medicine*, 4th ed., p. 263. Philadelphia: W. B. Saunders Company.

Weatherall, D. J. (1991), 'Gene therapy in perspective'. *Nature* 349(6307), 275–276.

Weaver, D. D. (1989) *Catalog of Prenatally Diagnosed Conditions*. Baltimore: The Johns Hopkins University Press.

Young, E. W. D., and Stevenson, D. K. (1990), 'Limiting treatment for extremely premature, low-birth-weight infants (500 to 750 g)'. *American Journal of Diseases of Children* 144(5), 549–552.

Chapter 8

Rehabilitation of the dyspraxic dysphasic adult

Margaret and Robert Fawcus

The visible physical sequellae of damage to the left motor cortex or related areas of the brain are devastating in themselves, but in about a third of cases of stroke or head injury a right hemiplegia is accompanied by some degree of language disorder. The effect upon an individual ranges from minimal interference to a near total loss of communicative skills. The dysphasia can clear within weeks or disrupt both written and spoken communication for the remainder of a person's life. In the main these effects are dependent upon the severity and site of the cerebral damage, but they are also significantly affected by environmental factors, including rehabilitative intervention.

One of the most impressive features of the dysphasic man or woman is their resilience. It is remarkable that the overwhelming majority of patients, in our experience, do not succumb even in the face of a daunting catalogue of misfortunes. These typically include paralysis of the right limbs; significant deterioration in speech, language, reading and writing skills; loss of employment; the breakdown of relationships and a not unexpected high incidence of depression.

Prior to the cerebral insult they have each had their share of the gifts and experiences of the remainder of the adult population. The range of occupations of those who have attended the City Dysphasic group over the past twenty years covers virtually every aspect of modern life, from accountants and architects through to zoo keepers. Attempts to establish the efficacy of therapeutic procedures are seriously hampered by the multiplicity of attendant factors, both medical and social.

Our original dysphasic group was set up in 1970 as part of a speech therapy training establishment because we were seriously concerned that such patients were receiving limited help from the standard pattern of provision. Many individuals at the time received no help at all, most were seen for no more than thirty minutes a week and few had opportunities to receive speech therapy for longer than twelve months (cf. Rossiter, 1987).

From the first three members – a merchant banker, a street trader and an accountant – the group steadily grew to include an even wider educational and social mix. From the beginning we set up small integral groups which changed in composition to reflect the specific activity to be undertaken and the linguistic capacities of the members. A patient who encountered considerable difficulty with spoken language but who exhibited greater facility in writing would join different groups for these activities. The advantage of growing numbers was that it was usually possible to accommodate individuals in working groups which closely matched their capabilities.

Of the hundreds of dysphasic adults who have attended for intensive speech therapy at the City Dysphasic Group, we have elected to describe the adaptive behaviour of one small sub-group. In addition to hemiplegia and a serious level of difficulty with speech, language, reading and writing, each of these individuals exhibits a marked degree of articulatory dyspraxia (apraxia of speech). Dyspraxia represents a disorder at the programming level of production, as opposed to dysarthria which is due to lesions at a lower level of neuromotor organisation.

A dyspraxic child or adult may have no observable paralysis of limbs or speech musculature but displays disorganisation and limitation of skilled behaviour patterns (Huskins, 1986; Square-Storer, 1989). The site, nature and severity of the cerebral lesion tends to dictate the type of dyspraxia. The most severely affected cases of articulatory dyspraxia have great difficulty in producing phonation or even basic articulatory movements. In an attempt to reproduce gestures or signs a dysphasic with ideomotor dyspraxia will show struggle, frustration and inaccuracy as he or she attempts a pattern of hand movements.

The emphasis in aphasia rehabilitation traditionally centred on the need to restore speech. Inability to achieve this goal represented failure for the patient and therapist alike, and led to the belief that speech therapy was of limited value to the more severely impaired dysphasic patient (Sarno et al, 1970). If, however, we shift the emphasis towards the development of nonverbal communication skills, then we begin to see possibilities for successful intervention. As Kraat (1985) says, 'this broadened concept of what constitutes communication behaviour allows us to tap a rich flow of information that is passed from one person to another in a conversational exchange'.

Argyle (1972) and many others have demonstrated the role of non-verbal behaviour in human communication, and have made us aware of its importance in conveying information and expressing attitudes. Parallel with these studies, there has been an increasing recognition that signing is an effective form of communication for the deaf, and should not be regarded as a language system inferior to the spoken language of the hearing world. The Makaton vocabulary, based on British Sign Language (Walker, 1973), has gained rapid ground internationally in work with both the mentally and physically handicapped non-speaking population. As Kraat (1985) observed, however, 'until recently, researchers in communication disorders and communication development tended to ignore the non-verbal or non-linguistic aspects of communication'.

A number of therapeutic approaches have focused attention on the development of non-verbal skills in the dysphasic patient.

Skelly (1979) reported on the use of AMERIND (American Indian Hand Talk) as an augmentative form of communication for patients with severe language impairment following cerebral vascular accident or head injury. AMERIND, having developed as a form of communication between tribes who did not share a common spoken language, required that 'hand talk' had to be sufficiently clear that the majority of viewers could easily guess its meaning. This 'transparency' tended to preserve a simplicity of structure in the system but limited the levels of abstraction and symbolism. This is of particular importance for the dysphasic patient who has problems in dealing with the abstractions of language and auditory and visual symbols. Clinical evidence suggests that signs can be recognised by dysphasics with all levels of linguistic impairment.

Whilst Skelly (1979) and Stuart-Smith and Wilks (1979) have reported on the successful acquisition of a signed vocabulary, clinical experience suggests that not all patients acquire signs in a reliable and recognisable way. Furthermore, the successful use of signs in the clinical situation is often not reflected in their use in the home situation (Kraat, 1990).

The dual problem of a hemiplegia which affects the preferred hand and limb dyspraxia may result in signs that are incomplete and imprecise. Gainotti and Lemmo (1976) have commented on the dysphasic's difficulty in reproducing gestures because of a 'true dyspraxia' rather than to any lack of understanding of the gestures themselves. A failure to produce signs that are not recognised, and therefore not responded to, will soon discourage the dysphasic patient from further attempts at using signing.

The advent of PACE therapy (Promoting Aphasics Communicative Effectiveness) (Davis, 1983) had a profound effect on the management of the severely impaired dysphasic patient. The overall purpose is to achieve a natural communication interaction, in which the burden of communication is shared between patient and therapist. Davis claims that 'PACE focuses the patient and clinician on ideas to be conveyed rather than on the struggle for linguistic accuracy'. He describes the four principles of PACE:

1. The equal participation of clinician and patient as senders and receivers of messages;

2. The exchange of new information between clinician and patient;

3. The choice by the patient of the communicative modality;

4. The provision of feedback on the extent to which messages have been conveyed successfully.

Our work on total communication has been developed within a small group of patients who present on a continuum between global aphasia and moderately severe Brocas's dysphasia. A number have been handicapped by both articulatory and limb dyspraxia. Many of these patients have experienced months and even years of communicative failure, and whilst they may sometimes show evidence of anger and frustration, a number tend to demonstrate a passive acceptance of a non-communicating role.

The first step in the rehabilitation process is to maximise the use of non-verbal behaviours, such as facial expression, and head nods, which are frequently intact even in the severely impaired dysphasic patient. It is the therapist's responsibility to make the dysphasic person aware of the potency of non-verbal communication in the natural situation. Few normal speakers are aware of the extent to which non-linguistic behaviours convey information and express feelings, and this is no less true of the dysphasic and his friends and relatives. A heightened awareness of the function of non-verbal communication can aid both the dysphasic and his listener. The therapist must model the use of such communicative behaviours and encourage their use within the group. The aim is to create a situation in which the patient is willing to communicate feelings:

'What do you think of Mrs Thatcher? What would you do if your husband came home drunk . . . or the dog had torn up your slippers?'

We begin signing by expressing various sensory experiences of pleasure or pain. Group members may be asked to imagine that they have a very bad headache or toothache. What would they do if something made them very angry or frightened? How would they react if they were watching something exciting or something very boring? It is obvious that optimal emotional expression will occur only if the clinician can develop a sufficiently dynamic atmosphere and encourages communicative initiative within the group. We aim to create a group of dysphasic people who want to communicate, argue or interrupt. Wilcox and Davis (1977) listed the following speech activities which occur in normal human interaction: Requesting, asserting, questioning, greeting, thanking, ordering, arguing, advising, warning and congratulating.

These activities rarely occur in the normal speech therapy session. As Green (1982) says, 'Certain speech acts predominate to the near exclusion of others' (e.g. confrontation naming and picture description) and these are often far removed from the realities of normal human interaction.

All the patients within our group have been able to recognise, promptly and confidently, a 'lexicon' in excess of a hundred signs (which included both AMERIND and signs created by the therapist and members of the group). The majority have been able to execute the signs when presented with the stimulus word or picture. Skelly (1979) has suggested that resistance to the use of signing may be overcome by reminding patients of the several occupations where signing is used. Whilst we seldom meet such resistance, we have shared the pre-occupation of Green (1982, 1984), Davis and Wilcox (1981), and others that such learnt communication skills are not used spontaneously outside the therapy situation.

Whilst, initially, we used only AMERIND signs, we came to the conclusion that some of the signs could have been more iconographic. In addition, we found Skelly's suggested agglutinations were sometimes unnecessarily clumsy. Increasingly, we have discussed and devised 'new' signs within the group, which have involved members in creative decisions. Interestingly, some of these have been almost identical to the AMERIND signs.

It has been encouraging and rewarding to see patients gain greater confidence when they are involved in creating their own signs, and this has inevitably led to the development of a much less constrained approach to non-verbal communication. The natural consequence of this development has been the increasing use of pantomime which Duffy et al (1975) defined as 'the propositional use of non-verbal behaviour to convey meaning'. It is important that the mime springs from the patient's own needs and desires to communicate. The thrust in therapy is increasingly towards a more client-centred approach: a less prescriptive model of therapy. There is a growing awareness that the patient should decide what he wants to say and how he is going to say it. This approach encourages a more active, independent and far less passive role in therapy. It enables the dysphasic to become more assertive and confident in making his or her feelings and needs known. The small group situation is invaluable in allowing the dysphasic to experiment with different forms of communication and providing opportunities for successful communication.

Whilst the emphasis has been on the development and use of signing and mime, we would regard drawing, 'sky-writing' or any other communication attempt as acceptable: 'normal people are naturally multi-modality communicators' (Green, 1982), and it would therefore seem entirely appropriate to allow the dysphasic to make use of any effective form of communication. The therapist has a role in shaping behaviours towards successful communication by reinforcing every communicative attempt, however incomplete or partially successful it may be.

Failure to understand the task fully, difficulties in the retrieval of the appropriate symbolic behaviour, and articulatory and limb dyspraxias may all interfere with or limit such attempts, but positive responses from the clinicians and other members of the group will give the patient confidence to make further efforts. Whilst the group setting undoubtedly helps the transfer of the new skills, it is vital that relatives, friends or other care-givers should understand what is being attempted and become involved in the process.

Fawcus and Fawcus (1990) described a study of the efficiency of message transfer between therapist and carer via the dysphasic dyspraxic patient. Because of our interest in functional aspects of rehabilitation it was decided to take the experiment into the patient's home rather than set up an artificial message transfer situation within the department. The study developed from work with a specific group of patients with severe to moderate Broca's dysphasia, a number of whom had varying degrees of articulatory dyspraxia. In view of the frustrating limitations on communication in most of the group, a total communication approach to therapy had been adopted. At the time of the study, none of the four patients selected had any functional speech. They had all been diagnosed as severely dyspraxic, and all four were far beyond the period of spontaneous recovery. With one exception, limited to one specific word on two occasions, none of the subjects used speech to convey their messages.

Each subject was presented with a series of messages to be conveyed to the carer when the subject returned home from the City Dysphasic Group. In order to ensure that there was no way of 'leaking' the message, it was presented verbally to each subject. Care was taken to see that the message was fully understood. There were doubts about the ability to retain the message and this was a potential weakness of the study. From the results achieved, however, it did seem that the messages were remembered. In any future study, arrangements might be made to transfer the message to someone more immediately available. Ten messages were given to each patient, where possible on successive therapy occasions. The carers were presented with a form, which had to be completed for each message.

In evaluating the subjects' performance we looked at the extent to which the message was conveyed correctly, by counting the number of elements in each sentence that had been transferred to the carer. Secondly, we looked at the non-verbal strategies that had been employed in conveying those elements. It was also decided that the time taken to convey the message should be recorded. Just over half the messages (52%) were delivered in under two minutes and 7% took over ten minutes to convey to the carer.

BA (A*) and JP (D*) each achieved a total of 67% of message elements correctly transmitted. FO (C*) scored 58% and HC (B*) 88%. If the success rate had been scored in terms of establishing context and the transmission of major elements, each participant's performance would have achieved much higher scores. A* to D* refers to an earlier publication, Fawcus and Fawcus (1990): its use is continued in Figure 1.

The following accounts of the four participants plus TS are added to provide a fuller picture of the problems faced by the dyspraxic dysphasic patient and the strategies which they have employed to achieve communication.

On referral, WA had already developed good communication skills. He was a retired accountant in his late sixties who had suffered a major cerebral haemorrhage two years before. He exhibited a right hemiplegia but was and

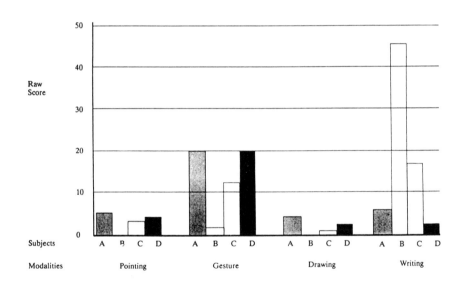

Figure 1: Modality scores in message transfer study

SAMPLE MESSAGES	ELEMENTS
The little girl has four candles on her cake.	5
Maggie is going to the dentist at four o'clock today.	5
Jean has left hospital.	3
Please telephone Maggie tomorrow.	4
Bob and the family are going to Scotland on 8th April.	6

remains extremely active. He takes every opportunity to travel around London, visiting museums, galleries and botanical gardens. In spite of the paralysis in his right leg he walks briskly and copes easily with buses and the Underground system.

After seven years, his speech is still limited to one expletive and a recurrent utterance, 'di di di'. The final syllable is expressed with appropriate stress and intonation to match his intention, and with the added bonus of facial expression and fluent gesture he achieves a remarkably high level of communication. His ability to employ appropriate stress and intonation make even a telephone conversation possible with a practiced listener.

Much effort was expended over the first year to develop his spoken output. He was usually committed, attentive and unusually patient but little gain was observable and he finally decided that there was no point in continuing the struggle. He similarly decided at a later stage that he would prefer to attend far less frequently as he had achieved as much as possible from the group. His facility in drawing and gesture, supported by writing, made him an effective communicator, in spite of his minimal speech.

In the latter stages he was introduced to the possibility of using a word processor to assist his written output. His degree of dysgraphia was initially such that he could usually write the first letter of a word but the remainder tended to include random letters. He could read individual words and very basic material with a high level of accuracy but was, much to his chagrin, unable to read a book or a newspaper.

His writing ability improved slowly but surely and, when confronted by a computer, he was able to identify words on the screen and to achieve an increased number of appropriate letters in a word. Because of his high degree of mobility it was decided to see if his communication skills could be extended by the use of a low cost, hand-held computer. The Psion Organiser has three accessible memories, some of which can contain up to 128K. The keyboard is small and not easily managed by an individual with a total paralysis of the muscles of his preferred hand. WA rapidly developed a technique reminiscent of a virtuoso cellist, using his thumb to switch on the computer and his little finger to press the 'exec' key. His index finger could be used to select individual memory banks. He showed no difficulty in recognising words and phrases on the small Liquid Crystal Display which serves as a screen.

WA was not able to key in words with sufficient accuracy, so we built up series of words and phrases on a PC with the assistance of his wife. He was able to reject and modify and also offer new suggestions using drawing, gesture etc. to make his requirements known. It was then possible to download the material into the memory banks of the Psion. This was an important facility because battery failure or inadvertent key entries could easily result in the loss of material.

His enthusiasm was such that he mastered the selection of the different memory banks with great facility. The spellchecker offering 23,000 words increased his self esteem but proved too demanding for effective communication and he was never observed to use it independently.

HC, at the age of 44, was involved in a tragic accident in which all her immediate family were killed and she herself was left speechless and hemiplegic. She had the support of a good network of friends with whom she lived until she moved into a flat where she has since lived independently.

On referral, she presented with a severe apraxia of speech, with occasional spontaneous (but unreliable) use of 'yes' and 'no'. She had received four months of intensive speech therapy in a rehabilitation unit and her prime method of communication was writing, using her non-preferred hand to write single words. In these early stages her written output was agrammatic. She had begun to use gesture to communicate but was unable to produce more than about five or six monosyllabic utterances.

HC had followed a professional training and was, in her own words, 'independent and determined'. She commenced speech therapy at the City Dysphasic Group some nine months after her accident; at that time her comprehension of the spoken word was functionally adequate, but she tended to misinterpret complex commands. She showed some difficulty in reading but was beginning to complete crosswords independently.

Two years after the accident she took part in the message transfer study. At that time she was still unable to use speech as a means of communication, but had developed such an effective written output that she conveyed virtually all the messages in this form. Although she could make competent use of gesture and mime in group activities, writing remained her preferred mode of communication, no doubt because she found that this was the most accurate and reliable way to convey information.

Subsequently she entered a stage in which she began to use the spoken word more spontaneously, but with limited intelligibility. She tended to back up these attempts with the written word sometimes producing both modes concurrently. Her speech has continued to improve and her confidence has been reinforced by increasing success leading to a reduction in the need to rely on writing. From single word utterances she began to link words and recently returned from a holiday in Australia, triumphantly reporting that she had on one occasion put eight words together.

HC has gradually carved out a new life style which appears to offer her satisfaction and a sense of fulfillment. She remains hemiplegic but is mobile and fiercely independent. She has, over the past year, been learning to use a word processor, and this is facilitating improvement in her written language.

FO, a fifty eight-year-old manager of a supermarket, suffered a stroke which left him wandering inexplicably around a railway station some fifty miles from London, totally speechless. He was admitted to Addenbrookes Hospital and investigations showed evidence of total obliteration of his left frontal lobe. He returned to London after six months and was referred to the City Dysphasic Group.

He presented as a shy, nervous man who displayed understanding of simple written and oral commands but failure to comprehend more complex material. He exhibited severe apraxia of speech, having regained no meaningful spoken utterances, and his written output was limited to the ability to copy words and phrases. He was introduced to the AMERIND gestural system but his limb dyspraxia made even the most basic gestural manoeuvres very difficult.

After one year of attendance he was reported to be gaining in confidence, and using signs both within and outside the group. He was actually observed to be assisting other less able members on a number of occasions. After a further year he was continuing to progress with signing, with modest gains in the production of a few spoken words. There was also clear improvement in reading and writing, and even in drawing, which had been hampered significantly by limb dyspraxia and associated visuo-perceptual problems.

```
Lynn  food  tea in Church Hall on Saturday
 W     G    W      G              W

Dad took my photo on Tuesday
 G        G        W

Squirrel eating nuts upside down in garden
 D       G      G      G          P

My dog is fifteen
 P   W   G

Pack clothes for holiday
 G    G        G

Blow cake candles on my Birthday Saturday
 G    G     G       P    W        W

Smashed my finger in shopping trolley
 G       P   P        G        G
```

By the time of the message transfer study, a year later, he was able to achieve a score of 58%, conveying information to a relative primarily by means of gesture and writing.

JP, aged 30, had two strokes in her late twenties. On referral she had no communication strategies beyond pointing, indicating 'yes' and 'no'. She had no written language, and the acquisition of signing was hampered by her limb dyspraxia.

Three years of imposed silence had had its effect psychologically. Fortunately, with the interest and encouragement of her mother, and the facilitating environment of the group, she has gradually become a reasonably successful communicator, who will persevere in getting her message across. She now travels alone and communicates outside the safe environment of the group.

As an extension of this study, Subject JP continued to convey messages, which her mother recorded for us. She revealed an ability to convey a wide range of messages, although agrammatically. Her mother added the appropriate function words in many cases. It seemed that the success with the original 10 messages had made her realise her considerable potential for communication. Some of the messages conveyed are recorded below, with pointing, gesture, drawing and writing being indicated by their initial letters: It was interesting to note an increased use of writing in these messages. Since they followed immediately after the research series, one is tempted to conjecture that this was related to her growing confidence in experimenting with multimodality communication.

We have chosen to add one further patient to the original series. TS joined the City Dysphasic Group more recently and it was decided to include an account of his difficulties and his adaptive behaviour because they illustrate the profound effects of restricted comprehension (Lawson and Fawcus, 1991).

TS suffered a cerebrovascular accident in his fifty-fifth year. This episode had a devastating effect on his ability to comprehend speech and his sole spoken utterance was an expletive. His severe communication difficulties placed him in a socially isolated position. He belonged to a close family but his intense misery and frequent angry outbursts placed a considerable strain on relationships. His hemiplegia made his former hobbies, which included fishing, gardening and motor cycling, virtually impossible.

He spent three months at a rehabilitation centre and when discharged was beginning to employ pointing, gesture and drawing in order to communicate; he had made some attempt at writing. He could write his own name and occasionally names of members of his family. He was described as depressed, quick to anger and essentially negative about communicating. He managed to convey, mainly through facial expressions, that he regarded himself as beyond help. His wife wrote 'when he came out of hospital he was a very angry and bitter man. He swore at me and wiped the floor with me for months. I cried every day because I thought I'd never be able to cope . . . . The only things that stimulated his mind were visual things, such as places and faces on television.'

One year post onset he was referred to the City Dysphasic Group and entered a new experimental subgroup. By this time he had lost many of the gains made in the rehabilitation centre. His comprehension of the spoken word was still virtually nonexistent. He could write his own name but little else and showed few successful communication strategies.

There were, however, some positive aspects: in the first place he showed some understanding of single, concrete words; secondly he showed normal non-verbal behaviour (particularly in the form of facial expression) and, finally, he was a positive group member, showing a caring attitude toward other members. He would demonstrate his approval of a successful speech therapy session by hand gripping and hugging the therapist.

His poor auditory comprehension presented problems in a group situation, but was overcome to some extent by accompanying speech with gesture and by writing down key words. He gradually began to 'read' gesture, which made communication easier. At this stage his only way to obtain any meaning from a social situation was to watch facial expression, actions and gestures.

He was undoubtedly helped by the group setting where he saw communicative strategies being modelled. His own initial attempts at communication were encouraged and reinforced.

He began to discover that he could use both facial expression and drawing to good effect. His role as a non-speaking individual had been thrust upon him precipitately and completely, and it took a long time for him to become aware of his full potential as a communicator and to adjust to his new role.

As his drawing improved it became an increasingly effective strategy for conveying his ideas. On one occasion, when he had been absent from the group because of illness, he indicated that he had been in hospital by drawing himself in bed complete with a drip! Comparison of his early and more recent drawings demonstrates the improvement in his ability to convey information. He has an eye for detail which has helped. It is easy to forget that he is using his non-preferred left hand.

Eight months later, he was using gesture, mime, pointing and drawing and had begun to use writing, and these communication strategies had generalised to his home environment. The use of mime enabled TS to explore ways of expressing more complex ideas. The burden of communication still rested quite heavily on the 'conversational' partner, but he was becoming quite resourceful and would persevere in the face of initial failure. His wife reported the following example:

> T led me by the hand into the lounge and pointed to the garden. I asked what he had seen. In the air he wrote R and stroked his chest. I knew he'd seen a robin.

A year later, in June, 1990, his wife wrote:

> He writes words which I can understand. He draws excellently. The gestures are quite good. He now says words like 'Hello', 'Park', 'Car', 'Tea', 'Key' and 'Money'.

Despite his lack of speech, he has developed into a successful and increasingly confident communicator. He now understands the gist of what is said to him, and it is possible to enjoy a 'conversation' with him, in which he can share the burden of communication. He can still lose his temper, but he is no longer the negative, passive and depressed person who joined the group two and a half years ago.

We could have selected many of the individuals attending the City Dysphasic Group to illustrate aspects of human vulnerability and resilience. This specific group of patients is drawn from those who have suffered the most radical loss of communicative abilities, but even in our high level groups we observe daily the tragedy of those who can no longer continue with a career for which they have trained or engage in past activities, such as reading, which they have formerly loved.

Between the group who display relatively little disturbance of linguistic abilities and those who have lost everything lie the majority of our patients who have significant levels of dysphasia affecting speech, reading and writing.

Our approach, with its emphasis on developing the full communicative potential of such patients, has been clearly influenced by Anne and Alan Clarke's philosophy which we first encountered at the Manor Hospital, Epsom in the 1950s.

Their recognition of the need to provide a facilitating environment in order to achieve the optimal potential of the cognitively impaired population can be seen as the foundation of the normalisation programmes which now play a major part in the care of the disabled.

Acknowledgements

We wish to thank all our patients who have taught us so much over the past twenty years since the Group began. Their patience, tolerance and good humour has been monumental and highly supportive.

We also wish to thank the Lord Ashdown Foundation, The Boltons Trust, Mason's Medical Foundation and many other charitable bodies for their continued support.

References

Argyle, M. (1972) *The Psychology of Interpersonal Behaviour*. London: Penguin.

Davis, G. A. (1983) *A survey of Adult Aphasia*. Englewood Cliffs: Prentice Hall.

Davis, G. A., Wilcox, M. J. (1981) Incorporating parameters of natural conversation in aphasia treatment. In Chapey, R. K. (ed) *Language Intervention Strategies in Adult Aphasia*.

Duffy, R. J., Duffy, J. R., Pearson, K. L. (1975) Pantomime Recognition in Aphasics. *Journal of Speech and Hearing Research*, 24, 70–84.

Fawcus, R., and Fawcus, M. A. (1990) Information transfer in four cases of severe articulatory dyspraxia. *Aphasiology*, 4, 2, 207–212.

Gainotti, G., Lemmo, M. A. (1976) Comprehension of Symbolic Gestures in Aphasia. *Brain and Language*, 3, 451–460.

Green, G. (1982) Assessment and Treatment of the Adult with Severe Aphasia Aiming for Functional Generalisation. *Aust. J. of Human Communication Disorders*, 10, 1.

Green, G. (1984) Communication in Aphasia Therapy: Some of the procedures and issues involved. *Brit. J. of Disorders of Communication* 19, 1.

Huskins, S. (1986) *Working with Dyspraxics*. London: Winslow Press.

Kraat, A. W. (1985) *Communication Interaction between Aided and Natural Speakers – A State of the Art Report*. Canadian Rehabilitation Council for the Disabled.

Kraat, A. W. (1990) Augmentative and Alternative Communication? Does it have a future in aphasia rehabilitation? *Aphasiology*, 4, 6, 321–338.

Lawson, R., and Fawcus, M. A. *A total communication approach with a man with chronic global aphasia*. (In press).

Rossiter, D. (1987) *Ever decreasing circles: a review of the speech therapist in relation to aphasia*. Paper presented at the British Aphasia Society Conference. Newcastle-upon-Tyne.

Sarno, M. T., Silverman, E., Sands, E. (1970) Speech Therapy and Language Recovery in Severe Aphasia. *Journal of Speech and Hearing Research*, 13, 607–623.

Skelly, M. (1979) *Amer-Ind Gestural Code Based on Universal American Indian Hand Talk*. New York: Elsevier.

Square-Storer, P. (1989) *Acquired Apraxia of Speech in Aphasic Adults*. London: Taylor and Francis.

Stuart-Smith, V. G., and Wilks, V. (1979) Gesture Programme: A Supplement to Verbal Communication for Severely Aphasic Individuals. *Aust. J. of Human Communication Disorders*, 7, 2.

Walker, M. (1973) An experimental evaluation of the success of a system of communication for the deaf mentally handicapped. Unpublished MSc Thesis, Guy's Hospital Medical School, University of London.

Wilcox, M. J., and Davis, G. A. (1977) Speech act analysis of aphasic communication in individual and group settings. In Brookshire, R. H. (Ed.) *Clinical Aphasiology Conference Proceedings*. Minneapolis, Minn.: BRK

Chapter 9

Vulnerability and resilience to early cerebral injury

Edgar Miller

One of the central issues when considering human resilience and vulnerability, and especially as manifest in the work of Ann and Alan Clarke, lies in the examination of the role of early experience. This is especially so in relation to adaptation to early adverse circumstances. From a neuropsychological perspective this line of work translates into a consideration of the effects of early brain damage, since this represents a potentially significant form of adverse event. This chapter attempts to offer a brief survey of what has been established about the consequences of early brain damage for psychological functioning.

The literature relevant to this field is now quite large and far too extensive to allow for a comprehensive discussion within present limitations on space. The aim will therefore be the rather more limited one of identifying the key points that need to be taken into account in any examination of this issue and to offer an indication as to how a synthesis of the diverse findings might be reached. Detailed justification for some of the statements made will not be possible, but it is hoped that the reader interested enough to want to take the matter further will find the necessary details within the cited references.

The 'Conventional Wisdom'

In general, there has been a common belief that young children, when compared with adults sustaining similar damage to the brain, show better recovery from the results of cerebral insult, or even complete sparing of any deleterious effects. Within childhood, it is assumed that the younger the age at injury, the better the outcome, and the protective effect of younger age at injury has even been extended to comparisons within the adult age range (e.g. Miller, 1979, 1984). So prevalent has this view been in some settings that it merits being regarded as the 'conventional wisdom'. In effect this chapter is an examination of the validity of this piece of conventional wisdom.

As Finger and Wolf (1988) have argued, the general view of better recovery, or even total sparing from effects, after early brain insult has been in existence for some time. This idea was certainly expressed in the 1860s and 1870s on the basis of animal research by such authorities as Vulpian and Stoltmann. Corresponding views were expressed by Bastian on the basis of clinical studies in the late 1890s. However, it is interesting to note, in view of later aspects of this discussion, that Bastian (1898) did qualify his opinion by indicating that it is 'by no means a rule free from exceptions'.

Within the present century, a very influential set of studies were published by Margaret Kennard (1936, 1940, 1942). In her experiments Kennard placed lesions in the motor cortex of both infant and adult monkeys and studied the resulting impact on motor behaviour. She concluded that damage in infancy did not produce the same drastic impairments as apparently similar lesions in adult subjects and also claimed that the consequences of early lesions were often very small. This work has led to the general principle of better recovery from brain injury in early life being referred to in some quarters as the 'Kennard principle' (Schneider, 1979; Simon and Finger, 1984; Taylor, 1984).

There is also much evidence from studies of human clinical populations that could be regarded as consistent with the Kennard principle. For example, it appears to be possible for those who have suffered extensive left hemisphere damage in very early life to grow up with relatively little in the way of language impairment. On the other hand, adults sustaining lesions of a broadly similar extent are likely to remain markedly aphasic for the rest of their lives. Much of the evidence relevant to this point is documented in Satz and Bullard-Bates' (1981) review of childhood aphasia. Even within the age range associated with childhood there are indications that those sustaining the injury at the earliest ages have the better outcome (e.g. Woods and Teuber, 1978).

In the case of closed head injury, the long-term outcome appears to be less satisfactory in adults than in children and, even within adult life, there is an association between age and outcome (e.g. Levin et al, 1984; Miller, 1979;). There is also evidence to support the contention that adults who have had the corpus callosum sectioned (for the relief of epilepsy) show a number of impairments when specialised testing based on the careful presentation of stimuli to one hemisphere or the other is employed, as in the brief tachistoscopic presentation of visual stimuli to left or right visual fields (e.g. Gazzaniga and Sperry, 1967). Such impairments are not manifest to the same degree in those born with agEnesis of the corpus collosum (Jeeves, 1981).

Plasticity at the behavioural level has also been assumed to be mirrored by plasticity at the neuronal level. Phenomena such as compensatory hypertrophy, axonal sprouting (whereby undamaged neurons develop more elaborate axonal processes) and denervation sensitivity (whereby unaffected neurons compensate by becoming more sensitive to incoming stimulation) are physiological mechanisms considered to underlie adaptation to injury (e.g. Liedermann, 1988; Miller, 1984). It is then further assumed that these physiological mechanisms operate more efficiently within the younger brain.

As this brief summary has shown, there is evidence consistent with the idea of better response at the behavioural level to brain insult in early life (the 'Kennard principle'). There are even some indications of apparent total sparing after very early damage from what might be regarded as the usual consequences of such injury. In addition, underlying compensatory physiological mechanisms have been demonstrated which might underpin recovery and which may be more readily manifest in the younger organism.

Unfortunately, as is all too common in psychological research, this simple picture turns out not to be quite so straightforward on closer examination. The following sections set out reasons why the Kennard principle must be treated with some caution and offer some indications as to the lines along which a better understanding of the phenomena might be achieved.

Before going further, it is worth noting that the issues involved are of much more than academic significance. Understanding the factors involved in early recovery is likely to lead to better advice being given to parents unfortunate enough to have brain damaged children and to much more effectively designed programmes to ameliorate the effects of this damage.

Problems with the Kennard principle

Whilst evidence of the kind considered so far is consistent with the Kennard principle, and much similar evidence could be cited, there are difficulties in accepting the principle as it stands. These are of three types conceptual, methodological and empirical. The methodological difficulties relate to the need to take into account a number of other factors which may affect the relationship between age and recovery. Failure to control for these factors argues against taking much of the evidence at face value because findings may be biased or contaminated. Empirical problems arise out of detailed findings which are not easy to reconcile with the Kennard principle.

A basic conceptual issue centres around the use of age as a crucial variable, as in claiming that adaptation to the deleterious effects of brain insult is better when that insult occurs earlier in life. Age is not in itself a causal variable. It is therefore not so much age as mere passage of time that results in changed manifestations of recovery as the organism gets older. Age can only be important in that it gives an opportunity for other factors to operate. A full understanding of the phenomena must require the identification and exploration of these other factors that require time in which to operate.

St James-Roberts (1981) has pointed out a number of methodological problems inherent in studying the effects of early versus late brain injury. Early and late damaged groups are often not comparable, for a number of reasons. For example, in many studies the length of follow-up to ascertain recovery is not comparable in groups with early and late lesions. Infant-damaged subjects are often followed for a considerable length of time whilst the adult group is studied over a much shorter period. In defence, it might be argued that infant-damaged groups have to be followed for long periods to see what the impact is likely to be at maturity, whilst adult groups need only be followed until recovery has flattened off. However, it is difficult to determine when recovery is complete, and in many investigations it is still possible that further slow recovery might occur in the adult groups. This would close the gap between adult and infant damaged subjects.

In the case of human studies, investigators have to rely for obvious ethical reasons on the experiments provided by nature in terms of various forms of pathology. As a general rule, pathologies encountered in adults are different from those occurring in children and adult pathologies are more likely to be malignant or progressive. Obtaining child and adult samples with lesions comparable in site and extent, as well as in the nature of pathology, is virtually impossible. Again the uncontrolled factors involved are generally such as to give the appearance of poorer recovery in adults.

Yet another factor that might bias findings concerns the adoption of compensatory strategies. Lesions in the young may give the impression of better recovery, or even sparing, for reasons other than that the underlying impairment produced by the lesion actually recovers so much better. It might be that the younger organism is just more efficient at developing compensatory strategies whereby the same behavioural goals can be achieved by different means and without depending to the same degree on abilities that have been directly affected by the lesion. This may be because such adaptive learning is truly better in the young, or simply because older subjects have had the opportunity to overlearn strategies which are now disrupted and which may still interfere with the learning of new ways of achieving the same ends. It is well established that post injury experience affects recovery (Will and Eclancher, 1984). There is also some indication from animal research that good recovery from early lesions may be mediated, under at least some circumstances, by learning compensatory strategies (Simon and Finger, 1984).

Turning to empirical investigations, a significant amount of evidence has now accumulated which either fails to support the Kennard principle or even, in a few instances, shows the reverse picture of better outcome in older subjects. Much of this has been reviewed elsewhere (e.g. Miller, 1984; Simon and Finger, 1984).

In the first place, even in Kennard's own work (Kennard, 1936, 1940, 1942) the picture was not as clear as has sometimes been assumed. The evidence she gives suggests that apparent initial sparing of effects after motor cortex lesions in infant monkeys was later followed by the development of some spasticity. It is also the case that a large number of animal studies have failed to find any sparing at all in the case of infant lesions. To cite but one example, Murphy and Stewart (1974) found no effect of age at which the lesion was placed on visual discrimination after posterior cortex lesions in rabbits.

Results even more difficult to square with the simple statement of the Kennard principle have been obtained. In this context, two major series of investigations are particularly worth citing. In a set of investigations using hamsters, Schneider and his colleagues carried out some intricate experiments (for a detailed account see Schneider, 1979). Lesions were placed within the visual pathways at infancy or later, and the effects of these were studied in relation to head turning behaviour in response to the presentation of food-related stimuli (sunflower seeds) to the left or right visual fields. Following bilateral lesions at the level of the superior colliculus, substantial sparing of the orienting response to food is found in infant subjects, thus providing some support for the Kennard principle.

In the case of unilateral lesions, the situation is more complex. If the eye on the same side of the lesion is also enucleated, head turning in the wrong direction (i.e. away from the food stimulus) can be found, but only in subjects with lesions placed in infancy. The result is contrary to the Kennard principle, and Schneider (1979) relates this maladaptive response to the development of anomalous connections within the visual pathways which only occur after lesions in infancy.

Goldman and her collaborators were concerned with the effects of prefrontal lesions in monkeys (for a more extensive summary see Goldman, 1974). She initially found that the impairment in carrying out delayed response tasks associated with dorsolateral frontal lesions in monkeys was nothing like so marked in animals operated on as infants; again, a finding consistent with the Kennard principle. However, extending this work revealed features not readily predicted on the basis of this principle. Lesions in the caudate nucleus in one-year-old monkeys produced behavioural impairments greater than those associated with prefrontal lesions at the same age and as severe as those produced by prefrontal lesions at two years. Lesions of the prefrontal cortex at two years had a bigger effect on delayed response performance than caudate lesions at the same age. Thus, damage to whichever of these two structures gives the biggest behavioural effect is determined by the age at which the lesion is placed. In particular, lesions of the caudate nucleus have a bigger impact if they occur at one year than if they occur at a later age; a finding which is clearly not compatible with the Kennard principle.

It must be emphasised that results from the Goldman and Schneider groups incompatible with the notion of better recovery after early damage are not isolated findings. Several other reports have appeared of experimental results which also clearly contradict the Kennard principle (see Will and Eclancher, 1984). To mention but one further example, Eclancher et al (1975) noted that rats subjected to amygdalectomy at seven days of age exhibited much more disturbed aggressive behaviour than those receiving similar operations at 90 days.

The above findings, based on animal research, typically give a clearer picture simply because reasonably precise experimental procedures can be used. Nevertheless, investigations based on human clinical material also yield findings which fail to match the Kennard principle.

One clear example of an anomalous finding in humans, at least as far as the Kennard principle is concerned, is provided by Woods and Teuber (1978), who looked at those who had suffered unilateral brain damage. Some cases showed a form of synkinesia known as 'mirror movements'. This refers to a phenomenon whereby movements of one limb, particularly the distal portions such as toes and fingers, are always accompanied by corresponding movements of the same parts of the other limb. For example, it may be impossible for the person exhibiting this phenomenon to carry out a task like fastening a button with one hand without the fingers of the other hand going through similar movements at the same time. This rare phenomenon can occur in childhood hemiparesis, but Woods and Teuber noted it to be related to the age at which hemispheric damage was sustained. The subjects who sustained the damage at the earliest age within the group (mean age of around six years) were those that had the highest prevalence of this form of maladaptive movement.

Other factors adversely affecting the brain in ways likely to result in diffuse damage or change have also resulted in findings difficult to reconcile with the Kennard principle. These are described in greater detail by Levin et al (1984) but include such things as early meningitis, hypoxia, cranial irradiation and malnutrition. In the case of hypoxia and/or ischaemia resulting in a persistent vegetative state, follow-up studies suggest that outcome is no better when this occurs in early childhood as opposed to adulthood. However, it might be claimed that this is of marginal relevance because the persistent vegetative state is an extreme condition and damage is so severe as to preclude the manifestation of a tendency to better recovery in younger subjects.

Other things are less easy to explain away by similar arguments. Wright (1978), reviewing the effects of meningitis, concluded that 'the younger the victim, the greater the impact of meningitis on his/her intellectual functioning'. Similarly, cranial irradiation in those with acute lymphocytic leukaemia has been associated with greater psychological impairment when administered between the ages of two and five years than when given at a later age. Consistent with this is the finding that malnutrition has a particularly deleterious effect on later functioning when experienced early in life (Dobbing, 1974; Winick, 1976).

The arguments and evidence considered in this section have deliberately emphasised the difficulties that can arise in accepting the Kennard principle. It has to be acknowledged that a range of evidence that could be considered consistent with that principle, and only very briefly outlined in the preceding section, has been ignored. This is because the aim has been to demonstrate that the Kennard principle does break down and fails to summarise what happens under at least some circumstances.

Towards a better understanding

In trying to make sense of the evidence concerning the effects of early brain damage, it is clear that there are many findings, probably a majority, that are reasonably consistent with the Kennard principle. It is possible that some of these findings might be misleading because the methodological complications accompanying research in the field, as described above, generally tend to operate in such a way as to over emphasise the extent of early recovery. As a result, much of the evidence consistent with the Kennard principle can only be accepted with caution. Nevertheless it would be misleading not to allow the real possibility that this principle offers a rough and ready description of what happens under many circumstances.

Looking at the issues from the other side, there are certainly far too many instances of apparently well-conducted investigations where the result either fails to add support to the Kennard principle, or even provides evidence which directly contradicts this principle. A rather more sophisticated understanding of the relationship between early brain damage and psychological outcome than that offered by the simple statement of the Kennard principle is therefore required.

One potential way forward is to enlarge upon the conceptual point made earlier about the limitations in using time as a variable. Time can only be of significance because the passage of time allows other things to operate. An appreciation of what these other things might be and the effects that they might have on recovery should enable the relationship between age and recovery to be better understood.

In looking at possible underlying mechanisms, research on animals is of great significance because it is possible to carry out reasonably precise interventions that might be capable of isolating critical variables. Work based on human clinical material is less able to be conducted so as to isolate the influence of potentially key variables and so is less likely to offer clear indications as to the fundamental mechanisms involved. Human research is, however, essential in indicating the degree to which ideas gained from animal research are likely to apply in the clinical context.

Work referred to earlier by Schneider, Goldman and their respective collaborators offers some helpful insights. In the experiments based on hamsters (Schneider, 1979), evidence was obtained that unilateral lesions placed in the visual tracts in infancy at the level of the superior colliculus are associated with the development of new pathways to the other hemisphere. This is not the case in adult hamsters subjected to comparable procedures.

A better ability in the infant brain to adapt to injury, both physiologically and anatomically, by such things as neuronal sprouting, may play an important role. That these changes should mediate better recovery is quite likely, but it would also not be surprising if anomalous connections should turn out to be maladaptive under some circumstances. This is what appears to have happened when Schneider's hamsters with unilateral lesions in infancy oriented in the wrong direction when presented with a visual stimulus associated with food.

The possibility must also be noted that novel neural connections developed as a result of early lesions need not have any functional significance at all, whether for good or ill. In an experiment bearing some relationship to Schneider's work, Heywood and Cowey (1986) placed lesions in the superior colliculus in rats at either one or five days old. Only those operated on at one day old developed novel retinal projections, yet these subjects performed at the same level on a visual discrimination as subjects who were operated on at five days and who developed no new projections from the retina.

Another insight into physiological adaptation is provided by Goldman's work (Goldman, 1974; Miller, 1984). Goldman has appealed to the concept of 'functional maturity'. She suggests that in the early stages of development not all structures within the brain may be fully mature, in that they can carry out the functions which they subserve in the mature animal. Different structures may become functionally mature at different ages.

Goldman indicates how the concept of functional maturity might be used to explain findings like some of those which her group has obtained with monkeys. Specifically, she supposes that in monkeys the caudate nucleus is functionally mature at one year, whereas the dorsolateral frontal cortex takes much longer to reach maturity. In adults it is the dorsolateral frontal cortex that mediates such things as delayed response performance, but in young animals such behaviour is mediated by the caudate nucleus until the frontal cortex becomes mature enough to take over this role. This hypothesis is consistent with the impact of caudate lesions administered at around one year of age on delayed response performance, which is greater than similar lesions placed at an age after the dorsolateral frontal cortex has matured.

Turning to the human situation, the same anatomical and physiological factors identified as potentially mediating recovery in animals could potentially also be in operation. For example, the relatively good development of language in children suffering early extensive damage to the left hemisphere is linked to development of speech in the right hemisphere (Miller, 1984). This in turn may be mediated by a superior ability in the young organism to develop new neural connections, although the necessary anatomical evidence to back up this contention is more difficult to obtain from human clinical material.

The definite trend towards very early diffuse injury, as produced by malnutrition or meningitis, to be associated with a poorer outcome than similar factors operating later on, can also be linked to brain development. In the human being, the period shortly after birth shows the greatest rate of physical development in the brain and it would not be surprising if the brain was especially liable to disruption and difficulties in adaptation during the major spurt in growth.

To some degree, the good development of language after very early left hemisphere damage does not fit in well with the enhanced susceptibility to the adverse effects of brain infection and malnutrition. Possibly this is because it is only one hemisphere that is damaged in the former. This may well allow relatively normal development of the unaffected hemisphere and so retain its ability to adapt to the need of taking over language functions.

Turning to a different type of explanatory mechanism, Miller (1984) concluded an examination of possible mechanisms underlying recovery after brain damage by suggesting that functional adaptation, or the ability to develop compensatory strategies, was an important mechanism underlying apparent recovery, at least in adults. The young are also likely to be able to adapt to impairments by developing alternative ways of achieving the same goals which avoid relying on the functions that have been impaired. As already described above, Simon and Finger (1984) have presented evidence indicating that such a mechanism does operate in young brain injured animals under at least some circumstances.

The development of compensatory strategies could produce results confirming the Kennard principle because younger subjects are better able to learn such strategies. This may be because of a generally superior learning ability or because they do not suffer the disadvantage of having also to unlearn well practised ways of achieving the goals which have been disrupted by the consequences of the injury. Such alternative strategies are unlikely to be optimal in that they will often not achieve the desired goal as well as the strategy that might be employed had there been no functional impairment as a result of brain injury. They may also not be optimal, in the sense that they may well be less suited to achieving related goals, or even interfere with their achievement.

An example may illustrate this point. A person whose tactile sensation in the fingers is impaired to some degree by brain injury may learn to tie shoelaces entirely under visual control and with no reference at all to tactile feedback. Having to tie shoelaces in the dark may then be adversely affected to an undue degree because of learning to ignore the small amount of tactile sensation remaining and which now offers the only means of carrying out the task. Similar patterns of benefit and loss could also result from the compensatory strategies adopted by younger subjects, thus producing effects which either correspond to or contradict the Kennard principle, depending upon the exact nature of the task that is examined and whether the strategy had been originally developed to achieve the particular goal embodied in the task.

It is unfortunate that the development of compensatory strategies after brain injury has not been well explored either in adults or children. This makes it impossible to do other than merely point this out as a possible mechanism that might mediate differential recovery between early and late brain damage.

Conclusions

There is much evidence that appears to support the notion of better recovery from brain damage if that damage is sustained early in life (the Kennard principle). Unfortunately, this evidence is subject to methodological limitations, and enough contradictory findings have been reported to demonstrate that the impact of age on recovery is rather more complex that the Kennard principle would allow. The greater ability of the young organism to adapt physiologically and anatomically, together with the development of compensatory strategies, appears to offer a way forward towards gaining a deeper and more satisfactory understanding of the processes involved.

References

Bastian, H. C. (1898). *Aphasia and Other Speech Defects*. London: H. K. Lewis.

Dobbing, J. (1974). The later development of the brain and its vulnerability. In Davis, J. A. and Dobbing, J. (Eds), *Scientific Foundations of Paediatrics*. London: Heinemann.

Eclancher, F., Schmitt, P. and Karli, P. (1975). Effets de lésions précoses de l'amygdale sur le développement de l'aggressivité interspécifique du rat. *Physiology and Behavior*, 14, 277–283.

Finger, S. and Wolf, C. (1988). The 'Kennard Effect' before Kennard: The early history of age and brain lesions. *Archives of Neurology*, 45, 1136–1142.

Gazzaniga, M. S. and Sperry, R. W. (1967). Language after section of the cerebral commissures. *Brain*, 90, 131–148.

Goldman, P. S. (1974). Recovery of function after CNS lesions in infant monkeys. *Neurosciences Research Program Bulletin*, 12, 217–222.

Heywood, C. A. and Cowey, A. (1986). The nature of visual discrimination impairments after neonatal or adult ablation of superior colliculus in rats. *Experimental Brain Research*, 61, 403–412.

Jeeves, M. A. (1981). Age related effects of agenesis and partial sectioning of the neocortical commissures. In van Hof, M. W. and Mohn, G. (Eds), *Functional Recovery from Brain Damage*. Amsterdam: Elsevier.

Kennard, M. A. (1936). Age and other factors in motor recovery from precentral lesions in monkeys. *American Journal of Physiology*, 115, 138–146.

Kennard, M. A. (1940). Relation of age to motor impairment in man and subhuman primates. *Archives of Neurology and Psychiatry*, 44, 377–397.

Kennard, M. A. (1942). Cortical reorganisation of motor function studies on series of monkeys of various ages from infancy to maturity. *Archives of Neurology and Psychiatry*, 48, 227–240.

Levin H. S., Ewing-Cobbs, L. and Benton, A. L. (1984). Age and recovery from brain damage a review of clinical studies. In Scheff, S. W. (Ed.), *Aging and Recovery of Function in the Central Nervous System*. New York: Plenum Press.

Liedermann, J. (1988). Misconceptions and new conceptions about early brain damage, functional asymmetry, and behavioral outcome. In Molfese, D. L. and Segalowitz, S. J. (Eds), *Brain Lateralization in Children Developmental Implications*. New York: Guilford Press.

Miller, E. (1979). The long-term consequences of head injury a discussion of the evidence with special reference to the preparation of legal reports. *British Journal of Social and Clinical Psychology*, 18, 87–94.

Miller, E. (1984). *Recovery and Management of Neuropsychological Impairments*. Chichester: Wiley.

Murphy, E. H. and Stewart, D. L. (1974). Effects of neonatal and striate lesions on discrimination in the rabbit. *Experimental Neurology*, 42, 89–96.

St James-Roberts, I. (1981). A re-interpretation of hemispherectomy data without functional plasticity of the brain. 1. Intellectual functioning. *Brain and Language*, 13, 31–53.

Satz, P. and Bullard-Bates, C. (1981). Acquired aphasia in children. In Sarno, M. T. (Ed.), *Acquired Aphasia*. New York: Academic Press.

Schneider, G. E. (1979). Is it really better to have your brain lesion early? A revision of the 'Kennard principle'. *Neuropsychologia*, 17, 557–583.

Simon, D. and Finger, S. (1984). Some factors affecting behavior after brain damage early in life. In Finger, S. and Almli, C. R. (Eds), *Early Brain Damage. Vol.2. Neurobiology and Behavior*. New York: Academic Press.

Taylor, H. G. (1984). Early brain injury and cognitive development. In Almli, C. R. and Finger, S. (Eds), *Early Brain Damage. Vol.1. Research Orientations and Clinical Observations*. New York: Academic Press.

Will, B. and Eclancher, F. (1984). Early brain damage and early environment. In Finger, S. and Almli, C. R. (Eds), *Early Brain Damage. Vol.2. Neurobiology and Behavior*. New York: Academic Press.

Winick, M. (1976). *Malnutrition and Brain Development*. Oxford: Oxford University Press.

Woods, R. T. and Teuber, H. L. (1978). Mirror movements after childhood hemiparesis. *Neurology*, 28, 1152–1158.

Wright, L. (1978). A method for predicting sequelae to meningitis. *American Psychologist*, 33, 1037–1039.

Chapter 10

Educating children with severe learning difficulties:
challenging vulnerability

Peter Mittler

Children with severe learning difficulties are perhaps the most vulnerable of all the minority and disadvantaged groups, by virtue of their limited understanding and ability to communicate, their restricted life experiences and their limited opportunities to participate in decision making and to have a say in their lives.

In a more sinister sense, they are vulnerable from the moment they are born if doctors persuade parents to allow an infant with, say Down's syndrome or spina bifida to die by withholding medical treatment essential to the baby's survival. Throughout the whole of their lives, they are vulnerable in a different sense to the abuse of power by professionals who are driven by a conviction that they know best what is good for them. They are also made more vulnerable by the widespread under-estimation by others of their capacity to learn and to make choices and participate in decision making.

Can education prevent or compensate for such vulnerability? During the past twenty years, dramatic improvements have been made in the education of children with severe learning difficulties. But will these improvements make children less vulnerable when they leave school and enter the adult world?

Will they be able to exercise choice and decision making, to have a say in their own lives and to take part in the life of their community? Can schooling really prepare these young people to challenge the discrimination, victimisation and poverty which many will experience in adult life?

Children with severe learning difficulties

The label of learning difficulties or an IQ result tell us next to nothing about the individual. Two people with the same IQ from an identical background and attending the same school or service can have totally different outcomes. Similarly, a diagnosis of Down's syndrome in no way predicts how a single affected individual will develop, or how they will respond to early intervention or special education.

With this caveat in mind, what information is available on the 24,000 children now attending day schools for children with severe learning difficulties?

Survey findings

In the late 1970s in North West England, a survey of 3,600 children in 70 schools for children with severe learning difficulties showed, according to teachers' reports, that 12 per cent were unable to walk or were otherwise immobile, eight per cent had little use of arms or hands, 16 per cent had some degree of visual impairment and seven per cent had hearing impairments. In addition, about a fifth had very little language comprehension; between a third and a fifth had not yet started to speak in single words and about half of those who had started to speak were unintelligible to those who knew them (Mittler and Preddy, 1981). On a more positive note, 90 per cent of pupils leaving school were continent, 78 per cent were fully mobile, 87 and 96 per cent had no visual or auditory impairments respectively and 97 per cent were free of epilepsy.

A more recent survey in South East England (Evans and Ware, 1987) reflects substantially higher rates of impairment, partly because more children with profound and multiple learning difficulties now survive as a result of improved medical care and partly because children who would previously have been sent to hospitals are now almost without exception attending day schools and living with their families or with substitute families.

Children with profound and multiple learning difficulties are defined in broad terms as those whose level of intellectual retardation is more than five standard deviations from the mean (where the mean is 100 and the SD is 15 points) or, expressed differently, children whose mental age scores are one quarter of their chronological age and who, in addition, have one or more significant additional sensory or physical impairments (Hogg and Sebba, 1986). A small proportion of these children are functioning at extremely low developmental levels, sometimes corresponding to only a few weeks of normal development. There are therefore real issues about what kinds of educational intervention are appropriate for such children. Fortunately, these issues are now beginning to be addressed (e.g. Presland, 1990).

Other recent evidence has focused on pupils with 'challenging behaviour', including stereotyped and ritualistic behaviour, non-compliance, self-injury and injury to others, and destructive and socially or physically disruptive behaviours. On the basis of a one in three national sample of schools for children with severe learning difficulties, Kiernan and Kiernan (in press) have estimated that an average school of 60 pupils would include five pupils with 'extremely or very difficult' behaviour and another nine 'less difficult' pupils. Projected to England and Wales, this would mean 2000 and 3400 pupils whose needs are exceptionally difficult to meet and whose teachers and parents receive little training or support.

Education for what?

A consideration of the characteristics of children attending special schools raises questions about the aims of education, its content and the methods of education for this group of children.

The Warnock report insisted that the goals of education were the same for all children:

> 'to enlarge a child's knowledge, experience and imaginative understanding and thus his awareness of moral values and capacity for enjoyment . . . to enable him to enter the world after formal education is over as an active participant in society and as an active contributor to it, capable of achieving as much independence as possible' (Department of Education and Science, 1978).

These are bold and imaginative aims, echoed in muted form perhaps by the 1988 Education Reform Act which refers to the need for schooling to 'promote the spiritual, moral, cultural, mental and physical development of pupils at the school and of society and to prepare pupils for the opportunities, responsibilities and experiences of adult life' (Department of Education and Science, 1989).

What can schools and schooling do to reduce the vulnerability of young people with severe learning difficulties and to strengthen the ability to cope with the demands which will be made of them when they leave school and enter the adult world?

Can schools, preferably in partnership with parents, help to develop the skills which are essential not merely to survival but to a good quality of life in the community? Should this extend to helping their students to be more assertive, to seek out opportunities to exercise choice and decision making, to form self advocacy groups and teach and support others? Is it the role of schools to teach students to protest against discrimination and under-estimation of their abilities or refusal by others to allow them to experiment and take risks? The ability to speak for oneself is not learned overnight or by simple exposure. The process needs to begin in early childhood, to continue throughout the whole period of schooling and to culminate in the participation of the student in what should be an extended process of decision making associated with transition from school to adult services. This is also an area of the curriculum that calls for the closest possible collaboration between parents, teachers and the young people themselves.

Schools cannot begin early enough to develop a 'curriculum for adult life'. A curriculum in the broadest sense, defined as 'all the learning experiences provided by a school', creates opportunities for choice and decision making from the earliest levels – choice between two drinks, two items of clothing, two stories, two toys. Such an approach involves the family from the start; indeed, they will often have initiated it themselves.

Until the advent of the national curriculum in 1990, schools for children with severe learning difficulties had been free to determine their own curriculum and to develop individual educational programmes to meet specific needs, based on assessment involving teachers, parents and other professionals. Several influential curriculum and organisational guidelines have been published (e.g. Coupe and Porter, 1986; Gardner, Murphy and Crawford, 1983) and some schools have published detailed accounts of their own curricula (e.g. Rectory Paddock, 1983).

The 1970s and early 1980s were characterised by a heavy reliance on behavioural approaches to teaching (Kiernan, 1985). The school-based INSET course known as EDY (Education of the Developmentally Young) (McBrien and Foxen, 1987) has been disseminated through a cascade model and has reached some 5000 staff of schools and adult services, as well as a small number of parents and health and social service professionals. These methods provided a powerful technology of how to teach at least certain skills but left the question of curriculum content relatively unanswered. It was only in the 1980s that schools began to reappraise their own curricula, to use behavioural approaches as a teaching methodology in those areas where they seemed appropriate and to develop other approaches where these methods did not seem relevant. The EDY materials are now being revised and updated in the light of these developments (McBrien, Foxen and Farrell, in press).

Curriculum models relying heavily on specification of behavioural objectives, task analysis, appropriate reward and step by step recording have been highly influential and successful. But it has always been clear that not all areas of the curriculum lend themselves to this approach which is necessarily restricted to what can be observed. More fundamentally, there are concerns that a behavioural framework does not allow enough scope for teachers to take their cue from the child's own preferences and interests (Wood and

Shears, 1986) and from the opportunities provided through social interactions between teachers and pupils and between pupils themselves.

The last few years have seen a growing emphasis on the social contexts of teaching and learning. This approach emphasises the importance of encouraging pupils to initiate communication and to develop a rich interactive dialogue with staff and other pupils, in place of the somewhat sterile question and single word response exchanges which were once common (Leeming, Swann, Coupe and Mittler, 1979). This work has been influenced by a better understanding of the social origins of human communication and the interrelationship between cognitive and communicative development in normally developing children (Smith, 1987; Coupe and Goldbart, 1988). This includes information from studies of parent-child interaction patterns, including 'proto-conversations' between mothers and babies, joint action routines and giving children time and opportunities to anticipate adult actions and demands through appropriate games.

A further encouraging development is the renewed interest in group work as a deliberate approach to helping children to learn from one another in cooperative activities where each is dependent on the other (Sebba and Ferguson, 1991). This is timely in the context of the emphasis on topic and cooperative work in the national curriculum programmes of study particularly at the primary stage. Farrell (in press) has argued that interactive and behavioural methods are by no means incompatible and that approaches which incorporate the best features of both are likely to be productive.

The Warnock Report and the 1981 Education Act

The Warnock report strongly endorsed the developments which were taking place in the education of children with severe learning difficulties and was unequivocal in its view that such work was fundamentally of an educational nature. The 1981 Education Act built on some of the foundations laid by the Warnock report and established important points of principle and practice. In particular, it laid a duty on all schools to identify and meet the special educational needs of their pupils and on Local Education Authorities to make provision to meet those needs which could not be provided by schools from within their own resources. Particular importance is attached to the full involvement of parents in the process of assessment and decision making. The Act also expressed a commitment to the education of children with special educational needs in ordinary schools, but this was subject to several qualifications – that it would not interfere with the efficient provision of education of other children and that it was compatible with the efficient use of resources.

How far have these changes specifically benefited children with severe learning difficulties?

Statements of special educational need

The purpose of the statement is to provide an official record of the process of identifying the needs of individual children with a view to specifying the additional resources which the LEA is required to provide to meet identified needs.

Unfortunately, statements have fallen far short of these aims. Where children with severe learning difficulties are concerned, many statements provide little more than a summary of what is already known about the child's limitations and conclude with a recommendation that these needs will best be met in a special school, nearly always a school for children with severe learning difficulties.

This contrasts sharply with the operation of Public Law 94–142 in the USA which prescribes an individual educational plan, including short term objectives, target dates and criteria for determining whether objectives have been attained. Although statements in the UK are nothing like as prescriptive as this, there is no reason why the annual reviews required by the Act should not include more detailed individual educational programmes.

There is much talk of the 'protection' afforded by a statement, in the sense that it is meant to guarantee the resources required to implement its recommendations. This may be useful for children with special educational needs in ordinary schools, provided that specific resources are identified – e.g. so many hours of additional help provided by a support teacher. But in the case of children with severe learning difficulties, the nature of additional provision is rarely spelled out in detail, since most of them are either in special schools already or will be recommended for them by the statement itself. The schools will make the best possible provision for such pupils in the light of individual needs and whatever resources are available to them. These needs are more likely to be identified during the course of diagnostic teaching within the school rather than as a result of special pedagogic insights deriving from the statementing process as such.

Information supplied by the government in answer to a Parliamentary Question indicates that some Local Education Authorities have been so slow in producing statements that many pupils already in special schools have not yet received a statement (Swann, 1988). This may not be a serious issue as far as the education of children in special schools is concerned, since teachers will in any case be doing their best to teach the child. But it would be a serious matter if the child needed resources which the school could not supply. Even where children do have a statement, there are unresolved issues about the legal responsibilities of the National Health Service to meet specific needs identified in statements drawn up by the LEA, even where health professionals have themselves participated in the process of assessment and decision making.

The same point applies to Social Services Departments and to relevant voluntary agencies.

As far as children with severe learning difficulties are concerned, there is little evidence that the statementing process has provided either protection or additional resources which the school would not have been seeking to provide without a statement. A statement would, however, be essential if the pupil were attending an ordinary school.

Education in ordinary schools

It is often said that the education of children with special educational needs is the central question of special education and of education itself. But how much progress has been made in achieving this goal where children with severe learning difficulties are concerned?

It is difficult to answer this question because official statistics are not available in relation to specific groups of children. Following the abolition of categories of handicap in the 1981 Education Act, the Department of Education and Science ceased to publish information on pupils with specific disabilities and confined itself to global data on children with statements, distinguishing only between those in special and ordinary schools. These global figures have been analysed in some detail by Swann (1988, 1991), who concluded that the proportion of the nation's children in all special schools remained remarkably constant at around 1.5 per cent for some years and has only recently been showing signs of a slight decrease. There is also evidence that, of all children with statements, the proportion in ordinary schools has been rising steadily and is now around 30 per cent.

The way in which statistics are collected thus makes it impossible to come to any conclusions on a national scale concerning the extent to which children with severe learning difficulties are being educated in ordinary schools. One interesting pointer is provided by a longitudinal study of all children with Down's Syndrome born in the Greater Manchester area between 1973 and 1980. The most recent report from this study indicates that six per cent of the 127 children in the study were attending units in mainstream schools and a further ten per cent were in ordinary classes (Turner, Sloper, Knussen and Cunningham, 1991). The rest were attending schools for children with moderate or severe learning difficulties. Children with Down's Syndrome constitute about a third of children attending schools for children with severe learning difficulties.

There are now a number of accounts of practice in particular Local Education Authorities, as well as studies of individual children. Can any conclusions be drawn from these studies?

Pre-school

In the first place, it seems clear that an increasing number of pre-school children with severe learning difficulties are being integrated into a wide range of pre-school services. These include LEA nursery schools and classes, Social Services day centres and a large number of voluntary pre-school playgroups. A number of children also attend nursery class of special schools.

Several studies have suggested that, whatever the social benefits of mainstream placements for the children involved, the staff are themselves lacking in information and support on how the needs of these children can be met (Clark, 1988; Robson, 1989). Information is needed, for example, on the results of inter-disciplinary assessments and whether Child Development Centres or Community Mental Handicap Teams have made suggestions for specific interventions. Here again, a recent HMI report highlights problems of communication and coordination among professionals, a shortage of resources in both health and social services and lack of opportunities for joint training (HMI, 1991a). These were precisely the problems identified by the Warnock Committee which led to their recommendation for a 'named person and single point of contact'.

Perhaps the most important single development in the pre-school sector is the expansion of Portage schemes into most parts of the country, as a result of special government grants earmarked for this purpose. Although the Portage association has still not published any large scale evaluation of the effectiveness of this approach, a national overview report by Her Majesty's Inspectors is most encouraging (HMI, 1990). We do not know, however, whether children who have been on Portage programmes show longer term benefits once they reach school or whether their prospects for education in ordinary schools are any different from those of other children.

Primary schools

A growing number of young school age children with severe learning difficulties are attending ordinary infant schools, often as an initial placement on reaching the age of five. Both they and pre-school children should have a statement specifying what additional resources are needed to meet their needs, whatever school or establishment they attend, but little information on the adequacy of these statements is available.

One of the earliest reported schemes was the London Borough of Bromley which catered for all its five- to seven-year-old children in special classes attached to ordinary infant schools, after which they were sent to special schools (Pierse, 1973).

There are also reports from a few areas of attempts at full classroom integration in the child's neighbourhood primary school. For example, Overdale school in Stockport succeeded in placing five children in their nearest primary schools but each of these children needed a full time special support assistant, all supported in turn by a peripatetic specialist teacher. Evaluations of the scheme suggested that the attitudes of all staff and parents concerned were very positive but the scheme proved too costly to extend to the whole school (Sloper and Elliott, 1990, Day, 1990). Of the many accounts of individual children, that by Hulley (1985) of the integration of his severely handicapped nine-year-old daughter in an ordinary class is amongst the most impressive and carefully documented. See also Hulley, Hulley, Parsons, Madden and Swann (1987) for a more detailed account including perspectives of the child's classmates.

Parts of Oxfordshire currently have a well publicised scheme, in which classes of children from a hospital school were transferred with all their staff to a local primary school. Nineteen children were originally not considered suitable for transfer and remained in the special school (Kidd, 1985), but these too were later transferred. These children were mostly being taught in a special class but were spending increasing periods of time in mainstream classes. A more recent account from a different part of Oxfordshire has recently been published by Wilson (1990), who provides a detailed account with timetables of a scheme in which the nature and degree of integration in a primary and secondary school was related to the individual needs of children.

Secondary and further education

The older the child, the lower is the probability of their attending an ordinary school. Impressively, the South Oxfordshire scheme established two classes in a local secondary school and a further class in the local College of Further Education. Another example of secondary integration is reported from a secondary school in Derbyshire where a class of children with severe learning difficulties has been successfully established for many years (Roberts and Williams, 1980). Colleges of Further Education have also increasingly tried to make appropriate provision for students with severe learning difficulties though progress has been very uneven throughout the country (Dean and Hegarty, 1984).

After reviewing reports of integration schemes in this country and abroad, Mittler and Farrell (1987) suggested a provisional model of integration which involves the education of all children with severe learning difficulties in special classes in specially resourced primary and secondary schools. Such a model would permit the total closure of the special school and the transfer of all staff to the designated ordinary schools. Although it falls short of full classroom integration in the child's own neighbourhood school, it does facilitate full locational and social integration for all children, including those with profound and multiple impairments. These special classes can also provide a base for planned functional integration in the appropriate ordinary class of the designated schools. Such a model does not preclude full classroom integration in the neighbourhood school for all those children for whom it is feasible.

Although the number of children involved in such schemes is very small compared to the 24,000 or so children with severe learning difficulties in special schools, the fact that even one child can be successfully integrated in an ordinary school suggests that it could be attempted on a much larger scale, provided that such schemes are properly planned and resourced.

Link schemes between special and ordinary schools

Although there has not been much progress in moving towards integration in the full sense, schools for children with severe learning difficulties have in fact been spearheading close working links between special and ordinary schools.

These are carefully planned, regular, time-tabled weekly links, in which individual children but more often whole classes accompanied by their teachers and support workers join forces with a selected class in a nearby ordinary school and take a full part in relevant activities. Jowett, Hegarty and Moses (1988), who carried out a national study of such link schemes, reported that four out of five schools for children with severe learning difficulties were involved in such schemes in the mid 1980s. These developments generally spring from the initiative of the headteachers and staff of the schools involved. The question now is whether such link schemes will survive in the harsher climate created by the Education Reform Act.

Partnership with parents

The Warnock Committee's emphasis on partnership with parents has fallen on particularly fruitful ground in schools for children with severe learning difficulties. In fact, it is probably no exaggeration to say that such schools have pioneered new approaches and gone further along the road to partnership with parents than other sectors of special or mainstream education (Mittler and McConachie, 1983; Topping, 1986).

But volume of publications is not necessarily an indication of the national spread of such partnerships or of their quality. There are indications that their potential is not always developed to the full. For example, in their survey of school leavers and their families in North West England, Cheseldine and Jeffree (1982) found that although schools were teaching young people basic cookery, parents were reluctant to allow their children to cook at home. At the same time, they expressed concerns about how the child would cope when they were no longer able to provide a home.

It seems that, despite a general commitment to parental involvement, schools may be missing out on opportunities to forge a working partnership with parents in which there are agreements concerning allocation of responsibility for meeting the child's needs in different contexts and also for ways in which parents can help the child to generalise at home and in community settings skills which are also being taught at school. Making toast and a pot of tea is an obvious example but there are many other areas of experience where collaboration between parents and teachers would be productive – using money in 'real shops', using public transport, eating out, attending local recreational facilities and perhaps above all in the area of personal relationships and sex education. Now that the demands of the national curriculum make it difficult for teachers to incorporate these activities into a crowded timetable, partnership with parents becomes even more important.

Implications of the 1988 Education Reform Act

What implications does the 1988 Education Reform Act have for the progress that has been made and remains to be made in the education of children with severe learning difficulties? At a time when policy changes from month to month, it is difficult to draw up a balance sheet and to anticipate the future, all the more so as initiatives lie less with government and Local Education Authorities and more with individual headteachers and their governors. It may be better to err on the side of optimism and to put on one side the anger and despair felt by many professionals and parents in the long period when it seemed that special educational needs were being totally overlooked in the rush to reform. This neglect is still an ever present danger and demands eternal vigilance.

A broad, balanced and relevant curriculum?

The authors of the ERA have stated officially that 'the principle that each pupil should have a broad and balanced curriculum which is also relevant to his or her particular needs is now established in law' (Department of Education and Science, 1989).

This is a strong affirmation of entitlement, coming into the category of 'SEN friendly'. It is reinforced by constant reiterations by ministers and HMI, as well as the National Curriculum Council and the School Examination and Assessment Council, of the theme that the national curriculum is for all pupils and that there should be the minimum of exemptions and modifications. Can this rhetoric be translated into practice?

The arrival of the national curriculum has been accepted as a major challenge by teachers in special schools for children with severe learning difficulties, united in their determination to prevent children and schools being excluded from the national curriculum and regarded as ineducable and schools being relegated to their pre-1971 status. On the positive side, teachers are determined to maintain the progress and momentum of the last ten years. How are they setting about this?

ACCESSING THE CORE AND FOUNDATION SUBJECTS

Firstly, a number of working parties have been set up with the aim of making each subject more accessible to pupils with severe learning difficulties. The National Curriculum Council is funding the dissemination of materials produced by a group of teachers based at the Cambridge Institute of Education (e.g. Sebba and Ferguson, 1991).

A team of Manchester teachers seconded to the University is producing a series of guidance documents designed to make the curriculum accessible to all. The lead document (Fagg, Aherne, Skelton and Thornber, 1990) delineates in considerable detail how each of the components of 'broad, balanced and relevant' can be interpreted along cross-curricular lines within the framework of a school for pupils with severe and complex learning difficulties and how it would affect three individual pupils with varying needs, including one with profound and multiple learning difficulties. Subsequent documents provide a detailed analysis of the core subjects of English, Maths and Science, breaking down the programmes of study, statements of attainment and attainment targets into smaller steps. Working downwards from the statement of attainment, suggestions have been made for a series of preliminary steps, leading right down to those that might be within the reach of pupils with profound and multiple learning difficulties and at the earliest stages of development. Subjects include maths (Aherne and Thornber, 1990), science (Fagg and Skelton, 1990), communication (speaking and listening) (Aherne and Thornber, 1990), literacy (reading, writing, handwriting and spelling) (Ackerman and Mount 1991), and Technology (Mount and Ackerman, 1991).

Breaking down national curriculum subjects into smaller steps is not possible or appropriate for all subjects or activities but the approach does provide one way forward in at least some areas of the curriculum. This approach could also be used for younger children in infant schools or for other children with delayed development. Using such milestones as part of a record of achievement, parents, other teachers and pupils themselves can celebrate progress, rather than being consigned for long periods or for the whole of their school careers to a line below the official starting point of the national curriculum. The fact that these milestones do not form part of the statutory orders need not prevent teachers developing them now (Mittler, 1991).

PLANNING A WHOLE CURRICULUM

Teachers are currently struggling to integrate three elements – the child's individual educational programme, the school's pre-existing curriculum and the national curriculum. A major obstacle to such integration is lack of time, exacerbated by lack of resources.

Although it is frequently stated that the national curriculum is not the whole curriculum, teachers are understandably concerned about many activities which are essential to meet the needs of pupils with severe learning difficulties but which do not fit comfortably either within the programmes of study for the ten foundation subjects and religious education or the numerous cross-curricular themes, skills and dimensions which are now seen to be essential – e.g. personal and social education, careers education, health education, economic awareness, environmental education, citizenship, as well as strands concerned with equal opportunities, gender and multi-cultural experiences. Writing as the head of a school which has a long established tradition of curriculum development and innovation, Coupe (1991) believes that it is possible to develop a whole curriculum approach which integrates the national curriculum with existing good practice.

At the same time, the extent to which the whole of the national curriculum is relevant or necessary is being increasingly questioned (e.g. Emblem and Conti-Ramsden, 1990; Tye Green School, 1990). Since this curriculum was never devised with the needs of children with severe learning difficulties in mind, why, it is argued, should there be such strong opposition to the possibility of exemptions, modifications and even exclusions, provided that parents, teachers and the LEA are satisfied that the proposed curriculum is broad, balanced and relevant to that pupil, as required by the Act?

Any modification of the child's curriculum would need to be discussed by all concerned as part of the annual review of the statement required by the 1981 Education Act. The full and informed participation of parents is therefore essential if there is any question of reducing the child's entitlement.

So far, no information is available on the extent to which statements are being modified in the light of the national curriculum. The law assumes that all children are on all relevant and age appropriate programmes of study and that they will be assessed both through Teacher Assessment and Standard Assessment Tasks unless specifically exempted through the statement.

ASSESSMENT

The 1988 Act requires that children should be assessed each year on all the national curriculum attainment targets which they are being taught in the context of programmes of study to record these results and to pass them both to the parents and to the LEA. Two assessments are required – Teacher Assessment every year and Standard Assessment Tasks at the end of each key stage at seven, 11, 14 and 16.

Within special schools, neither teachers, parents nor children have anything to fear from Teacher Assessment since teachers have been carrying out regular, ongoing, formative assessment for many years. There is no reason why results reported to parents should not provide more information than is required by the regulations; for example, they need not be confined to a simple level of attainment, since these might remain at level 1 for many years, but can record the more detailed statements of attainment and even the very small steps within a level.

Concern has focused largely on the Standard Assessment Tasks rather than Teacher Assessment. As a result of criticisms that SATs were unmanageable, they have been greatly slimmed down and will only be assessing nine rather than 36 attainment targets. At Key Stages 1 and 2 (for seven- and 11–year-olds) SATs will be required only for a small sample of Attainment Targets in English, Maths and Science and not for the other foundation subjects, for which 'non-statutory SATs' will be available for those teachers who want to use them – starting with Technology. Since most special schools will not be using SATs formally before the summer of 1992, it is too early to evaluate their relevance or appropriateness to children with severe learning difficulties. The 1991 SATs, though slimmer, are somewhat more prescriptive and focus more on specific core subjects, in contrast with the cross-curricular thematic SATs used in the 1990 trials.

The government has also performed a welcome U-turn on Records of Achievement (Department of Education and Science, 1990). These will now be required for all children but are already alive and well in most schools for pupils with severe learning difficulties. Records of Achievement celebrate all areas of achievement, including the pupil's interests, hobbies and community activities, and are not restricted to the national curriculum attainment targets alone. Furthermore, pupils themselves play a major part in preparing these Records of Achievement which remain their personal property.

PROSPECTS FOR INTEGRATION

Serious concerns have been expressed about the extent to which even the limited progress towards integrated education can be maintained in the future. Now that schools are forced to publish their results and to compete with one another for pupils and resources, will ordinary schools be less inclined to welcome pupils with special educational needs in general and those with severe learning difficulties in particular? Will the children be able to cope with the demands of the national curriculum in ordinary schools? What are the prospects of securing and funding the support staffing which is an essential component of integration for children with severe learning difficulties? Even without full integration in special or ordinary classes, how will the regular link schemes which are now a feature of most special schools be funded under Local Management of Schools? Are children who are already partially or wholly integrated at risk of being excluded from ordinary schools and returned to special schools?

These are real fears, arising in part from failure at all levels to develop clear policies to maintain and fund good practice. As part of its introduction of Local Management of Schools, the government is insisting on the production of clear policy statements by LEAs, setting out a strategic view of their plans for integration and for delegation of funding for pupils with special educational needs (Department of Education and Science, 1991). The government itself seems to disclaim responsibility for policy initiatives and places the entire onus on schools and on the greatly weakened Local Education Authorities.

Prospects for adults

After this review of progress and prospects for children of school age, what are the prospects for adolescents and adults achieving the Warnock aims of 'entering the world after formal education is over, as an active participant in society and as an active contributor to it . . .'?

The answer to this question varies greatly from one part of the country to another, depending on the effectiveness of local planning and policy implementation, the quality of the collaboration between the different statutory and voluntary agencies involved and between all of these and families and above all the young people themselves. But compared with the transformation in the quality of work in the schools since 1971, adult services have lagged badly behind. Reviewing the main services, it is hard to be optimistic about the future.

On the positive side, many more Colleges of Education are now providing for the needs of these young people, at least for two or three years, though provision is extraordinarily patchy across the country. A recent HMI (1991b) report on transition from school to adult provision is severely critical of the absence or poor quality of liaison between staff of the different agencies and the low level of curriculum planning across the 14–19 age group and beyond. On the other hand, many more young people attending both school and college have had successful work experience programmes, often with the help of funding from the Technical and Vocational Education initiative and the support of the Manpower Services Commission and then Training Agency.

Against this, there is little national evidence of higher quality services in Day Centres, now attended by some 55,000 people daily receiving around £2 per week or less pocket money. The centres are very badly staffed, so that individual service programmes are few and far between. A national report from the Social Services Inspectorate (1988) reflects a lack of recognition and support from senior management, resulting in underfunding, low levels of training and poor morale among staff. Reform of day service provision is long overdue but very low on the priority list at any level of central or local government.

Considerable progress has been made in the use of ordinary housing, with three to five adults living together, with as much support as they need provided by or through Social Services Departments or voluntary agencies. It remains to be seen whether these developments will survive the much postponed 'Care in the Community' proposals. There has also been good progress in the field of supported employment following on the initiatives taken by MENCAP in the Pathway scheme.

Whether the large scale relocation of hospital residents into the community is seen as a benefit or as a burden depends again on local variations. In some areas, people have been relocated with their consent and participation, on the basis of an agreed resettlement plan involving all the agencies, using earmarked funding. In other areas, there has been 'discharge without regard', with people abandoned unsupported and without adequate housing or occupation.

An examination of the quality of provision for adults with learning difficulties suggests a picture of gross underfunding, poor communication between the different service agencies involved, a failure to apply knowledge already available and above all low priority attached to a devalued group of citizens.

Conclusions

The education of children with severe learning difficulties has changed out of all recognition during the past twenty years. Indeed, this sector has pioneered many developments and been in the forefront of innovation in the field of special education. But the rapid changes which are now taking place in the field of education as a whole are forcing these schools to take stock and to question the direction and the priorities of their work. They have already responded well to the challenge of integration into ordinary schools, only to find that the curriculum of all schools is itself being radically restructured, not always in directions which are necessarily in the interests of children with severe learning difficulties. This challenge is now being met by teachers determined to ensure that their children are not again excluded.

On the other hand, the poor quality of services and support for adults with learning difficulties raises new questions about the role of special schools. How can their experience and expertise be shared with colleagues working in adult services? What would persuade policy makers and planners to devote a greater share of resources to adults? What more can teachers do to work in partnership with parents to press for the needs of adults to be given greater priority? Above all what more can schools and parents do to empower people with learning difficulties themselves to play a greater part in determining their own future?

References

Ackerman, D. and Mount H. (1991), *Literacy for All*. London: Fulton.

Aherne, P. and Thornber, A. (1990), *Communication for All*. London: Fulton.

Cheseldine, S. and Jeffree, D. (1982), 'Mentally handicapped adolescents: a survey of their abilities'. *Journal of Mental Deficiency Research* 25, 49–59.

Clark, M. (1988), *Children Under Five: Educational Research and Evidence*. London: Gordon Breach.

Coupe, J. (1991), Teaching and learning: retrospect and prospect. In Segal, S. and Varma, V. (eds.) *Prospects for Pupils with Learning Difficulties*. London: Fulton.

Coupe, J. and Porter, J. (eds.) (1986), *The Education of Children with Severe Learning Difficulties*. Beckenham: Croom Helm.

Coupe, J. and Goldbart, J. (eds.) (1988), *Communication Before Speech*. Beckenham: Croom Helm.

Day, E. (1989), Attitudes of school staff towards the integration into ordinary schools of children with severe learning difficulties. Unpublished M.Ed dissertation: University of Manchester.

Dean, A. and Hegarty, S. (eds) (1984), *Learning for Independence*. London: Further Education Unit, Department of Education and Science.

Department of Education and Science (1978), *Special Educational Needs: Report of the Committee of Enquiry into the Education of Handicapped Children and Young People*. London: HMSO.

Department of Education and Science (1989), *National Curriculum: From Policy to Practice*. London: HMSO.

Department of Education and Science (1990), *Records of Achievement*. Circular 8/90.

Department of Education and Science (1991), *Local Management of Schools: Further Guidance*. DES Circular 7/91.

Emblem, B. and Conti-Ramsden, G. (1990) 'Towards level 1: illusion or reality?' *British Journal of Special Education*, 17, 88–90.

Evans, P. and Ware, J. (1987), *Special Care Provision in the Education of Children with Profound and Multiple Learning Difficulties*. Windsor: NFER-Nelson.

Fagg, S., Aherne, P., Skelton, S. and Thornber, A. (1990), *Entitlement for All in Practice: Towards a Broad, Balanced and Relevant Curriculum for Pupils with Severe and Complex Learning Difficulties.* London: Fulton.

Fagg, S. and Skelton, S. (1990), *Science for All.* London: Fulton.

Farrell, P. (in press), 'Behavioural and interactive teaching for children with severe learning difficulties: match or mismatch?' *Educational and Child Psychology*

Gardner, J., Murphy, G. and Crawford, N. (1983), *The Skills Analysis Model: An Effective Curriculum for Children with Severe Learning Difficulties.* Kidderminster: British Institute for Mental Handicap.

Her Majesty's Inspectorate of Education (1990), *Portage Projects: A Summary of 13 Projects Funded by the Education Support Grants.* London: Department of Education and Science.

Her Majesty's Inspectorate (1991a), *Interdisciplinary Support for Young Children with Special Educational Needs.* London: Department of Education and Science.

Her Majesty's Inspectorate (1991b), *Transition from School to Further Education for Students with Learning Difficulties.* London: Department of Education and Science.

Hogg J. and Sebba, J. (eds.) (1986), *Profound Retardation and Multiple Impairment* (vol 1). Beckenham: Croom Helm.

Hulley, T. (1985), *Samantha Goes to School.* London: Campaign for People with Mental Handicap.

Hulley, B., Hulley, T., Parsons, G. and Swann, W. (1987), Samantha. In Booth, T. and Swann, W. (eds.) *Including Pupils with Disabilities: Curricula for All.* Milton Keynes: Open University Press.

Jowett, S., Hegarty, S. and Moses, D. (1988), *Joining Forces: A Study of Links Between Special and Ordinary Schools.* Windsor: NFER-Nelson.

Kidd, R. (1985), Bishopswood special school: a recent initiative. In Orton, C. (ed.) *Integration in Action: The Way Forward.* London: Centre for Studies in Integrated Education.

Kiernan, C. (1985), Behaviour modification. In Clarke, A., Clarke, A.D.B. and Berg, J. (eds.) *Mental Deficiency: The Changing Outlook.* London: Methuen (4th edn.)

Kiernan, C. (1991), Research: progress and prospects. In Segal, S. and Varma, V. (eds.) *Progress and Prospects for Pupils with Learning Difficulties.* London: Fulton.

Kiernan, C. and Kiernan, D. (in press) 'Challenging behaviour for pupils with severe learning difficulties.' *Mental Handicap Research.*

Leeming, K., Swann, W., Coupe, J. and Mittler, P. (1979) *Teaching Language and Communication to the Mentally Handicapped.* London: Methuen.

McBrien, J. and Foxen, T. (1987), The EDY inservice course for mental handicap practitioners. In Hogg, J. and Mittler, P. (eds.) *Staff Training in Mental Handicap.* Beckenham: Croom Helm.

McBrien, J., Foxen, T. and Farrell, P. (in press), *EDY Trainee Work Book and Instructors' Handbook* (Revised Edition). Manchester: Manchester University Press.

Mittler, P. (1991), Foreword to Ackerman and Mount, *op.cit.*

Mittler, P. and Farrell, P. (1987), 'Can children with severe learning difficulties be educated in ordinary schools', *European Journal of Special Needs Education*, 2, 221–236.

Mittler, P. and McConachie, H. (eds.) (1983) *Parents Professionals and Mentally Handicapped People: Approaches to Partnership.* Beckenham: Croom Helm.

Mittler, P. and Preddy, D. (1981), Mentally handicapped pupils and school leavers: a survey in North West England. In Cooper, B. (ed.) *Assessing the Handicaps and Needs of Mentally Retarded Children.* London and New York: Academic Press.

Mount, H. and Ackerman, D. (1991) *Technology for All.* London: Fulton.

National Development Group for the Mentally Handicapped (1977) *Day Services for Mentally Handicapped Adults.* Pamphlet 5. London: Department of Health and Social Security.

Pierse, A. (1973), 'A bold experiment in Bromley'. *Special Education*, 62, 12–14.

Presland, J. (1990), *Paths to Mobility in Special Care*. Kidderminster: British Institute for Mental Handicap (2nd edn.)

Rectory Paddock School (1983), *In Search of a Curriculum: Notes on the Education of Mentally Handicapped Children*. Orpington, Sidcup, Kent: Wren Publications.

Roberts, L. and Williams, I. (1980), 'Three years on at Pingle School'. *Special Education: Forward Trends*, 7, 24–26.

Robson, B. (1989) *Pre-school Provision for Special Needs*. London: Cassell.

Sebba, J. and Ferguson, A. (1991), Reducing the marginalisation of pupils with learning difficulties through curriculum initiatives. In Ainscow, M. (ed.) *Effective Schools for All*. London: Fulton.

Sloper, T. and Elliott, C. (1990), Evaluation of Overdale project for integration of children with severe learning difficulties into mainstream schools. Unpublished report. Manchester University: Hester Adrian Research Centre.

Smith, B. (ed.) (1987), *Interactive Approaches to the Teaching of Children with Severe Learning Difficulties*. Birmingham: Westhill and Newman College.

Social Services Inspectorate (1988), *Inspection of Day Services for People with a Mental Handicap*. London: Department of Health.

Swann, W. (1988), 'Trends in special school placement to 1986'. *Oxford Review of Education*, 14, 139–161.

Swann, W. (1991), *Variations between LEAs in levels of segregation in special schools, 1982–1990: a preliminary report*. London: Centre for Studies in Integrated Education.

Topping, K. (1986), *Parents as Educators*. Beckenham: Croom Helm.

Turner, S., Sloper, P., Knussen, C. and Cunningham. C. (1991), 'Factors relating to self sufficiency in children with Down's syndrome'. *Journal of Mental Deficiency Research*, 35, 13–24.

Tye Green School (1990), 'Broad, balanced . . . and relevant? *Special Children*, 44, 11–13.

Wilson, D. (1990) Integration of a special school. In Baker D. and Bovair, K. (eds.) *Making the Special School Ordinary?* (vol. 21). London: Falmer.

Wood, S. and Shears, B. (1986) *The Education of Children with Severe Learning Difficulties: A Radical Critique*. Beckenham: Croom Helm.

Chapter 11

Resilience and vulnerability in child survivors of disasters

William Yule

Introduction

Human beings are above all adaptable. We learn, we develop, we adapt. When our resources are insufficient to adapt to environmental demands, we experience stress. Usually, we adapt, to a greater or lesser extent, even to severe stressors. Like some other contributions to this text, this chapter addresses the question of why some children who experience a stressor – in this case a major disaster – appear to adapt well, while others do not. What factors are associated with a high risk of poor adaptation, and what factors are associated with a low risk? What is understood by vulnerability and resilience in children who have survived a major, life-threatening disaster?

Forty years ago, in the aftermath of World War Two, child mental health professionals did not dwell for long on the effects of war on children's development. If anything, negative effects were underplayed. The patriotic picture of strong community spirit in the face of civilian bombing was emphasized and little was written about fears and phobias. Enuresis was noted among evacuees, but little was said about the effects of separation from parents. Studies of the child survivors of the Nazi concentration camps seemed marginalised.

Instead, the post-war child development literature was dominated by psychoanalytic theories which, even today, despite much empirically based criticism and revision, still influence social policy in relation to child welfare. In the early 1950s, there was a general belief that not only was much of children's development influenced by their early experiences, it was set and largely unmodifiable. Such theorising fitted well with the parallel view of the biological basis of intelligence and its imperviousness to environmental modification that dominated educational theorising, particularly in relation to the mentally handicapped. Jack Tizard's (1964) classic experiment at Brooklands demonstrated dramatically and humanely that developmentally appropriate care improved performance and the quality of life in severely retarded children. Barbara Tizard's (1977) later study of the effects of late adoption also showed the power of good experimental design in challenging the then current orthodoxy in relation to substitute care. Ann and Alan Clarke (1976) drew on their own and other's work to mount a serious challenge to the notion of irreversible influences in early childhood. Since then, a more balanced approach has been adopted by leading researchers, trying to identify both risk and protective factors in children.

In this spirit of greater optimism about the effects of major stressors on child development, it is still, nevertheless, important to acknowledge that children do get harmed by such stressors. In this chapter, I will argue that adults have, until very recently, been unwilling to acknowledge the depth of suffering experienced by many children following severe traumas. As a result, while there are now many descriptive studies of the effects of disasters on children, there are few methodologically sound ones that contribute to our understanding of the mechanisms involved (Garmezy, 1986). Some of the more recent, more adequate studies will be briefly described. Age and sex differences in reactions will be examined. Models from adult psychopathology will be examined for their relevance to understanding risk and protective factors in childhood and I will draw on my recent experience with child survivors to consider which suggestions seem to apply to children. Finally, in as far as one can at this stage, I will consider implications for prevention and intervention.

Some disasters involving children

Just after school started on the morning of 21st October 1966, a huge coal tip slid down a mountainside in Wales and engulfed the primary school in Aberfan, killing 116 children and 28 adults. One hundred and forty-three primary school children survived. Scarcely a family in the tightly knit community was unaffected by the disaster. Offers of help poured in, but plans to study the psychological effects of the disaster were strongly resisted. Lacey (1972) reports on 56 children treated at the local child guidance clinic over the following four years:

> 'Symptoms varied but the commonest were sleeping difficulties, nervousness, lack of friends, unwillingness to go to school or out to play, instability and enuresis. Some of the children too, had shown some of these symptoms before the disaster, but they were said to be very much

worse after it. Broadly speaking, the children who were most affected were those with other anxiety creating situations in their backgrounds' (Lacey, 1972, p 259).

Lacey goes on to describe how some anxious parents became overprotective of their children. Fears of the dark and nightmares caused sleep problems. Bad weather upset the children as a period of bad weather had preceded the tip slide. Children rarely spoke spontaneously of their experiences. Three children played games of 'burying' in the sand.

Twenty-two years later to the day, on 21st October 1988, the cruise ship, *Jupiter*, sailed from Athens to take a party of around 400 British school children and their teachers on an educational cruise of the eastern Mediter-ranean. As they left harbour, it was beginning to get dark. Some of the groups were lining up for the evening meal, some were attending a briefing lecture on what they were to see on the trip. Just out of the harbour, the *Jupiter* was struck amidships by an Italian tanker and holed.

At first, no one realised the seriousness of their predicament, but very quickly the *Jupiter* shipped water and began listing badly to the port and aft. Children were told to assemble in a lounge on an upper deck, but many were unfamiliar with the layout of the ship. As the vessel listed at 45 degrees and then worse, they found it very difficult to get around. Children became separated from friends and teachers. Many were able to jump across to tugs that had come along side, but sadly two seamen assisting in the transfer were fatally crushed between the ship and the tug. Many children saw their dead bodies.

Other children, some of whom were non-swimmers, clung to the railings on the topmost deck under the lifeboats and had to jump in the water as the *Jupiter* went down, its funnel hissing and spurting out soot and smoke. Children and staff clung to wreckage in the dark oily water until rescued. Some of those swimming in the water were terrified lest they were run down by the rescue craft. It was many hours before it was realised that all but one child and one teacher had survived. After spending a sleepless night on a sister ship moored in Piraeus harbour, the children were flown back to a barrage of publicity the next day. Although the tour company offered to arrange counselling for any of the children who requested it, schools varied enormously in how they dealt with the aftermath. Some were very sympath-etic and arranged individual and group help; others wanted to forget the whole episode and discouraged children from even talking about it.

How far has our understanding of the effects of disasters on children progressed in the 22 years between the tragedy at Aberfan and the sinking of the *Jupiter*? What do we now know about the phenomenology of the psychological sequelae? How can we identify those survivors at most risk of developing major problems? What is known about intervention and treatment? It will be argued that it is no coincidence that research was resisted at Aberfan or that some schools tried to put the shutters down after the *Jupiter* sinking. It is now well documented that adults deny the severity of the effects of disasters on children and that problem must be borne in mind when evaluating the evidence presented below.

Measuring children's reactions – the Rutter rating scales

Reports of the effects of disasters on children have been fully reviewed elsewhere (Yule, 1991a). Here, I would like to emphasize that when disaster strikes, people on the spot naturally do their best to cope with the immediate crisis and often give second place to conducting research into what is happening. Moreover, when they do try to evaluate their interventions, they understandably use methods with which they are familiar, rather than measures that are relevant. Thus, Galante and Foa (1986) studied children badly traumatised by the massive earthquakes in a remote mountainous region of central Italy in November 1980. They set up treatment groups for 300 first to fourth grade children who were first rated on an Italian translation of the Rutter (1967) behaviour rating scale for completion by teachers. Detailed notes were taken of the content of discussion during the group meetings that were spaced over a one year period, and the Rutter scales were completed again at the end of the period, some 18 months after the earthquake.

The authors were disappointed that many of their predictions relating the teachers' ratings to indices of trauma and bereavement were not substantiated in their data. However, the Rutter scales were developed as screening instruments for use in general population studies and were not intended to screen out specific or rare conditions; nor can teachers be expected to report on the subjective experiences of the children.

Rutter's screening scales were also favoured by McFarlane in his large scale studies of the effects of the February 1983 bush fires in South East Australia (McFarlane, 1987; McFarlane, Policansky and Irwin, 1987). The children studied were aged five to 12 years and lived in one rural community in which large tracts of agricultural and forest lands were burnt, a quarter of a million livestock perished, 14 people died and many homes were burnt out or partially devastated. As has been found in other studies that attempt to research survivors, many teachers were unwilling to participate fully and while McFarlane tried to get repeated measures two, eight and 26 months after the fire, the attrition rate in his sample was very high. Teachers argued that it was not in the children's interest to remind them of what had happened. However, since the children need not have known that the teachers were rating their adjustment, the teachers' reluctance to cooperate tells us more about their own difficulties in acknowledging the children's suffering.

In the immediate aftermath of the fire at two months, the children were rated as less disturbed than a comparison group studied elsewhere. However, by eight months, both parents and teachers report significant increases in the numbers of children at high risk of psychiatric disorder and these high rates were maintained at 26 months. In fact, close inspection of the data show that teachers lagged behind parents in reporting problems and overall the study demonstrates a consistent increase in reported morbidity from eight months after the disaster. McFarlane et al (1987) concluded that the delayed recognition of problems suggests that many problems do not spontaneously resolve.

In a related paper, McFarlane (1987) reports his investigations of family reactions and functioning and their relationship to children's adjustment. Again keeping the caveats about sample attrition and inappropriate measures in mind, the questions he poses are very apposite in trying to understand why some children are affected more than others and why some remain affected for longer. He concludes that at the eight month follow up, the families showed increased levels of conflict, irritability and withdrawal, with maternal overprotection being quite common. The adjustment of the parents themselves were important determinants of the adjustment of the children. In particular, he comments that '. . . families who did not share their immediate reactions to disaster may have had more trouble with their long-term adjustment . . . and experienced a greater degree of estrangement'. Equally important, the child's reactions to the fire affected the adjustment of the family, emphasizing the reciprocal interactions among members of a family system.

Interviews and specially constructed scales

Pynoos and his colleagues have undertaken among the most systematic studies of children suffering Post Traumatic Stress Disorders (PTSD) following a variety of trauma from witnessing a parent being murdered or raped to themselves surviving an attack from a sniper in their school playground (Pynoos and Eth, 1986; Pynoos, Frederick, Nader, Arroyo, Steinberg, Eth, Nunez and Fairbanks, 1987; Pynoos and Nader, 1988). They sampled 159 children (14.5% of those attending the school) who were exposed to a sniper attack on the school in which one child and a passer by were killed and 13 other children were injured. Many children were trapped in the playground under gunfire and others were trapped in classrooms. Many were separated from siblings and, of course, parents. The siege lasted a number of hours.

Pynoos and his collaborators used a structured interview to obtain information on the children's reactions and codified this into a PTSD Reaction Index. On average the children were 9.2 years old at the time of the trauma. Nearly 40% of the children were found to have moderate to severe PTSD approximately one month after the event. A particularly striking finding in this study was the very strong relationship between exposure and later effects, in that those children who were trapped in the playground scored much higher than those who had left the vicinity of the school before the attack or were not in school that day.

At fourteen month follow-up, Nader, Pynoos, Fairbanks and Frederick (1990) report that 74% of the most severely exposed children in the playground still report moderate to severe levels of PTSD, contrasted with 81% of the unexposed children reporting no PTSD. Earlier PTSD Reaction Index scores were strongly related to those obtained at follow-up. In a more detailed analysis of the data, Nader, Pynoos et al (1990) investigated the effect of the survivors' knowledge of the victim on their PTSD Reaction Index scores. They found that only among the less exposed children did greater knowledge of the victim increase the strength of the emotional reaction to the trauma. In other words, the level of exposure to the life threatening trauma was more important than other factors such as knowledge of the victim. In this study, the moderating effects of families' reactions was not reported but the strength of the relationships noted between level of exposure and subsequent reactions challenges McFarlane's (1987) claim that most effects are mediated by parental reaction.

Yule and Williams (1990) report their experiences in assessing and treating children who survived the capsize of the *Herald of Free Enterprise* in Zeebrugge harbour in March 1987. They assessed 13 of the then known 22 surviving children under the age of 16 years. At six to nine months post accident, over half the children were reported by parents to be showing significant disturbance, while only two of eight children rated by teachers were said to be disturbed. The authors used the Rutter parent and teacher rating scales and, despite the small numbers, concluded that these screening scales were not sensitive to the subjective distress that is the hallmark of PTSD. In interviews, children revealed much more pathology than was known to parents or teachers.

After getting to know the children better, the authors were able to ask the children to complete Horowitz's Revised Impact of Events Scale (Horowitz, Wilner and Alvarez, 1979). Children as young as eight years found the scale meaningful and on that basis it was concluded that the children scored higher than adult patients attending Horowitz's clinic for treatment. At 12 to 15 months post accident, the children repeated their ratings and it was found that the overall level had scarcely dropped.

Returning to the aftermath of the sinking of the *Jupiter*, Yule and Udwin (1991) offered to help the survivors at one school. They screened all 24 survivors on three scales – the Impact of Events Scale, Birleson's Depression Scale (Birleson, 1981; Birleson, Hudson, Buchanan and Wolf, 1987) and the Revised Children's Manifest Anxiety Scale (Reynolds and Richmond, 1978). On the basis of their scores 10 days after the sinking, ten girls aged 14 years were thought to be at high risk of developing problems. When help was offered on an individual or group basis, and without saying which girls were considered to be at high risk, eight of the 10 high risk group came forward for help on the first day. The other two attended the second meeting. Only five others ever attended any group meeting. This was a highly significant relationship between scores on the screening scales and later help seeking, and the authors conclude that the battery shows considerable promise in identifying children who most need help after a disaster.

Following on Dollinger, O'Donnell and Staley's (1984) study of children hurt in a lightning strike on a playing field, Yule, Udwin and Murdoch (1990) asked all fourth year girls in one school which had had a party of 24 aboard the *Jupiter* when it sank to complete the Revised Fear Survey Schedule for Children (Ollendick, Yule and Ollier, 1991). Effectively, there were three subgroups of girls – those who went on the cruise and were traumatized, those who had wanted to go but could not get a place, and those who showed no interest in going in the first place. However, this latter group could not be considered as an unaffected control group as the whole school was badly affected by the aftermath of the disaster. Accordingly, fourth year girls in a nearby school also completed the fear schedule, along with the depression and anxiety scales.

Two sets of results should be noted. Firstly, the girls on the cruise were significantly more depressed and anxious than the other groups five months after the disaster. Indeed, there is a strong suggestion of an exposure/effect gradient on these two measures, reminiscent of that reported by Pynoos et al (1987). Secondly, the fear survey items were rated as being related to the events on the cruise or not. There was agreement among the authors that 11 items were related and 33 were unrelated. It was found that there were no differences across the four exposure groups on unrelated fears. By contrast, on related fears, only the girls who experienced the traumatic events showed a significant increase in reported fears. Thus, the authors took the opportunity of the disaster to examine the effects on children's fears and conclude that the effects are specific to stimuli present and thereby provide more confirmatory evidence of the conditioning theory of fear acquisition.

Later, 334 of the children – both boys and girls – who survived the Jupiter sinking completed the same screening battery. The results confirmed across the larger group that the survivors were significantly more depressed and anxious than matched controls. The findings in relation to related versus unrelated fears were confirmed in this larger sample. A new finding was that, overall, girls scored higher than boys on all the measures (Yule, in press).

The adolescents who were on board the *Jupiter* were mainly in their fourth and fifth year of secondary schooling at the time of the sinking. This meant that they were preparing for the GCSE examinations and there was considerable concern as to how their experiences might interfere with their academic attainment in these public examinations. Surprisingly, there appears to be only one attempt at studying the effects of a disaster on school performance, following a tornado that hit Wichita Falls in April 1979 (Martin and Little, 1986). Unfortunately, the analysis of school records was difficult to interpret and no attempt was made to relate school performance to emotional effects on the children. Thus, Tsui, Dagwell and Yule (in preparation) examined this in one school party that survived the *Jupiter* sinking. As the results are very much relevant to issues of risk and protective factors, this study will be considered in more detail later in the chapter.

Summary

As the methodology used improves, successive studies have shown that, following disasters, children's and adolescents' reactions are closely similar to those shown by adults. The failure to appreciate this earlier was largely due to investigators not asking the children about their own reactions. General screening scales of child psychopathology have limited value in quantifying traumatic reactions in children, largely because they are completed by parents or teachers. Specialist interviews and measures of intrusive thoughts, depression or anxiety seem to be of greater value.

Risk and protective factors

There is an increasingly large and sophisticated literature discussing risk and protective factors in relation to general child psychopathology (Garmezy and Rutter, 1985; Kimchi and Schaffner, 1990; Garmezy and Masten, 1990; Masten and Garmezy, 1985). While it remains useful to talk about risk and protective 'factors', it is recognized that a distinction must be made between a risk factor and a risk index and that in general the aim is to identify protective mechanisms or processes. Moreover, it is recognized that no factor operates in a vacuum and that there is always an interaction between the demands placed on the individual and that individual's constitution and previous learning. Kimchi and Schaffner (1990) note that constitutional factors are relatively more important in modulating stress in infancy and early childhood, whereas intrapersonal factors, such as characteristic attribution of locus of control, play a greater part in adolescence.

In their review, Kimchi and Schaffner (1990) conclude that resilient children are best characterised as active, affectionate, good natured, alert, responsive, sociable, and easy to deal with. As infants, they elicit attention and warmth from their caregivers. Resiliency, then, is associated with flexibility in coping and with 'outgoing social personality at all ages'. Put in a different framework, resilient children are more likely to be extrovert in personality.

It is impossible to separate out the risk and protective factors associated with gender from the child rearing approaches. Resilient girls are seen as coming from families in which there is an absence of overprotection and an emphasis on independence. Resilient boys are seen as coming from families in which there is greater structure, rules and parental supervision, and more emphasis on emotional expression. Of course, many of these generalisations come from studies of risk and protective factors in delinquency and may not apply to all forms of psychopathology.

Again, in general, high intelligence and good school attainment are seen as providing protection against stressors. A secure attachment with at least one adult caregiver is widely recognized as being protective early on, while later, good sibling relations and good friends are also seen as protective. Kimchi and Schaffner (1990) point out that good school experiences can counteract domestic stress.

Garmezy and Masten (1990) consider that the concept of stress '. . . implicates four factors: (1) the presence of a manifest stimulus event; (2) the event is one capable of modifying the organism's physiological and psychological equilibrium; (3) the disequilibrium is reflected in a state of arousal marked by neuropsychological, cognitive and emotional consequences for the individual; (4) these changes, in turn, disrupt the adaptation of the person' (p.462/3). The individual responds to stress by coping, but how one copes is determined by an appraisal of what the demands are and whether one is able to meet these. Thus, increasingly it is recognized that whatever the objective, stimulus properties of a stressor, the individual's coping will be affected by how that individual appraises the threat. Hence, an increased interest in cognitive coping strategies and attributional processes.

Risk, protection and disasters

Two general reviews of the adult literature will suffice to point out the main milestones in relation to risk and protective factors and the effects of disasters. Gibbs (1989) surveys factors in the survivor that mediate between disaster and psychopathology. She notes that there are conflicting findings on whether age is a risk factor, notwithstanding that the American Psychiatric Association's DSM-III-R (1987) clearly regards children and old people as being more susceptible to the effects of disasters. In general, she concludes that females are more vulnerable to the effects of disasters than males. However, she notes that following the Yom Kippur war, Milgram and Milgram (1976) reported increased anxiety in boys but not in girls. Again, Burke et al (1982) found that first grade (presumably six-year-old boys) were more affected by floods and blizzards than girls, whereas Burke (1986) reported that in fifth grade, girls were more affected than boys.

In an earlier, more comprehensive review, Rachman (1980) examined various sets of factors that were found to be related to difficulties in 'emotional processing'. By emotional processing, he meant the person's ability to adjust to the major threats experienced in traumas and disasters. Poor emotional processing was evidenced by

'. . . the persistence or return of intrusive signs of emotional activity (such as obsessions, nightmares, pressure of talk, phobias, inappropriate expressions of emotion that are out of context or out of proportion, or simply out of time.) Indirect signs may include an inability to concentrate on the task at hand, excessive restlessness, irritability'.

These signs of problems in emotional processing bear a strong resemblance to what the American Psychiatric Association recognized as Post Traumatic Stress Reaction with its three cardinal groups of symptoms – troublesome re-experiencing of the trauma; avoidance and emotional numbing; and increased physiological arousal. As I have shown elsewhere, these symptoms are also common in children and adolescents who have survived disasters (Yule, 1991a).

Rachman (1980) considered that there were four groups of factors that increased the risk of difficulties in emotional processing: factors of state, personality, stimulus, and associated activity. Where survivors are highly aroused, suffer sleeplessness and are tired, they will have greater difficulties in processing the emotions aroused by the disaster. Fortunately, Rachman notes, '. . . most people successfully process the overwhelming majority of the disturbing events that occur in their lives' (p 56), but here we are considering their reactions to major stressors.

Of primary importance for this chapter are Rachman's conclusions relating to personality factors in survivors. Children who have a high level of self-efficacy and are broadly competent should have fewer problems than those who do not possess these attributes. Difficulties in emotional processing are therefore related to '. . . a sense of incompetence, high levels of neuroticism, introversion' (p. 56). From a methodological point of view, even when evidence for this is forthcoming *after a disaster*, it is difficult to disentangle how far the scores reflect the effects of the disaster and how far they truly reflect pre-morbid personality. Studies such as those of McFarlane (1988) of adult firefighters clearly show that those most affected by the fire had higher scores on introversion and neuroticism, although the scores were obtained after the fire. There are no studies to date of personality in child survivors.

Arising from these observations is the controversy over the relative importance of the stimulus characteristics of the disaster and predisposing factors in the person. Rachman (1980) concludes that disasters that are sudden, intense, dangerous, give rise to feelings of uncontrollability and involve fears that are phylogenetically 'prepared' – such as fears of dark, suffocation or drowning – and will give rise to greater difficulties in emotional processing. Thus, a knowledge of the nature of a disaster may guide those managing the rescue services in estimating the likely levels of psychosocial morbidity later.

Where a group of people experience a similar intensity of exposure to danger, then in follow-up studies pre-morbid personality and post-disaster life events are bound, statistically speaking, to appear to relate more strongly to the outcome measure than is the exposure to the disaster. Only by considering the interrelationship among pre-morbid and exposure indices across different disasters can one come to a better understanding of the interactions.

Summary

In one of the better descriptions of psychological processes mediating reactions to disasters, Rachman (1980) highlights factors in the disaster and factors in the survivor that contribute to ease or difficulty in emotional processing. These findings are largely based on adult survivors and point to the importance of pre-existing personality and temperament. Gibbs (1989) suggests that children are at greater risk of traumatic reactions than adults, but concludes that the evidence on gender effects is unclear.

Risk and protection in child survivors

Let us now consider the meagre evidence in relation to child survivors.

Age

To date, there are insufficient studies to examine whether children of different ages are at different risk of developing post-traumatic stress disorders. Anecdotal and descriptive studies (Yule, 1991a) suggest that children under the age of six are more likely to get involved in repetitive play and repetitive drawing of the trauma, and this may be the developmental equivalent of re-experiencing the trauma, although they do also suffer from nightmares. I have seen some children who were below the age of two years, and hence nontalking, at the time of a severe trauma who over the subsequent four years did not show signs of stress reactions. Again, I have seen one prelinguistic boy who had vivid recollections of what happened, even though his parents swear they never discussed it with him. It is probably the case that with very young children, the reactions of the parents are as important as the experience of the trauma itself, but this needs to be examined properly.

Sex

Burke et al (1986) rated stories written by fifth grade flood victims ten months after the storms. Girls showed significantly more evidence of disaster-related material and more distress. This was in contrast with their earlier study of the same children five months after the disaster when boys showed higher anxiety. Milgram and Milgram (1976) studied fifth- and sixth-grade children two months after the Yom Kippur war and found boys to have higher anxiety scores than girls.

In contrast, the study of 334 of the *Jupiter* survivors (Yule, in press) found that on the Birleson Depression Inventory (Birleson, 1981), both boys and girls scored significantly higher than controls, and that girl survivors scored higher depression scores than boys. On the Children's Manifest Anxiety Scale (Reynolds and Richmond, 1978), again both boys and girl survivors scored higher than controls, and again boy survivors scored lower than girls. In contrast, neither boys nor girls showed any increase over controls in their reporting of fears that were unrelated to the accident, but both sexes showed significant increases in related fears. Once again, girl survivors reported many more related fears than did boy survivors.

Ability

Tsui, Dagwell and Yule (in preparation) studied the end of term examination results of 24 girl survivors of the *Jupiter* and the remainder of their fourth year (14–year-old) age group from the same school. They found that the 24 who went on the cruise were above average in attainment during the three years prior to the cruise, suggesting some bias in selecting children for the trip. Compared to another 24 who were also above average, and who remained high performers after the accident, the cruise survivors' attainment plummeted significantly to merely average levels one year after the accident. Two years after the accident, in their GCSE results, the survivors still performed less well than expected, although the difference was no longer as marked.

For the purposes of the present chapter, two other factors need to be emphasized. It will be remembered that on the basis solely of completing screening questionnaires ten days after the accident, Yule and Udwin (1991) had identified 10 girls as being at higher risk than others. When the pre-disaster attainment of these girls was examined, it was found that they had significantly *lower* pre-accident attainment. Thus, lower attainment can be seen as a high risk factor and higher attainment, and by implication higher ability, can be seen as protective factors in this group.

School factors

The *Jupiter* disaster gives the opportunity to compare how different schools reacted to the disaster and whether that is related to outcome. At five months, most children completed a screening battery measuring self reports of depression, anxiety, intrusive memories and fears. Yule (in press) presents preliminary findings contrasting one school that accepted and organized outside help immediately with one similar school that resisted all offers of help. The pupils in the former school showed slightly lower scores on depression and anxiety and highly significantly lower scores on Horowitz et al's (1979) Impact of Events Scale. Similarly, pupils in the cooperative school reported significantly fewer related fears five months after the accident. This provides some suggestive evidence for the value of early intervention as well as suggesting that how schools react to disasters is important in maintaining the distress.

Family factors

As noted earlier, McFarlane (1987) noted that families were also affected by the bush fires. In particular, there were increased levels of conflict and increased maternal overprotection. Where parents had difficulties processing their own emotional reactions, they were less successful in helping their children. Those families who found it difficult to share their immediate reactions had more difficulties coming to terms with the disaster.

This accords well with Yule and Williams' (1990) observations of families who survived the *Herald of Free Enterprise* and Yule's (1991a) general observations on children who survived the *Jupiter* sinking. In general, teenagers found it very difficult to confide their inner feelings to their parents, in part to protect the parents from getting upset. Since they also found it difficult to confide in teachers and peers, for many it was difficult to share their distress.

Prevention and intervention

Whatever safety improvements are made, whatever improvements are developed in relation to accuracy of long range weather forecasting, there will always be disasters and many will involve children. It has been argued that one reason we understand so little about the effects of disasters on children's adjustment and development is that adults deny that there are long term effects. The results of recent descriptive studies with improved methodologies confirm that children's reactions are not merely transient adjustment reactions but rather can be severe disorders that last many years and affect all aspects of children's functioning. In major disasters, as many as 50% of children may be distressed a year later. Disasters, then, are an important cause of childhood psychopathology and cannot be ignored.

As was illustrated above, with some foresight, it is possible to mount descriptive, evaluative and experimental studies in the wake of a disaster – studies that illuminate process and outcome. Moreover, it must be recognised that pathology can also follow 'small' disasters – accidents on school outings, accidental and deliberate deaths within the school. Schools, then, should be a focal point in the community's plans to deal with the aftermath of disasters.

There are many sources, such as Ayalon (1988), that give basically sound suggestions for dealing with the emotional effects of disasters on children. However, these tend to be aggregated wisdom rather than empirically tested approaches. Whilst early 'debriefing' of survivors is now widely offered, it is still far from clear when this should be offered, by whom, on what form and how soon after the disaster. While children may be encouraged to share their feelings through talking, play and drawing, we must be cognisant of Rachman's (1980) and Saigh's (1986) warning that exposure sessions that are too short may sensitize children rather than help them habituate their anxiety. It is clear from work with adults that intense and long exposure sessions can speed emotional processing (Richards and Lovell, 1990; Richards and Rose, 1991) and more trials of these techniques are needed with children and adolescents.

Schools, then, need to realise that, remote as it may be, a disaster could happen to them. They need to have contingency plans for seeking support from local mental health agencies. Recognising the need for children and parents to be reunited as soon as possible after a disaster, someone needs to ask how this is best effected. After the *Jupiter* sinking in Athens harbour, the children were all flown home as soon as possible. Whilst they were thereby reunited with their parents, they were also removed from all sights of the sea in which the boat went down. Three years on, many still have strong fears of water, the sea and boats. What might have been the outcome had the parents been flown out to Athens for the reunions? Behaviour therapy principles would suggest that exposure to the feared stimuli in the presence of a safety signal would have speeded habituation of anxiety.

Schools need to decide who is to talk with the children and how. They need to accept that children will be upset, but they need to develop procedures for dealing with this rather than telling the children merely to stop talking about it (as has happened in recent cases). Contingency planning does not increase the probability of a disaster happening, but may improve our ways of reacting and hence reduce the levels of distress in the children. Factors such as type and severity of disaster may give a rough indication of how many children may be adversely affected. Factors such as sex, premorbid adjustment and ability may help identify those children at greatest risk of having difficulties processing the resulting difficult emotions. The screening battery used by Yule and Udwin (1991), although it needs much more work on it, may be a useful interim guide that can be applied within the first few weeks after a disaster does strike.

Now that the importance of disasters in causing psychopathology in childhood has been recognised, and now that it has been seen that the issues raised can be analyzed within the mainstream framework of risk and protective factors, perhaps we can look forward to even more good studies that will guide public policy in coping with the psychosocial aftermath of future catastrophes.

Almost by definition, disasters are unpredictable. It follows that it is very unlikely that a disaster will strike a group of children whose premorbid development and personality are well documented. Should that happen, as almost happened in the case of the Three Mile Island Nuclear accident, every effort should be taken to capitalize on the opportunity for worthwhile research. Instead, research will have to proceed on an iterative, incremental basis, taking what opportunities occur. There is an urgent need to develop better, more appropriate, standardized interview schedules which can provide valid information on post-traumatic reactions as well as broader psychopathology. Better measures of pre-disaster adjustment, life events and the post-traumatic course of disorders are needed. Controlled treatment trials should be undertaken with older children. The range of reactions of children under eight years of age still needs to be better described, and this should be seen as a challenge to all interested in developmental psychopathology. As this chapter has argued, little is yet known about the risk and protective factors moderating children's reactions to disasters, but disasters will, sadly, continue to provide a natural laboratory in which such moderating variables can be better studied.

References

American Psychiatric Association (1987) *Diagnostic and Statistical Manual of Mental Disorders* (Third Edition – Revised). Washington, DC: APA.

Ayalon, O. (1988) *Rescue! Community Oriented Preventive Education for Coping with Stress.* Haifa: Nord Publications.

Birleson, P. (1981). The validity of depressive disorder in childhood and the development of a self-rating scale: a research report. *J. Child Psychol. Psychiat.* , 22, 73–88.

Birleson, P., Hudson, I., Buchanan, D. G. and Wolff, S. (1987) Clinical evaluation of a self-rating scale for depressive disorder in childhood (Depression Self-Rating Scale). *J. Child Psychol. Psychiat.* , 28, 43–60.

Burke, J. D., Borus, J. F., Burns, B. J., Millstein, K. H. and Beasley, M. C. (1982) Changes in children's behavior after a natural disaster. *American Journal of Psychiatry*, 139, 1010–1014.

Burke, J. D., Moccia, P., Borus, J. F. and Burns, B. J. (1986) Emotional distress in fifth-grade children ten months after a natural disaster. *Journal of the American Academy of Child Psychiatry*, 25, 536–541.

Clarke, A. M. and Clarke, A. D. B. (1976) *Early Experience: Myth and Evidence*. London: Open Books.

Dollinger, S. J., O'Donnell, J. P., and Staley, A. A. (1984). Lightning-strike disaster: Effects on children's fears and worries. *J. Consult. Clin. Psychol.* , 52, 1028–1038.

Galante, R., and Foa, D. (1986). An epidemiological study of psychic trauma and treatment effectiveness after a natural disaster. *J. Amer. Acad. Child Psychiatry*, 25, 357–363.

Garmezy, N. (1986). Children under severe stress: Critique and comments. *J. Amer. Acad. Child Psychiat.* , 25, 384–392.

Garmezy, N. and Masten, A. (1990). The adaptation of children to a stressful world: Mastery of fear. Chapter 17 in L. E. Arnold (Ed.) *Childhood Stress*. New York: Wiley International.

Garmezy, N., and Rutter, M. (1985). Acute reactions to stress. In Rutter, M., and Hersov, L., (Eds.), *Child and Adolescent Psychiatry: Modern Approaches* (2nd Edition). Oxford: Blackwell.

Gibbs, M. S. (1989) Factors in the victim that mediate between disaster and psychopathology: A review. *Journal of Traumatic Stress*, 2, 489–514.

Horowitz, M. J., Wilner, N., and Alvarez, W. (1979). Impact of events scale: A measure of subjective stress. *Psychosom. Med.*, 41, 209–218.

Kimchi, J. and Schaffner, B. (1990) Childhood protective factors and stress risk. Chapter 18 in L. E. Arnold (Ed.) *Childhood Stress*. New York: Wiley International.

Lacey, G. N. (1972) Observations on Aberfan. *J. Psychosomatic Res.* , 16, 257–260.

McFarlane, A. C. (1987). Family functioning and overprotection following a natural disaster: The longitudinal effects of post-traumatic morbidity. *Austral. New Zeal. J. Psychiat.* , 21, 210–218.

McFarlane, A. C. (1988) The longitudinal course of post-traumatic morbidity: The range of outcomes and their predictors. *Journal of Nervous and Mental Disease*, 176, 30–39.

McFarlane, A. C., Policansky, S., and Irwin, C. P. (1987). A longitudinal study of the psychological morbidity in children due to a natural disaster. *Psychol. Med.* , 17, 727–738.

Martin, S. and Little, B. (1986) The effects of a natural disaster on academic abilities and social behavior of school children. *B. C. J. Special Education*, 10, 167–182.

Masten, A. S. and Garmezy, N. (1985) Risk, vulnerability and protective factors in developmental psychopathology. Chapter 1 in B. B. Lahey and A. E. Kazdin (Eds.) *Advances in Clinical Child Psychology*, Volume 8. New York: Plenum.

Milgram, R. M. and Milgram, N. A. (1976) The effects of the Yom Kippur war on anxiety level in Israeli children. *Journal of Psychology*, 94, 107–113.

Nader, K., Pynoos, R. S., Fairbanks, L. and Frederick, C. (1990) *Childhood PTSD Reactions one year after a sniper attack.*

Ollendick, T. H., Yule, W. and Ollier, K. (1991) Fears in British children and their relationship to Manifest Anxiety and Depression. *J. Child Psychol. Psychiat.* , 32, 321–331.

Pynoos, R. S. and Eth, S. (1986) Witness to violence: The child interview. *J. Amer. Acad. Child Psychiat.* , 25, 306–319.

Pynoos, R. S., Frederick, C., Nader, K., Arroyo, W., Steinberg, A., Eth, S., Nunez, F., and Fairbanks, L. (1987). Life threat and post-traumatic stress in school-age children. *Arch. Gen. Psychiat.* , 44, 1057–1063.

Pynoos, R. S. and Nader, K. (1988) Psychological first aid and treatment approach for children exposed to community violence: research implications. *J. Traumatic Stress*, 1, 243–267.

Rachman, S. (1980). Emotional processing. *Behav. Res. Ther.*, 18, 51–60.

Reynolds, C. R. and Richmond, B. O. (1978) What I think and feel: A revised measure of children's manifest anxiety. *J. Abnorm. Child Psychol.* , 6, 271–280.

Richards, D. and Lovell, K. (1990) Imaginal and in-vivo exposure in the treatment of PTSD. Paper read at Second European Conference on Traumatic Stress, Netherlands, September 1990.

Richards, D. A. and Rose, J. S. (1991) Exposure therapy for post-traumatic stress disorder: Four case studies. *British Journal of Psychiatry 158*, 836–840.

Rutter, M. (1967). A children's behaviour questionnaire for completion by teachers: Preliminary findings. *J. Child Psychol. Psychiat.* , 8, 1–11.

Saigh, P. A. (1986). In vitro flooding in the treatment of a 6–yr-old boy's post-traumatic stress disorder. *Behav. Res. Ther.* , 24, 685–688.

Tizard, B. (1977) *Adoption: A second chance.* London: Open Books.

Tizard, J. (1964) *Community Services for the Mentally Handicapped.* Oxford: Oxford University Press.

Tsui, E., Dagwell, K. and Yule, W. (1991) Effect of a disaster on children's academic attainment.

Yule, W. (1991a) Work with children following diasters. Chapter in M. Herbert (Ed.) *Clinical Child Psychology: Social Learning, Development and Behaviour.* Chichester: John Wiley.

Yule, W. (in press) Post-traumatic stress disorder in child survivors of shipping disasters: The sinking of the *Jupiter. Psychotherapy and Psychosomatics.*

Yule, W. and Udwin, O. (1991) Screening child survivors for post-traumatic stress disorders: Experiences from the *Jupiter* sinking. *British Journal of Clinical Psychology*, 30, 131–138.

Yule, W., Udwin, O. and Murdoch, K. (1990) The *Jupiter* sinking: Effects on children's fears, depression and anxiety. *J. Child Psychol. Psychiat.* , 31, 1051–1061.

Yule, W., Williams, R. (1990) Post-traumatic stress reactions in children. *Journal of Traumatic Stress*, 3 (2), 279–295.

Part 4

Responses to Psychosocial Stress

Chapter 12

A useful old age

Don C. Charles

In my early work in developmental psychology I was concerned with the ways in which children judged to be mentally deficient had managed by young adulthood to cope with life in greatly varied, but frequently quite successful, ways. It was in this context that I first encountered Ann and Alan Clarke and came to know them as the warm, stimulating and supportive persons they are, and to know their continuing research and writing on the context and details of human 'vulnerability and resilience'.

My own interest in aspects of continuity and discontinuity in ability and performance over time persisted and extended to the lives of average as well as gifted and creative persons, and extended beyond maturity into old age. For about three decades I have been primarily concerned with these late years, especially with the (frequently negative) probabilities of late-age change, as well as with the (frequently positive) possibilities of achievement and rewarding life experience: in other words, with the vulnerability and resilience of the late decades.

One of the surprises of the late 20th century has been the unprecedented and generally unpredicted lengthening of life expectancy in old age. Past the middle of the century, life expectancy *at birth* did increase significantly and dramatically. But in the last few decades, life expectancy in the late years suddenly began to lengthen for a variety of not-entirely-agreed upon reasons – medical, economic and cultural. The result is not just that more people reach their sixties and seventies, but that in the developed world the fastest-growing segment of the population is the over 85 group.

What I want to consider here is the use to be made of these almost-unexpected late years. What are the possibilities: that is, what capabilities do old people have? What factors influence competence and vitality? Then I would like to examine the late years of some noteworthy persons in science, the arts and other fields of endeavour. The central question is: What are the possibilities and probabilities of useful, productive, and creative late years, for persons who have been useful, productive and creative in their earlier years?

What is old? In the United States, the answer has been easy: 65. But this figure is based not on physiological or psychological data, but on political decisions originating in the 19th and 20th centuries, culminating in age 65 for eligibility for Social Security and, in the past at least, mandatory retirement.

Despite longer life, social trends have been towards earlier and earlier voluntary retirement. In the USA in 1970 about 80% of males and 42% of females below 65 were employed, with about 25% and 10% after. The projection for 1990 was for only 16% of males and fewer than 8% of females to be employed after 65. Significant numbers of workers are retiring in their 50s and even 40s (Clark and Spengler, 1980).

Retired people travel, volunteer, garden, watch television – the list of activities is as varied as the persons concerned. But to learn about possible productivity and creativity in the late years it is necessary to look at persons exceptional enough to make reports of their lives, so I have chosen some of these persons to study and have arbitrarily set approximate age 70 as the beginning point. To see what *has* been accomplished by some may suggest something of what *could* be done by many.

I have used three terms that need some consideration (I hesitate to 'define' them): 'Productive', 'creative', and 'useful'. What do they mean in the context of this look at the activities of some old people?

Productivity

Productivity is fairly easy. When a person is engaged in any activity that effects positive results in society, I see that person as productive, whether the activity is looking after young children or experimenting in a laboratory. As is usually the problem in the behavioural and social sciences, it is not always easy to define or quantify a behaviour we readily recognize.

Creativity

There have been about as many definitions of creativity as there have been persons interested in it. Terms frequently used by discussants, such as 'inventive', 'original', or 'unique' simply leave us with more defining to do. Discussing creativity in science, Medawar (1990) provides a definition: 'Creativity is the faculty of mind or spirit that empowers us to bring into existence, ostensibly out of nothing, something of beauty, order, or significance'. Then he comments 'But this is a romantic illusion in that the act does not arise out of nothingness' (p. 83). After commenting on various theories he concludes '. . . the element of mystery is with us still' (p. 89). Rather than quote another array of definitions, I shall look at the most useful criterion used in research: identification of creative persons through an evaluation by competent judges of their produced work.

What distinguishes the creative person? Various studies have eliminated measured intelligence and achievement scores, school grades and other objective measures as predictors or indicators (MacKinnon, 1986). Obviously, if one is to become a creative engineer, it is necessary to be bright enough to become an engineer in the first place, and to acquire the basic knowledge and skills of the discipline. But with that as base, higher IQ, grades, or test scores are irrelevant to creative productivity.

The differences between creative and non-creative persons seem to be basically in what we call 'personality'. Donald MacKinnon found creative architects, for example, to be clearly and significantly different from their less-creative peers. They were more deviant, independent, individualistic, demanding, and generally unconcerned with the impression they made on others (MacKinnon, 1962).

Research exists in a social context, and is about as subject to fashion, especially in the social and behavioural sciences, as is skirt length. Creativity (and to some extent, giftedness in general) has been out of fashion for about two decades. Research flourished in the 1950s and early 1960s; giftedness, creativity, and its correlates, scientific and technical education, were overhauled and by the middle of the 1960s quantities of interesting and valuable research were appearing. Then came the social upheavals of the period. Associated with many positive and valuable changes in society, there developed what I choose to call 'Evangelical Egalitarianism', a commitment to the notion that except for trivial physical differences, everybody is, or ought to be, exactly like everybody else (except for athletes of course); any other belief is 'elitism'. In this social context, research on creativity has withered and virtually disappeared, but older studies remain.

Usefulness

This term is perhaps so general as to produce more confusion than clarity; still, it is closer to what I want to communicate than any other word that I have been able to generate.

There is of course a tremendous range in the behaviour of old people: there are great numbers who do little but sit and watch television, others who pursue golf or bridge relentlessly, some who contribute quietly to family or community, and a few who continue their earlier productive lives. It is this latter group that I wish to examine, out of my own intrinsic interest and in a hope of making some inferences of value for people in general.

Before proceeding to illustrative cases it would seem desirable to review briefly some of the changes – physical, intellectual, personality – that occur in the late years. We may infer from these universal changes something of the level of behaviour and performance that is possible, and thus likely.

The nature of senescence

The biologist Alex Comfort (1956) defined senescence as a change in the behaviour of the organism with age, leading to decreased power of survival and adjustment.

In so intellectual a process as creativity, why be concerned about the functioning of various body systems? It is the body that does the work: one has only to consider one's own functional effectiveness after a week of illness or wrenched knee to understand the effect of negative physical change on any performance.

Neural

On the negative side it must be observed that loss of brain cells begins early in life, and continues and accelerates in the late years; traumas such as strokes of course inflict specific damage. This neural loss is a factor in the general slowing of both motor and cognitive processes. On the positive side, the human brain has what the neurologist Oliver Sacks describes as 'almost unlimited neural group power', and he comments that even in long and very productive lives, 'There is no reason why a human being cannot evolve, individuate, renew himself mentally right up to the end of his life (as great artists such as Shakespeare and Beethoven did)' (Sacks, 1990, p. 68).

Sensory

Visual acuity declines from its peak in childhood, exacerbated by cataracts or other disorders. Change of point of good focus is universal but is mostly a nuisance leading to bifocal use. Colour vision deteriorates somewhat but not to a significant degree in most persons. Barring trauma or chronic ailment, most people manage well with their less-efficient but still functional old-age vision. Hearing declines from its peak in childhood, and presbycusis – loss of high-frequency hearing – is universal and annoying in the difficulty it causes in hearing in noisy setting. Modern electronic devices can provide some help, but are avoided by many old persons.

Motor

Decline in motor efficiency is also universal, but the rate varies greatly. Response speed and coordination peak early in life; most athletic records are held by persons in their teens and twenties. From that point on decline is inexorable, but in a world where few of us survive on the basis of our motor skills, function is adequate for most purposes of life to a very old age in active and healthy individuals.

Intellectual

Research in this area is usually divided into intellectual performance measured in some fashion to predict academic performance, and research on specific functions, especially memory.

When I entered the developmental field some decades ago, 'everybody knew' that intelligence followed the same path as physical characteristics, peaking in late adolescence and declining thereafter with an acceleration downward in late maturity (old people were not studied at all). This inference was made from cross-sectional studies with little or no controls on education or other experience of subjects. As groups of subjects first studied as children matured and aged, longitudinal studies, some with careful controls, began to change the picture. From several decades of accumulated research we can summarize present knowledge: First, when declines occur, they occur late in life – even in the 70s. Second, declines are generally small enough to question whether there are real-life effects. Third, generational (cohort) effects are generally greater than age effects. And finally, changes are complex: different kinds of intelligence show different patterns of growth and decline. Relevant research is summarized in Dixon, Kramer, and Baltes (1985) and in Cerella, Poon, and Williams (1980).

A major concern in cognitive research has been memory. A comment frequently heard from persons at every level of maturity is 'I must be growing old, I'm becoming so forgetful'. This expectation probably stems in part from knowledge or observation of losses caused by Alzheimer's disease or by senile dementia. Is memory really lost in old age? Certainly laboratory studies demonstrate some loss of efficiency in memory, but in everyday life the most noticeable effect is a slowing of the brain's processing, so both intake and retrieval take more time; thus we recall the elusive name an hour – or a day – after we need it. A nuisance, but not a traumatic loss.

There are some other functional changes. Some theorists believe that apparent cognitive defects in ageing may result from models on youth-centered formal thinking. Instead, Labouvie-Vief and Blanchard-Fields (1982) suggest that with age there is a growth of more complex and highly-differen- tiated skills, 'a mature level of cognitive differentiation characterized by an autonomous, socially-oriented and dialectical mode of reasoning' (p. 183). Information-processing theorists hypothesize that thinking becomes more abstract in nature and more concerned with deriving inferences than with reproducing details (Labouvie-Vief and Schell, 1982). We may observe, then, that current theory and research is focused not on discovering the nature and extent of decline, but on identifying changes in the nature and complexity of thought processes in the late years.

Personality

To many developmentalists, the most intriguing question about personality is the degree to which it is consistent or changes over time.

In recent years, medical and psychological researchers have placed increasing emphasis on the role of genetic factors in behaviour ranging from traits like aggressiveness to disorders like manic-depressive psychosis. Genetic factors would of course predispose consistency. But genetic influences provide only a structure that is to a small or greater extent modifiable by life experiences.

A number of longitudinal studies suggest that there is marked consistency in basic personality factors such as aggressiveness, activity level, and vigour. The long-term Baltimore study showed for example considerable stability in introversion-extroversion, tendency to neuroticism, and to a lesser degree, 'openness to experience'. The latter trait would seem to be highly relevant to creativity (Chiriboga, 1987). While the various longitudinal studies are somewhat restricted by limited subject selection in generalizing to the total population, they are generally relevant to the kinds of persons we are concerned with here.

Influence of life experience

A safe inference from several decades of gerontological research is that health and an adequate income are prerequisite to a satisfying old age. In health, there are generally agreed-upon effects of smoking and dietary practices. Exercise clearly affects physical function and vitality, but activity in general is not supported as a predictor of longevity in current research (Lee and Markides, 1990).

From a number of longitudinal studies on widely varying populations, it seems clear that intellectual and cognitive function is significantly affected by experience: education, occupation and general level of intellectual activity and involvement are positively related to adequacy of function in old age. In addition to general descriptive studies, research on specific cognitive functions shows that declines observed in abilities that have been regularly used begin at a later age and are less drastic than are the abilities that have been used less frequently. There is, in addition, evidence that old persons can improve markedly in specific cognitive functions in response to varied intervention techniques (Denny, 1982).

Inferences

The rather positive tone of the foregoing is not to suggest that decline and negative change do not characterize the late years. Rather, current knowledge makes it clear that a great many persons experience after late maturity – the 50s and 60s – a period of life with adequate health and physical functions, high intelligence, and with personal and social competence intact.

What, then, is the use to be made of these late years? What has been accomplished by aged persons who, in earlier life, have been useful, productive and creative?

Productivity

Other than pure speculation or inferences of real-life behaviour from laboratory research on cognitive and other capacities, the only source of evidence on what *can* be done is what *has* been done. Such evidence of course depends on published accounts of the lives of persons who have been noteworthy for one reason or another.

The classic study in this genre was H. C. Lehman's *Age and Achievement* (1953). His approach was to select men who were noteworthy in science, scholarship, and the arts, gather data on their quantitative productivity by decade of life, in some cases extending into the 80s, and examine the total productivity by decade of life. He then asked experts (e.g. physicists) to cite the most important work of the individual so he could identify the decade of life in which the most significant work was done in various fields.

Lehman's work was important and occasioned much interest and comment, and generated inferences about age effects on productivity, but was flawed by his failing to consider the effect early death of some subjects had on late group productivity.

Dennis (1966) corrected the flaws of the earlier research and examined the productivity of 738 persons who lived to age 79 or beyond. Again, subjects were engaged in scholarship, science and the arts; they were all persons for whom complete work records existed, generally therefore limited to persons born after 1600.

Studying only persons who survived to age 80, Dennis found differences in productivity among his occupational categories. Scholars (historians, philosophers, and others) average about 20% of their life productivity in their 70s. Scientists (the usual categories, plus inventors and mathematicians) did in general about 15% (with a range of 13% to 21%) of their life work during the eighth decade. Dennis' arts category was broad, his seven occupations as diverse as architects, librettists, and poets. Their 70s produced about seven percent of their life work, ranging from four percent for architects to 10% for opera composers. Looking at his data in another way, he figured the output of the most productive decade; using this as 100% he could find the relative output of each decade. For his scholars, the 70s were about 85% as productive as their best younger period. For scientists, the late period was a little better than half as productive. Workers in the arts were again more variable, ranging from nine percent to 43% as productive in this late period as in earlier ones, averaging less than 25% as efficient as in earlier life.

Ageing psychologists

In the course of working on histories of my interest areas in psychology, I was somewhat surprised to note how many distinguished psychologists continued professional activity into late life. To get a clearer view of this late work I chose to study a group of psychologists born in the nineteenth century, who had lived to at least age 70. The choice of names was personal, based on my own view of their importance in the developing field they pioneered. Most of my information on their lives came from obituaries published in professional journals, but some biographies and autobiographies existed, as well as newspaper reports on more widely known individuals, like John Dewey. All subjects were of necessity male; while there were eminent women early in the field (e.g. Mary Calkins) I could find no published information on their late lives.

My primary concern was what use they made of their lives after about age 70; did the individual continue working in psychology, with or without pay? Did he enter a new professional activity, or develop or expand a hobby? If he retired, how did he spend his time? Other activities of interest were noted. There were 16 cases in all. The earliest born was G. Stanley Hall (1844) and the latest was Harry Helson (1898). These men survived from nearly 80 years to well beyond 90.

Of greatest note was their devotion to work: nearly 90% of them continued beyond age 70 to a high level of scientific and professional involvement, while some developed new careers and one developed a hobby to a noteworthy level; only one dropped from public view.

Why work? To many persons in society the sight of someone who is 'retired' going off to work every day without pay (frequently true of professors) is ludicrous. Why do it? I asked two colleagues in their 70s who follow this regime. One, an internationally known biological scientist, continues because he is fascinated by his life work, and wants to keep learning and producing more as long as he is able. The other, equally noted in a different field, replied, 'What else would I do – watch daytime television?' These are probably the major reasons: fascination with the subject of life work, or lack of interest developed in life in anything other than work.

Two examples of work commitment in the group I studied include E. G. Boring and Harry Helson. Boring had no interest in life, other than his family, in anything but his discipline, but he allowed himself at 65 to reduce his (self-reported) 4000–hour year by buying a farm and cutting trees during part of the summer. Helson, Boring's student, learned the work lesson well from his mentor. He reported his motto to be 'You must continually concentrate on work; you can have only one hobby, work' (Bevan, 1979, p. 157).

Multiple careers characterized the life of Walter Miles. He retired from teaching at Yale at age 67. He then did three years of research at Istanbul; after this interlude he became scientific director at the United States Submarine Base at New London, Connecticut, which position he held until age 80. Still another pattern was that of Joseph Jastrow who after retiring from the University of Wisconsin at age 64 moved to the New School for Social Research in New York, where he continued for 17 years. Coupled with his work there was his emergence as a communicator of popular psychology. He published eight books, wrote a regular syndicated newspaper column, became a popular speaker and later presented a weekly radio program (Charles, 1989).

Again, I emphasize that these lives demonstrate the *possibilities* of old age, and not the *probabilities* for the general population.

The larger picture: productivity, quality, and creativity

Going beyond the 'counting' aspect of the studies just discussed, what can we learn of the quality or creativity of work at different ages?

Although Lehman failed to take into account the ages at which his productive subjects died, one aspect of his work is relevant here. From historical and contemporary sources he determined the age at which the most significant or creative work was done. In more than a dozen fields of endeavour – physics, medicine, invention, and philosophy for example – the decade of the 30s was clearly the most important one, especially for subjects born in the 19th century or later. Corrected for early deaths of many subjects, it would probably have been in the 40s. Significant and creative work *continued* into old age, but it neither peaked nor began there.

Dennis did not evaluate quality, only productivity. But for what it is worth, he found the decade of the 20s to show little productivity; except for some of the arts, even the 70s out-produced the twenties. For almost all fields, the decade of the 40s was either the most productive or was only slightly below the peak.

In my own psychologist study, I found little evidence of creativity in the late years. For the most part, it was a 'dotting of i's and a crossing of t's', a working out of some details neglected in the earlier development of a theory or simply a continuation of work in progress. Lewis Terman illustrates well the continuity aspect. At the time of his death in 1956, near age 80, he was working on the fifth volume of his 'Genetic Studies of Genius', as he called the longitudinal study he began in the 1920s, when he was in his 40s.

Robert Yerkes had a distinguished career as an early psychobiologist and was also active in professional and public affairs such as military science and the National Research Council. After age 67 he produced no more scientific work but was noteworthy for his public and professional contributions.

I would have to summarize the late work of these distinguished psychologists by describing them as useful, but not as creative or distinguished in the fashion of their earlier work.

Performance in selected areas: Cases

The following individual cases follow no systematic, historical, or disciplinary plan; I selected them as 'for instances' because their late-life performance seemed to me to illustrate well a range of qualitative characteristics of the old-age work of noteworthy practitioners in various fields.

Writers

Sophocles was one of the great tragedians of the fifth century BC. He wrote over a hundred plays, of which a handful survive. When he was 89, his son tried to have him declared incompetent but he read a draft of his last play, *Oedipus at Colonus* to the court, which promptly released him. The subject matter of the play suggests his apprehension about forces of decay at work in Athens, and perhaps reflects that in his own person.

A number of 19th century American poets lived to old age. Ralph Waldo Emerson lived in good health to age 79 but produced little of value after his early 60s; Walt Whitman, visiting him in his late years, regarded him as a kind of national monument. Longfellow similarly lived to be very old, and wrote some retrospective and reflective verse in his late years. Whitman himself survived into his 70s; his late-life poems were, for the most part, gloomy reminiscences unlike his early and noteworthy work.

William Butler Yeats was one of the great poets of the twentieth century. He died relatively 'early' – at 73 – but at age 68 he felt himself failing (mostly sexually) and had new sex glands transplanted by a medical charlatan. He felt that he was rejuvenated and called himself 'the wild wicked old man' and wrote what are regarded as some of his best poems in a new style, direct, earthy and passionate (Cowley, 1980).

Thomas Mann was productive and creative over his entire long (80 years) life, from *Buddenbrooks* (1901) to *Doctor Faustus* (1947) and some later essays. The critic Robertson Davies comments, 'The work of writers over 70 often shows a decided cooling, but it may gain a compensatory silver radiance; and of course like Thomas Mann's, their last work may rank with their finest' (Davies, 1990, p.218).

Marcia Davenport has been an important figure in music and literature for more than 50 years. At mid-century she was a best-selling novelist. Recently, at 87, she commented on quitting fiction-writing in her 60s. She observed that fiction is, or should be, a work of imagination. 'And the imagination is a faculty that diminishes with age!' (Paris, 1991, p.83). To support her contention that fiction is the art of middle age, she cited writers whose best work was done before 60 (many of these writers died before 60): Balzac, Stendahl, Flaubert, Dickens, Thackeray, the Brontes, Jane Austen, George Eliot, Hemingway, Fitzgerald, and Thomas Wolfe.

P. G. Wodehouse was born and raised in England and India, but spent his later years in the United States. He was a kind of writing machine, producing between 1900 and 1975 about 50 books, hundreds of short stories, and about 50 plays and lyrics for musical comedies. Nearly 40 of his books were published between age 70 and his death at 94. He illustrates well the phenomenon of continuity in work; his famous 'Jeeves' character appeared regularly with little change in his books from 1917 to 1971. His work was light and amusing and changed little from youth to old age (Donaldson, 1982).

Painters

P. Auguste Renoir, while identified with Impressionism, constantly experimented with every aspect of painting and graphic art in general. His enormous output continued into old age (he died at 87). Crippled in his late years, he continued to work with a brush strapped to his arm.

Goya retired at 72 as official painter of the Spanish court. From then on to his death at 80, he painted for himself in a different style (the 'black paintings') and then worked with lithography using a new technique. At 80 he drew a caricature of himself as an ancient man with white hair and beard, propped up on two sticks, with the legend 'I am still learning' (Cowley, 1980, p.17).

Henri Matisse, another major 20th century artist, lived from 1869 to 1954 and was productive until the end. After a serious illness in 1940, he worked for the most part in bed, making drawings for books and designs for tapestries. He turned next to murals and stained glass, and in late years with failing vision he made paper cut-outs.

Titian, who lived to age 80, produced qualitatively different work from the middle 70s on. This 'late style' has been seen as special since the 16th century. Critics do not agree whether this different work was really a new approach for him; some judge that those works were really just unfinished projects which gave the painting in effect a soft focus. One critic labels them 'the senile sublime' (Rosand, 1990).

Picasso, who lived into his 90s, demonstrated a succession of styles from 1900 to 1970. Certainly he was one of the most creative and original painters of his time. Although his late work was uneven, his imaginative and technical mastery continued; how new, creative, and important his late work was is not agreed upon. One body of opinion suggests that he had lost touch with the contemporary world and was plunging into a kind of retrospective working of his former inventions, but that his late works 'show no diminution of his wit, his imagination, his technical mastery, or his vision of the world as a stage with himself as the leading player' (Marks, 1984, p.675).

Georgia O'Keefe, another long-lived painter, developed her style of abstraction early in her career, and even to the untutored eye (including my own) looking at a retrospective exhibition, that style of handling paint seems remarkably consistent and recognizably her own over the decades. Her subject matter changed with her life circumstances – flowers, the American desert, abstract-appearing work stimulated by ground patterns seen from the air – but her productivity, technical competence and manner changed little to very old age (Robinson, 1989).

Musicians

Conductors: Symphony and opera conductors seem collectively to have some secret that gives them extremely long lifetimes with undiminished vigour and competence. A few examples may represent a large group.

Arturo Toscanini made his conducting debut in 1886 and became one of the world's preeminent directors. By 1937 his status was such that the NBC Symphony was created for him. He led this group until 1954 when he was 87; rerecordings of his original 78s are now made on CD and are highly sought after.

Sir Thomas Beecham conducted major orchestras from 1899 to 1960 when he was 81. In addition to conducting he founded orchestras of his own in London. Leopold Stokowski, flamboyant in musical interpretation as in life, conducted various major orchestras continuously from 1909, when he started with the Cincinnati group, to 1973 in London.

Eugene Ormandy, conducting from 1924 to 1980, and George Szell, leading the Cleveland orchestra for 24 years, are other examples.

The most recently deceased of this long-lived group is Herbert von Karajan. He was music director at one time or another of nearly every major symphony and opera house in Europe – Berlin, Vienna, La Scala – and was a major musical figure for 60 years despite health problems after age 75. One obituary described him as the 'general music director of Europe' (*New York Times*, 1989).

These men all developed their musical styles relatively early in their careers, and then maintained their interpretations into very old age. Given their long tenures, they all directed some 20th century music, but generally they were not pioneers or enthusiasts for the new (like Pierre Boulez, for example) in their late years.

Jazz Musicians: Jazz as an art form depends on creativity; without that it becomes popular music, entertainment. Not many jazz musicians have lived to a great age, given their life-styles, but some have lived and flourished into the late years.

Louis Armstrong was one of the most influential artists in the genre up to the middle of the century. A New Orleans waif born in 1900, he was untutored (his first wife taught him to read music) but between about 1925 and 1930 he helped change the nature of jazz, freeing it from the early form that evolved out of ragtime and marches. His innovations influenced not only other jazz musicians but composers of more formal music both in America and Europe. His style was inimitable and he maintained it for nearly 40 years after his peak; he was often referred to in his late years as an 'ageing vaudevillian'. Chatting with him in the middle 1950s, I mischievously inquired whether he wasn't going to get into be-bop and cool jazz, then replacing swing as the new movement. He snorted in disgust and assured me, 'You won't hear none of them flatted fifths from my horn'!

One of the founders of be-bop, the avant-garde of the 1950s, was Dizzy Gillespie, 73 at the time of writing and still doing one-night stands. The recipient of honorary degrees, awards, and honours, he is still playing bop, much as he developed it 40 years earlier. He observed recently, 'The hardest part of the music is improvising, and it gets harder the older you get' (Balliett, 1990, p.54).

Late work in the arts

Artists, unsurprisingly, are highly variable in their late-life creativity and productivity. But despite this variability – the work of Matisse comes to mind – the norm seems to me a maintenance of patterns, methods, styles developed in youth or early maturity, and practiced in many cases with little if any diminution of quantity or quality. In orchestra conductors, this seems more of a virtue than it is in, say, jazz musicians.

Conclusion

What can we infer from the available research data, individual examples and observations?

First, for most persons who enter old age in reasonably good health, the inevitable declines in physical, neural, sensory, and cognitive functions are not of a nature to prevent continued work, of whatever kind was practiced earlier. There will be slowing and reduced efficiency, but high quality work can be maintained. Motivation and experience are powerful factors.

Since the productivity and creativity of most people is neither noted nor reported, it is necessary to look at the exceptional. But from these models we may infer that it is possible, and even likely, that maintenance and continuity of whatever kind will continue much as it did before, regardless of what magic number we use to designate 'old'.

Creativity is somewhat different and harder to evaluate than productivity. In the first place, most people are not very creative at any time of life. For those who have been demonstrably so, the data from studies, lives of exceptional persons, and general observations suggest to me that *continuity* of produced work is the norm. That is, the style, manner of work, uniqueness and quality have their origins in youth or early maturity, and may be maintained into the late years. But newness and departure from past approaches is unlikely. The field of endeavour is a factor, of course; academicians are more likely to wind down finishing old work than are some artists who in a few cases may embrace new techniques or approaches in old age.

If these observations are sound, it would seem reasonable to expect that with good health, old age may be a highly useful period of life, continuing earlier work, completing unfinished projects, and maintaining the kinds of creative contributions made earlier, even if newness and novelty are rarely apparent. The recognition of these possibilities should encourage ageing persons to continue their useful contributions, and should be considered in retirement planning.

The motives and feelings that colour the work of these late years were expressed by Oliver Wendell Holmes, Jr., the 'Great Dissenter' of the Supreme Court. In a radio address on his 90th birthday (March 8, 1931) he observed:

> The riders in a race do not stop short when they reach the goal. There is a little finishing canter before coming to a standstill. There is time to hear the kind voice of friends and to say to oneself: 'The work is done'. But just as one says that, the answer comes: 'The race is over, but the work never is done while the power to work remains'. The canter that brings you to a standstill need not be only coming to rest. It cannot be,

while you still live. For to live is to function. That is all there is in living (Lerner, 1943, p.451).

References

Baker, T. (1984) *Baker's Biographical Dictionary of Musicians*. New York: Schumer Books.

Bailiett, W. (1990) 'Portrait of Dizzy Gillespie' *New Yorker*, September 17, 45–58.

Bevan. W. (1979) 'Harry Helson (1898–1977)', *American Psychologist*, 92, 153–160.

Cerella, J. A., Poon, L. W., and Williams, D. M. (1980) 'Age and the complexity hypothesis', in Poon, L. (ed) *Aging in the 1980s*. Washington, DC: American Psychological Association, 169–189.

Charles, D. C. (1989) The old age of some eminent psychologists, *Educational Psychology Review*, 1 (4) 369–380.

Chiriboga, D. (1987) 'Personality in later life', in P. Silverman (ed) *The Elderly as Modern Pioneers*. South Bend, Indiana: Indiana University Press, 133–157.

Clark, R. and Spengler, J. (1980) 'America's elderly in the 1980's', in *Population Bulletin*, 35 (4). Washington, DC: Population Bureau, Inc. United States Department of Health, Education and Welfare, 213–221.

Comfort, A. (1956) The Biology of Senescence. London: Routledge and Kegan Paul.

Cowley, M. (1980) *The View From Eighty*. New York: Viking.

Davies, R. (1990) 'The young visitors', in Grant, J. S. (ed), *The Enthusiasms of Robertson Davies*. New York: Viking, 218–223.

Dennis, W. (1966) 'Creative productivity between the ages of twenty and eighty years'. *Journal of Gerontology*, 21, 1–8.

Denny, N. W. (1982) 'Aging and Cognitive Changes', in Wolman, B. and Stricker, G. (eds.) *Handbook of Developmental Psychology*. Englewood Cliffs, New Jersey: Prentice-Hall.

Dixon, R. A., Kramer, D. A., and Baltes, P. B. (1985) 'Intelligence: its lifespan development', in Wolman, B. P. (ed) *Handbook of Intelligence: Theories, Measurements and Applications*. New York: Wiley, 261–296.

Donaldson, F. (1982) *P. G. Wodehouse*. New York: Knopf.

Kramer, A. (1987) 'Cognition and Aging', in Silverman, P. (ed.) *The Elderly as Modern Pioneers*. South Bend, Indiana: Indiana University Press, 114–157.

Labouvie-Vief, G. and Blanchard-Fields, F. (1982) 'Cognitive aging and psychological growth', *Aging and Society*, 2, 183–209.

Labouvie-Vief, G. and Schell, D. A. (1982) 'Learning and memory in later life; a developmental view', in Wolman, B. and Stricker, G. (eds) *Handbook of Developmental Psychology*. Englewood Cliffs, New Jersey: Prentice-Hall, 828–846.

Lee, D. and Markides, K. S. (1990) 'Activity and mortality among aged persons over an eight year period'. *Journal of Gerontology*, 45, 539–542.

Lehman, H. C. (1953) *Age and achievement*. Princeton, New Jersey: Princeton University Press.

Lerner, M. (1943) *The Mind and Faith of Justice Holmes*. Boston: Little, Brown.

MacKinnon, D. T. (1962) 'The nature and nurture of creative talent', *American Psychologist*, 17, 484–495.

MacKinnon, D. T. (1965) 'Personality correlates of Creativity', in Aschner, J. J. and Bish, C. E., (eds) *Productive Thinking in Education*. Washington, D. C.: The National Education Association, 161.

Marks, C. (1984) *World Artists*. New York: Wilson.

Medawar, P. B. (1990) 'Creativity, especially in science', in Medawar, P. B., *The Threat and the Glory*. New York: Harper-Collins, 83–90.

New York Times (1989) Herbert von Karajan. Section A, 1+, July 17.

Paris, Barry (1991) 'Marcia Davenport', *New Yorker*, April 22, 42–88.

Robinson, R. (1989) *Georgia O'Keefe, A Life*. New York: Harper and Row.

Sacks, 0. (1990) 'Letter on neurology and the soul', *New York Review of Books*, 37 (19) December 6, 90.

Chapter 13

Troubled and troublesome:
perspectives on adolescent hurt

Masud Hoghughi

Alan Clarke came to Hull as the Professor of Psychology at the start of my third year. He massively encouraged and nurtured my already strong interest in clinical psychology. After qualifying as a clinical psychologist, I went to work at Aycliffe, where I am now the Director. Alan's unusual application of scientific psychology to clinical problems, and a strong methodological rigour always imbued with compassion and humanity (who else can make mental handicap so interesting?) was immensely attractive and encouraging. Indeed, his influence was so great that I chose to start my clinical training in a mental handicap hospital, although I recognised subsequently that the approach he encouraged was applicable in all clinical settings. Since leaving Hull, I have fortunately kept in touch with him and Ann Clarke and have continued to receive their always considerable kindness and wise counsel.

The impact of their writings on long term effects of early experience (1976) with their apparently common sense suppositions, and immense interest in human problems, can be seen in the work of those who know them. Few populations so starkly pose issues of vulnerability and resilience as those with whom I work. There is little question of their vulnerability to multiple hurt. But, equally, many show immense fortitude in the face of circumstances that would destroy most of us. Thus, the Clarkes' thesis about early experience is borne out, particularly in their emphasis on humane nurture for the hurt, fundamentally illustrating the theme of this book on *Vulnerability and Resilience*.

This paper may be somewhat unconventional because it is written from the perspective of a practitioner at the 'sharp end'. However, unusually for a practitioner in this field, I also have strong research and teaching commitments which have allowed me to examine the potential and limitations both of theory and practice in my area. As a practitioner-academic my ideal is gradually to arrive at a 'practice theory' which utilises available empirical knowledge to develop a structured and systematic way of addressing daily issues of practice. This paper is part fulfilment of that aim.

Aycliffe

Aycliffe, with 120 beds for boys and girls between the ages of eight and 18, is now the UK and Europe's largest specialised facility for dealing with disordered adolescents. The common denominator of the young people is that they have usually defeated every other form of intervention through gravely escalating disturbed behaviour. Aycliffe's motto is 'We don't say no, and we don't take no'. It is strongly organised on psychological principles, where multi-disciplinary staff activities are empirically based and rigorously monitored.

Classification of young people's problems

To identify behaviour as 'delinquent', or 'disordered' presumes some form of classification. There are a number of classifications of deviant or abnormal behaviour. Clinically, the most developed and widely used are DSM – III-R (American Psychiatric Association, 1987) and ICD-9 (World Health Organisation, 1984; Rutter and Gould, 1985). They are developed primarily by and for psychiatrists, using axes on which the diagnostic syndrome, physical disorders, psychosocial stressors and other related matters are identified.

Compared with the highly judgmental and idiosyncratic attempts of the past, they make a significant contribution to orderly classifications of disorders. They do not, however, take account of the logical and empirical difficulties of diagnoses in areas where no external validation of diagnostic judgment can be obtained (Rakoff et al, 1977). For this reason, and a number of others, they are seriously deficient in reliability and validity (Davison and Neale, 1986; Quay, 1986a; Cantwell, 1988).

In my context, though, the most serious shortcoming of the current diagnostic classifications is their lack of treatment utility for any but those abnormalities which have a significant physiological basis (e.g. psychoses), and, therefore, demand a physical response. When the disorder is palpably not physical – as in 'character', 'conduct' or 'personality' disorders, there are no specific treatments. The diagnosis, therefore, becomes no more than a theoretical, judgmental activity. Furthermore, the 'macro' diagnosis often cuts out the possibility of 'micro' treatment for some components of the behaviour (e.g. lying, aggressiveness) which, taken as part of a 'syndrome', would not warrant such treatment.

Alternative approaches to diagnostic classifications of adolescent disorders have, therefore, been proposed. These include the multivariate (e.g. Quay, 1986a), 'empirical' (e.g. Aschenbach and McConaghey, 1987), behavioural (e.g. Mash and Terdal, 1981) and eclectic (e.g. Schwartz and Johnson, 1985). Whilst these add something worthwhile to classification and assessment processes, they each present a range of other difficulties which reduce their utility. For these reasons (Hobbs, 1975; Hoghughi et al, 1980) I have supported a descriptive approach to problems which encapsulates the idea of change in youngsters, does not label in a damning and holistic way, and points to some treatment, however partial.

The Problem Profile Approach is a descriptive classification of problems generated by direct and persistent exposure to the need for comprehensive, focussed assessment of disordered youngsters, geared to treatment (Hoghughi, 1969). It is now extensively used in a variety of settings (Curran, 1983; Hoghughi et al, 1980; NACCW, 1988; Hoghughi et al, 1988). It includes six categories of difficulty or 'problem' areas. A 'problem' is defined as an 'unacceptable condition', so serious that it warrants intervention. Problem areas are as follows:

1. Physical – difficulties and disorders associated with physical functioning, including obesity, drug abuse, psychosis (because of its physical basis), epilepsy and eating disorders;

2. Cognitive – difficulties experienced in the area of intellectual and educational functioning, including mental handicap, reading retardation, memory and learning disorders;

3. Home and Family – the largest area of difficulties experienced by young people, ranging from poor home environment, material deprivation and adverse parental factors to aspects of parenting (such as abuse);

4. Social Skills – concerned with difficulties in making and maintaining relationships with peers and adults, such as peculiar presentation and unpopularity;

5. Anti-Social Behaviour – including all offences against person and property and such problems as deliberate self harm and temper tantrums;

6. Psychological – including unusual or abnormal personality features, such as impulsivity and neurotic reactions.

All young people present or suffer from these conditions at some point of their lives. The distinguishing mark of disordered and delinquent youngsters is the unacceptable number, intensity, duration and urgency of their difficulties. Any 'profile' drawn of the above problems is valid only at one time and one place, encapsulating the idea that young people change and those who deal with them also change their perceptions. So the problem profile changes with the behaviour and context of the young person. This obviates the need to use general diagnostic labels (such as 'conduct disordered'), which become lifelong millstones around young people's necks. A diagnostic label such as 'psychotic' can still be used, because there is usually lifelong persistence and some known treatments.

Having developed a comprehensive classification of children's difficulties, the issue was what should be done with them. Again, the position of Aycliffe as a 24–hour, 365–day facility demanded a whole new approach. Treating delinquent and disordered adolescents has been a battleground of ideologies since the beginnings of discourse in this area. Ideology has, indeed, dominated at the expense of empirical evidence (Hoghughi, 1983). Where evidence has been available, it has spawned approaches which bear little resemblance to their supposed theoretical foundations, but are rejected by the followers of other theories. Even where a single ideology prevailed, it was difficult to discern in the 1960s and 1970s exactly what was being attempted. Punishment, education, bits of social work, health care and psychiatry all intervened in a single child's life without any clear conception of where each fitted into an overall plan. Clearly, some attempt at integration seemed sensible.

Purpose of intervention

In discussions of disordered and delinquent youngsters, primary emphasis is usually placed on containment of disruptive and anti-social behaviour. Although understandable, this fails to recognise that a young person is a young person first and disordered, delinquent or anything else second. More often than not, young people have been devalued by experiences which have either failed to restrain from, or have positively pushed them into further disordered and delinquent behaviour.

The young people's lifestyle is not particularly surprising, fraught as it is with anxiety, fear, anger, frustration and short range consequences of their acts. Even when there is an 'anti-social personality dimension' in force (e.g. Farrington, 1989), the lifestyle of such young people is not subjectively associated with much happiness or sense of involvement with worthwhile and personally enhancing experiences.

Therefore, treatment must give them some sense of personal purpose which makes the treatment and its attendant demands worthwhile.

Equally, workers with delinquent and disordered youngsters must have some coherent conception of the underlying purposes of their technical and professional work. This encompasses four sets of interrelated imperatives, summed up in the acronym 'VCEE', for Value, Contain. Engage and Empower.

1. *Value*: The basis of dealing with young people at all is that they are important and to be valued for their own sakes as young people, particularly when they have often been unloved, deprived or damaged. Young people who are devalued believe themselves to be unworthy and cannot, in turn, value others, other than as 'things' and instruments of gratification;

2. *Contain*: Disordered and anti-social behaviour is disruptive and costly to society and the young person. It must, therefore, be contained;

3. *Engage*: Unless young people are to be treated through coercive use of physical measures, such as tranquillising medication or punishment, they must become involved with the people who are trying to motivate them towards behaving in a socially acceptable manner. They must, in other words, want to change.

4. *Empower*: All the foregoing are aimed at the final achievement of ability to choose, from an increasing range of options for self enhancement within socially acceptable limits, like other citizens. Adults are frequently afraid of giving power to young people, particularly the disordered, because they feel they cannot control the outcome. However, if the three earlier prerequisites have been achieved and the treatment is relevant and effective, gradual empowerment will ensure that young people do not have to engage in anti-social acts as ways of gaining power to sustain livelihood or sense of personal worth.

Needs

A natural extension of applying VCEE to young people is recognising that they also have needs arising from their personal condition. Needs are the 'gap between what is and what should be', as perceived by the young people or those who are close and competent to identify them. 'Need' is not an exact term because it frequently disguises special pleading and is not usually susceptible to external validation. However, there are no adequate alternative terms available.

Although there are various classifications of needs (e.g. Maslow, 1962) these are not universally accepted or adequately supported by empirical research. In practice, needs of young people fall broadly into physical, material, experiential and relational, with particular focus on issues of gender, ethnicity, culture and ability. Considerable information is now emerging on needs of delinquent, disordered and disabled young people (Brimblecombe, Hoghughi and Tripp, 1989; Hoghughi and Dunn, 1990; Kuh et al, 1988), which should help towards meeting them.

Tasks with troubled and troublesome youngsters

A conceptual map of intervention with 'problem people' is set out below.

This was first proposed in 1968 (Hoghughi, 1969) and has been in continuously refined practice since then. It is deemed to be a necessary precursor of good professional practice with any 'problem' person and an essential first step in the development of a scientific approach to *therapeutics* of which treatment of disordered and delinquent youngsters must be a part. It has the merit of being open-ended, atheoretical, relatively value-free and applicable to all disciplines. The steps to be covered include (1) the classification of young people's problems, (2) identifying the purpose of dealing with them, and (3) engaging in the tasks of management, care, assessment and treatment.

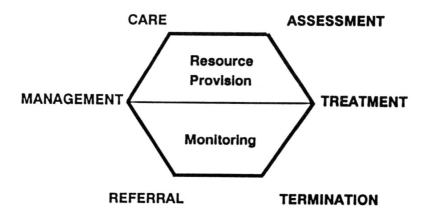

Figure 1

1. *Management* is primarily concerned with (1) curbing and containing unacceptable behaviour, and (2) creating a state of mutually easeful coexistence with the young person. Successful management obviously responds to specific problems and uses methods and techniques which are most appropriate to them. So, 'talking' may be appropriate to comforting a distressed young person, but not often to one who is in the habit of assaulting others. By now a considerable amount is known about less bad ways of managing disordered young people (Hoghughi, 1978; McArdle, 1988; Robertson, 1989; Treischman, Whittaker and Brendtro, 1969; Dangel and Polster, 1988). Some young people strain current knowledge to its limits, but usually an ethically acceptable management programme can be devised.

2. *Care* comprises a series of acts aimed at ensuring survival and optimum well-being in physical, emotional and social terms. Young people are subject to the general standards of care prevailing in the culture. Most societies do a reasonable job in this area as far as physical problems are concerned but much less so in terms of emotional and social needs. There are no known, generally accepted ways of fulfilling needs or of optimising young people's state (c.f. Kellmer Pringle, 1975), bearing in mind how much these are at the mercy of the general economic condition and the prevailing mood of society regarding disordered and delinquent young people.

3. *Assessment* is the essential prerequisite of any form of treatment. It is a purposive activity concerned with identifying the (problem) condition and what should be done about it. It is continuous and coterminous with treatment. It is a common human activity that everyone is doing all the time, and yet there are few people and places who carry out a rigorous, coherent, comprehensive assessment as a prelude to determining what should be done (Hoghughi, 1979a; Steinberg, 1986).

Traditionally, professional assessment has been done by psychiatrists and psychologists using diagnostic methods and nosological classifications (e.g. Rutter, Tuma and Lann, 1988). As already indicated, this approach is fraught with difficulties, particularly when so many of the problems do not have any 'psychiatric' treatments. Social work and probation use ad hoc and often idiosyncratic ways of assessing young people, permeated with half-baked psychodynamic interpretations of 'causes', whose relationship to the real difficulties of the young person may range from nil to considerable. The commonly messy and ineffective way in which young people's difficulties are treated is not, therefore, surprising (Hoghughi, 1978).

There is now considerable evidence that assessment can be carried out in a coherent, comprehensive and multi-faceted way (Hoghughi et al, 1980; Lazarus, 1976; Nay, 1979). Our approach is more comprehensive, simpler and more parsimonious than that of Lazarus, although the similarities are greater than the differences. As experience in a variety of settings has shown (Aufflick, 1983; Curran, 1983; Hoghughi and Nethercott, 1980; NFCA, 1990), Problem Profile Approach provides a helpful starting point towards identifying treatment, further supported by Government's adoption of the same broad approach in the development of a comprehensive guide to assessing children suspected of being physically or sexually abused (Department of Health, 1988).

> 4. *Treatment*. This is, or should be, the ultimate focus of all interventions with disordered and delinquent youngsters. It is concerned with 'reducing the number and intensity of unacceptable conditions'. It is different from 'management' in its focus of long term alleviation of problems rather than short term containment. Unfortunately, in practice the two have often been confused so that what should really be regarded as management is often billed as treatment.

The first element of treatment concerns the value basis, legislative force, theoretical orientation and ethical boundaries which enable or constrain treatment.

The second element concerns methods – systematic ways of dealing with a problem, deriving from the theoretical perspective. Surprisingly, despite the proliferation of treatment industries, until recently there has been no attempt to provide a generally accepted classification of treatment methods, with the possible exception of the response to Lazarus's 'Basic Id' (Keat, 1979; Lazarus, 1976). However, in a recent publication, (Hoghughi et al, 1988) we provide a classification of the major methods of treatment. These encompass (1) goods and service delivery, (2) physical methods (including medication and biofeedback), (3) behaviour modification (including a wide range of techniques from assertiveness training to token economy), (4) cognitive methods (including social skills training), (5) talking therapies (such as counselling and psycho-analysis), (6) group therapies, (such as family therapy), and (7) environmental therapies, (such as a therapeutic community).

The third level of specification of treatment concerns actions to be taken to meet the assessed difficulties. Based on our own practice, (Hoghughi et al, 1988) we suggest Individual Treatment Programmes which specify the problem, the aim of intervention, the preferred method and technique and details of who is to carry out the treatment, how, with what expected outcome and over what time span. As this suggests, for every problem there is often more than one method and technique of treatment which has been claimed to be effective by one worker or another. So, for example, in the treatment of aggressive behaviour, the use of tranquillising medication, various techniques of behaviour modification, social skills training, psychotherapy, family therapy and other group techniques, as well as environmental treatments have all been advocated as the 'treatment of choice'.

The claimed virtues of the available treatments cannot be addressed here. However, few of the claims are adequately supported by strong evidence. It is, therefore, sensible to be open-minded about relevant techniques although, undoubtedly, more or less sensible choices can be made depending on the condition and the research evidence, as well as on ethical, personnel and other costs of treatment (Hoghughi et al, 1988, Keat, 1979). One can be empirically selective without being close-minded. Indeed, the more professional the treatment environment, the wider the likely range of treatments used, if for no other reason than that young people with different 'packages' of problems, needs and personal characteristics, will respond better to some treatment techniques than others.

Troublesome adolescents

Against this conceptual background, the disordered adolescents with whom I now deal are marked by the two major characteristics of being both severely troubled and troublesome. The diagnostic systems available would variably label them as 'conduct disordered', 'unsocialised aggressive' or 'socialised delinquent'. Their behaviours include substance misuse; truancy; poor school performance; resistance to control and major conflicts at home; poor social relations with peers and adults; disruptiveness; running away; physical and verbal aggression and offences against person and property, as well as immaturity; impulse ridden, tense personalities with a good deal of free-floating anxiety and exceptionally poor levels of moral development and; fluid, negative self-concepts. Many of them conform to Robins' (1966) classical picture of 'Deviant Children Grown Up' into adolescence.

I adopted 'disordered adolescent' as a generic label to identify such youngsters rather than the more conventionally judgmental, damning 'delinquent' or ambiguous 'disturbed'. In clinical terms, once these youngsters are past 18, they would be called 'personality disordered' and, often with a bit more candour, 'psychopathic'. Professional wisdom suggests that though they badly need it, they could not be adequately treated (although recent evidence would suggest otherwise (e.g. Hollin, 1990)) and basically had to be kept out of harm's way until such time as they matured and grew out of their trouble.

The huge literature on delinquency and conduct disorder supports a widely held belief that there may be a genetic competent to such disposition

(Rutter et al, 1990), which Farrington calls 'anti-social personality' (Farrington, 1991). There may be some physiological peculiarities such as poor GSR, abnormal EEGs and high pain threshold associated with this conglomerate condition.

More importantly however, research shows that such youngsters come from variably disorganised or rigid and inconsistently punitive families, where the father is likely to have a criminal record, low income, low IQ and poor parenting practices. The children 'grow up' rather than are 'brought up', drifting into delinquency in the absence of strong prosocial pulls (Hoghughi, 1983). The identification and social processing of such youngsters is more often a matter of ideology than good sense or empirical evidence (Hoghughi, 1979b, 1983, Hollin, 1990). They receive doses of unpleasantness and restriction in attempts at control. When these attempts fail, as they often do, they deteriorate, frequently demanding heavier intervention to break down and reverse what becomes an increasingly anti-social and 'uncontrollable' cycle.

Over the past ten or so years, however, the picture of those who come to Aycliffe has changed. Although the strong propensity to anti-social behaviour remains, it is now very often overlaid with tension, anxiety, mild depression, tendency to angry and randomly directed aggression, and a quality of 'hopelessness' and despairing grievance which renders dealing with these people much more fraught and liable to breakdown (Hoghughi and Nethercott, 1980).

The troubled

From the above description, it is immediately apparent that we are not simply dealing with the traditional 'conduct disordered' or 'delinquent' youngsters. The quality of hurt and anger hints at layers of adversity presenting a picture of mixed 'conduct' and 'affective' disorders, fitting neither diagnostic category neatly and defying traditional explanations.

Recently, with greater awareness of child sexual abuse and some of its longer term consequences, we have begun to suspect that many youngsters' clinical problems may be associated with active abuse, of which the sexual sort is currently considered to be the most serious.

We have conducted a series of short range researches (Hoghughi and Richardson, 1990, Hoghughi, Bhate and Graham, 1991) which show the huge overlap between abused and abusive adolescents. Almost all Aycliffe's girls have disclosed sexual abuse and, in those who have not, the soft signs of abuse are evident. We also know that roughly 40% of our sexually abusive boys have themselves been abused.

Conduct disorder and child sexual abuse

The problem of child sexual abuse has 'hijacked' practically every other in clinical dealings with children and, to a lesser extent, young people. Since the Cleveland affair (which took place on our doorstep) every time a youngster presents a problem, the clinician considers the possibility of sexual abuse. There is also an extraordinary burgeoning of research interest in the area.

Unfortunately, other than cases of physical hurt and direct disclosures by children, the clinical signs of sexual abuse are often 'soft' and circumstantial. They can be accounted for by a range of other possibilities. Because of the quality of signs and symptoms and the high profile of the problem, there is a strong tendency both to over- and under-estimate the prevalence and symptomatology of abuse. It is tempting not only to reinterpret established views in the light of sexual abuse but also to bring in other clinical states as being 'caused' by it. This is aided by considerable writing (e.g. Wyatt and Powell, 1988) which shows significant relationship between sexual abuse and a wide range of subsequent difficulties.

A number of theoretical models and perspectives have been offered to explain the relationship between sexual abuse and different forms of disorder, of which Finkelhor's 'dynamic traumatisation' is the most suggestive. He classifies the main consequences of sexual abuse as guilt, powerlessness, betrayal and anger (Finkelhor, 1986, 1988), each with a cluster of related behaviours. These clusters include almost all behaviours associated with conduct disorder. It is, therefore, tempting to jump to the conclusion that conduct disorder is but one manifestation of the long term effects of child sexual abuse.

This is, however, too pat. Finkelhor's classification of behaviour is not strictly empirical, derived from multivariate analysis or research data. In any case, even if it could be shown that all sexually abused children behave in a disordered fashion, it would not follow that all disordered children had been abused. But even this cannot be done because the level of reliability and validity in identification of sexual abuse cannot be regarded as even approximately satisfactory. However, even when sexual abuse can be 'factually' established, its effects seem to be mediated by a range of other factors, such as the length, recency and severity of abuse, particularly when the relationship between the mother and daughter is a poor one. A range of other factors, such as the victim-abuser relationship, the context, the method of abuse, whether it was coercive or persuasive, and the age and cognitive ability of the victim are probably implicated. Given the variable effects of abuse, correlating different kinds of sexual abuse and their long term consequences has not been attempted and is likely to be very difficult in methodological terms.

In exploring these issues, we have compared the problem profiles of 'conduct disordered' and known sexually abused young people, both boys and girls. Our data show much greater similarity of features than differences. These include poor emotional relationships, stealing, running away, unprovoked lying, deliberate self harm, truancy, constant tension, indiscriminate sexual activity, fights and cruelty to people. The differences, as one might expect, are more serious anti-social acts for the conduct disordered and more self directed, affective difficulties for the abused. These are similar to Friedrich's (1988) findings.

Explanations

Clearly, sexual abuse does not affect every youngster in the same way. The question, therefore, of why some young people develop a pattern of conduct disorder in response to sexual abuse and some not still remains. The following preliminary ideas may go some way towards such an explanation.

1. There is no evidence or *a priori* reason why sexual abuse should be, despite claims to the contrary, any more traumatising than many other adverse human experiences.

2. The components of sexual abuse – made up of physical hurt, identity distortion and emotional damage – can be matched in intensity, extent and duration by many other traumata.

3. Using the current prevailing clinical paradigm of 'diathesis-stressor' (Davison and Neale, 1988), only some young people are likely to bear long term scars of the damage done by sexual abuse.

4. This depends on the degree of vulnerability of the victim. In other words, sexual abuse does not have an invariably adverse consequence, but adversity is related to the kind of personality to which it happens.

5. Whether response to abuse is 'acting out' conduct disorder or 'self-directed' affective disorder is probably mediated by an internalising/externalising switching mechanism, well established through varied researches (Aschenbach and Edelbrock, 1978; Hewitt and Jenkins, 1946; Quay, 1986a).

6. There is some vague speculation but not much evidence about the nature and exact processes which underlie the adoption of an 'externalised' rather than an 'internalised' response to adversity (e.g. Quay, 1986b). To show that 'externalising' children come from more chaotic

families, are socially less competent and respond less well to intervention is, after all, no more than to describe some sophisticated
correlations. The need for an explanation still remains.

7. A functional approach to internalised/externalised process would
suggest in survival terms that, at least in part, it either prevents
further damage or draws attention to itself, as a way of arousing
interest and possible help. So a girl who behaves anti-socially would
not only be discharging tension, anger, anxiety and other direct
consequences of abuse, but would also be creating the kind of fuss
that is bound to provoke a reaction from other people who might
then remove or otherwise attend to the person presenting the problem.

8. Gender is likely to play an important part. Both biologically and
culturally, girls are thought to be less aggressive. They may, therefore, respond to abuse, particularly coercive abuse, with 'internalis-
ing' self directed, mood and behaviour disorders, as has been shown
in a number of studies (e.g. Coute and Schuerman, 1988, Peters, 1988).
Boys, on the other hand, are more likely to become aggressive and
manifest the consequences of their hurt in an 'externalised' and
anti-social fashion.

9. Social factors also clearly play a part. A moody and withdrawn
reaction in a crowded and chaotic working class family is likely
neither to offer the protection of disguise and hiding to an abused
child nor to draw the attention of outsiders. Therefore, if a child were
seeking protection she would have to behave in an 'externalised'
male-like fashion. This might account for those girls who come
predominantly from poor working class homes and behave in a
seriously aggressive and disordered fashion, compared with the
better off, who are more likely to show a pattern of self-directed,
mood and affective disorder.

10. Clearly, the many genetic, psychological and social factors interact
along many dimensions and are, therefore, likely to result in widely
varying, mixed cases.

The gist of all this is that maladaptive behaviour (such as conduct and
affective disorders) essentially serves an 'adaptive function' of attracting
attention or withdrawing from the possibility of further hurt. Our current
view, backed up by mainly clinical evidence, albeit still slim and controversial, is that a considerable amount of disordered behaviour is probably a
mediated response to sexual abuse. Given that sexual abuse is unlikely to be
uniquely traumatising but that its force lies in combining physical and

emotional abuse, then we might consider that most of our young people are manifesting the consequences of long term abuse, be it physical or sexual. This does not mean that other variables, such as genetic abnormality and deviant socialisation, are not involved but rather that another helpful treatment perspective may be available.

So, where does this take us? It suggests that rather than coldly labelling young people's problems in order to curb their behaviour in often judgmental and punitive ways (Hoghughi, 1991), we might consider that their behaviour is an adaptation to long term hurt. We would then react differently compared with ineffective traditional approaches. We would work through young people's sense of loss, anger, powerlessness and betrayal. We would also encourage their acceptance that the world is existentially an unkind and unfair place, that being hurt is not a matter of desert, and thus help them gradually recognise that their experiences need not consign them to eternal, self-defeating strife.

References

American Psychiatric Association (1987), *Diagnostic and Statistical Manual of Mental Disorders* (3rd edn). Washington: APA.

Aschenbach, T. M. (1988), 'Interpreting assessment and treatment' in Rutter, M., Tuma, A. H. and Lann, I. S (eds) *Assessment and Diagnosis in Child Psychopathology*. London: David Fulton Publishers.

Aschenbach, T. M. and Edelbrock, C. (1978), 'The Classification of Child Psychopathology: a review and analysis of empirical efforts', *Psychological Bulletin* 85, 1275–1301.

Aschenbach, T. M. and McConachey (1987), *Empirically Based Assessment of Child and Adolescent Psychopathology*. London: Sage.

Aufflick, J. (1983), 'Learning to love', *Community Care*, March.

Brimblecombe, F., Hoghughi, M. S. and Tripp, J. (1989), 'A New Covenant with Adolescents in Crisis', *Children and Society*, Vol. 3, No. 2, 168–180.

Cantwell, D. P. (1988), 'DSM – III studies' in Rutter, M., Tuma, A. H. and Lann, I. S. (eds) *Assessment and Diagnosis in Child Psychopathology*. London: David Fulton Publishers.

Coute, J. R. and Schuerman, J. R. (1988), 'The effects of sexual abuse on multi-dimensional view' in Wyatt, G. E. and Powell, G. J. (eds) *Lasting Effects of Child Sexual Abuse*. Beverley Hills: Sage.

Curran, D. (1983), 'The Problem Profile Approach – a basis of inter-agency co-operation', *Social Work Advisory Group*, Vol. 19, January, Northern Ireland, Department of Health and Social Services.

Dangel, R. F. and Polster, R. A. (1988) *Teaching Child Management Skills*: New York: Pergamon.

Davison, G. C. and Neale, J. M., (1986), *Abnormal Psychology*, 3rd edn. Chichester: Wiley.

Department of Health (1988), *Protecting Children*, a guide for social workers undertaking a comprehensive assessment. London: HMSO.

Farrington, D. P. (1979), 'Delinquent Behaviour Modification in the Natural Environment', *British Journal of Criminology*, 19, 353–72.

Farrington, D. P. (1989) 'Implications of Criminal Career Research for the Prevention of Offending', paper delivered to International Conference on Juvenile Crime, Valencia, Spain.

Farrington, D. P. (1991), 'Psychological Contributions to the Explanation of Offending', paper given at First Annual Conference of Division of Criminological and Legal Psychology, British Psychological Society, Canterbury, Kent.

Finkelhor, D. (1986), *Sourcebook on Child Sexual Abuse* Beverley Hills: Sage.

Friedrich, W. N. (1988), 'The trauma of child sexual abuse' in Wyatt, G. E. and Powell, G. J. (eds) *Lasting Effects of Sexual Abuse*. Beverley Hills: Sage.

Friedrich, W. N. (1988), 'Behavior problems in sexually abused children: an adaptational perspective' in Wyatt, G. E. and Powell, G. J. (eds) *Lasting Effects of Child Sexual Abuse*. Beverley Hills: Sage.

Hewitt, L. E. and Jenkins, R. L. (1946), *Fundamental Patterns of Maladjustment, the Dynamics of their Origin*. Springfield, Ill.: State of Illinois.

Hobbs, N. (ed) (1975), *Issues in the Classification of Children*, San Francisco: Jossey Bass

Hoghughi, M. S. (1969), 'A conceptual model for a comprehensive child care system', *Child Care*, vol. 25, 2, 41–57.

Hoghughi, M. S. (1978), *Troubled and Troublesome*. London: Burnett Books.

Hoghughi, M. S. (1979a), 'Assessment: myth, method and utility', *Social Work Today*, Vol. 10, 29.

Hoghughi M. S. (1979b), 'The Aycliffe Token Economy', *British Journal of Criminology*, Vol. 19, No. 4, pp. 384–399.

Hoghughi, M. S. (1983), *The Delinquent: directions for social control*. London: Burnett Books/Hutchinson.

Hoghughi, M. S. (1991), 'The Last Resort', *Social Work Today*, Vol. 22, No. 21.

Hoghughi, M. S. (1991), 'Punishing Parents for their Children's Sins', *The Magistrate*, Vol. 47, No. 2, pp. 33–34.

Hoghughi, M. S., Bhate, S. and Graham, F. (1991), 'Sexually Abusive Adolescents', papers delivered to Division of Criminological and Legal Psychology Conference, British Psychological Society, Canterbury, Kent.

Hoghughi, M., Dobson, C., Lyons, J., Muckley, A. and Swainston, M. A. (1980), *Assessing Problem Children*. London: Burnett Books/Andre Deutsch.

Hoghughi, M. S. and Dunn, L. (1990), 'Needs of Disordered Adolescents', Aycliffe, Aycliffe Studies of Problem Children.

Hoghughi, M. S., Lyons J., Muckley, A. and Swainston, M. A. (1988) *Treating Problem Children: issues, methods and practice*. London: Sage.

Hoghughi, M. S. and Nethercott, S. M. (1980), 'Breakdowns in Care', Aycliffe, Aycliffe Studies of Problem Children

Hoghughi, M. S. and Richardson, G. (1990), 'Sexually abusive adolescents – the root of the problem', *Community Care*, 25 October, pp. 22–24.

Hoghughi, M. S. and Richardson, G. (1990) 'Sexually abusive adolescents – the legal sanction', *Community Care*, 1 November, pp. 21–23.

Hollin, C. (1990), *Cognitive Behavioral Interventions with Young Offenders*. New York: Pergamon.

Keat, D. B. II (1979), *Multimodal Therapy with Children*. New York: Pergamon.

Kellmer Pringle, M. (1975), *The Needs of Children*. London: Hutchinson.

Kuh, D., Lawrence, C., and Tripp, J. (1986), 'Disabled young people: making choices for future living options'. *Social Services Research* 15, 57–86.

Lazarus, A. (1976), *Multimodal Behavior Therapy*. New York: Springer.

McArdle, E. (1988), 'Management of Aggressive and Disruptive Behaviour', Aycliffe, mimeo.

Mash, E. J. and Terdal, L. G. (1981), *Behavioural Assessment of Childhood Disorders*. Chichester: John Wiley.

Maslow, A. H. (1962), *Towards a Psychology of Being*. Princeton: Van Nostrand.

National Association of Child Care Workers (1988), *The Problem Profile Approach: Basic Training Course*. Cape Town: NACCW.

National Foster Care Association, *A Problem Shared: a practical approach to difficult foster placements*. London: NFCA.

Nay, W. R. (1979), *Multimethod Clinical Assessment*. New York: Gardner Press.

Ollendick, T. H. and Hersen, M. (1984), *Child Behavioral Assessment*. New York: Pergamon.

Peters, S. (1988), 'Child sexual abuse and later psychological problems' in Wyatt, G. E. and Powell, G. J. (eds) *Lasting Effects of Child Sexual Abuse* Beverley Hills: Sage.

Quay, H. (1986a), 'Classification' in Quay, H. and Werry, J. (eds) *Psychopathological Disorders of Childhood*. New York: John Wiley.

Quay, H. (1986b), 'Conduct Disorders' in Quay, H. and Werry, J. (eds) *Psychopathological Disorders of Childhood*. New York: John Wiley.

Rakoff, V. M., Stancer, H. C. and Kedward, H. C. (1977), *Psychiatric Diagnosis*. New York: Brunner Mazel.

Robertson, J. (1989), *Effective Classroom Control: understanding teacher pupil relationships*, 2nd edn. London: Hodder and Stoughton.

Robins, L. N. (1966), *Deviant Children Grown Up*. Baltimore: Williams and Wilkins.

Rutter, M. and Gould, M. (1985), 'Classification' in Rutter, M. and Hersov, L. (eds) *Child and Adolescent Psychiatry Modern Approaches*. Oxford: Blackwell.

Rutter, M., Tuma, A. H. and Lann. I. S. (eds) (1988), *Assessment and Diagnosis in Child Psychopathology*. London: David Fulton Publishers.

Schwartz, S. and Johnson, J. H. (1985), *Psychopathology of Childhood*. New York: Pergammon.

Steinberg, D. (ed.) (1986), *The Adolescent Unit*. Chichester: Wiley.

Treischman A., Whittaker, J. and Brendtro, A. (1969), *The Other 23 Hours*. New York: Aldine.

World Health Organisation (1984), *International Classification of Diseases*. Geneva: WHO.

Wyatt, G. E. and Powell, G. J. (eds) (1988), *Lasting Effects of Child Sexual Abuse*. Beverley Hills: Sage.

Chapter 14

Implications of the Warsaw Study for Social and Educational Planning

Ignacy Wald and Anna Firkowska-Mankiewicz

After the Second World War the situation was ripe for a new view on mental handicap. The work of Alan and Ann Clarke, Jack Tizard, Neil O'Connor and Beate Hermelin created new standards of scientific analysis of the problem. Of special importance was the publication of the first edition of the classic text, *Mental Deficiency: The Changing Outlook*, edited by the Clarkes (1958). Research on these issues also brought new aspects to the studies of learning process and showed the impact of the social milieu on human development and behaviour.

The achievements played a significant part in the initiation of the Warsaw Study. It was started by the cooperation of workers in the following research centres: the Medical Sociology Unit of the Institute of Philosophy and Sociology at the Polish Academy of Sciences in Warsaw (Magdalena Sokolowska, Anna Firkowska-Mankiewicz, Miroslaw Czarkowski, Antonina Ostrowska), the Department of Genetics of the Psychoneurological Institute in Warsaw (Ignacy Wald) and the Sergievsky Centre at Columbia University in New York (Zena Stein and Mervyn Susser). Janusz Kostrzewski (Higher School of Special Pedagogics in Warsaw) and Lilian Belmont from the Sergievsky Centre acted as psychological consultants.

The city of Warsaw was selected because of its unique conditions. Seriously damaged at the end of the Second World War, it was rebuilt under a new political, social and economic system whose main ideology was the creation of equal living conditions for people, irrespective of their socio-economic status. During the city rebuilding a substantial uniformity of ecological and school factors was achieved. What effects did such a social change have on the intellectual achievements of school children coming from different social strata?

The Warsaw Study, designed to answer this question, was carried out in the years 1974–1977, in three consecutive stages.

Stage I

In stage 1 the sample under study consisted of the whole 1963 birth cohort of over 14,000 11–year-olds living in Warsaw at the time of testing.

The main groups of factors studied were the following:

- ecological variables describing 79 urban districts of Warsaw in terms of the degree of urban infrastructure development (density of population, number of schools, health service units, cultural facilities etc.) and in terms of social marginality (number of offenders, frequency of offences, etc.).
- school variables characterizing 209 Warsaw primary schools in respect of the school size, teachers' qualifications, efficacy of schooling, quality of school work, etc.
- variables concerning the socio-economic status of the family (including both parents' occupation and education).

The dependent variable – intellectual achievement – was measured using three tests: Raven's Progressive Matrices, a Vocabulary Test and an Arithmetic Test. A global index of intellectual achievement (based on standard scores in the three tests with a mean of 100 and SD = 15) was highly correlated ($r = .77$) with the Wechsler Intelligence Scale for Children (WISC). The mean value of the global index of 100 corresponded to IQ 112 (SD = 13) in the WISC. Considering that according to the US data the mean IQ has risen by 0.3 points per year since the standardisation in 1949 (Flynn, 1987), this seems not to be very surprising. However, we cannot be sure that the same process has occurred in Poland. It would be difficult to verify it because there are no suitable data.

It follows from the main results of stage I of the study, yielded by the step-wise multiple regression analysis, that the proportion of variance in the test scores accounted for by the socio-economic status of the family was several times higher than that explained by the combined ecological and school factors. In the portion of variance in test performance which could be explained by the variables under analysis, the socio-economic status of the family (SES) accounted for as much as 76 to 94 percent of the variance, while ecological and school factors accounted only for six to 24 percent of variance in the cognitive performance global index. Moreover, the relationship between the family's social and occupational status and the children's cognitive performance was found in the Warsaw research to be at least as marked as

Table 1. Correlations (Pearson's r) between some global indices of school factors, urban factors and SES of parents characteristics and test results in Raven's Matrices.

Developed infrastructure	.11
Social marginality	-.01
Overcrowding of school	-.01
Low educational effectiveness	-.10
General level of school work	.08
SES of parents	.32

Source: Sokolowska et al., 1978, p.175

in many other studies. The correlation coefficients obtained in our study (depending on complexity of SES and IQ indices) ranged from $r = 0.27$ to $r = 0.44$. These are even higher than those cited in Western literature, which most frequently attain values in the range between $r = .20$ and $r = .40$ (Jencks et al, 1972; Eysenck, 1979). Equally salient were differences in the test performance between children coming from families located at opposite extremes of the social hierarchy: namely, the mean value of the global index of mental performance of 87 in unskilled labourers' children was as many as 24 points lower than that in children whose parents were in professional occupations (mean value of global index of 111) – the distance approximates two standard deviations.

In the interpretation of the results obtained in Stage I of the Warsaw Study, presented here in a very brief and simplified way, it was pointed out that due to the social policy in Poland at that period a considerable uniformity of Warsaw urban and school milieus had been attained. However, the latter not only failed to decrease the traditionally reported gradient of the relationship between familial socio-economic status and the children's intellectual level, but had even resulted in a gradient sharper than that found in many studies carried out in Western countries (Firkowska et al., 1978; Sokolowska et al., 1978; Firkowska-Mankiewicz, Czarkowski, 1982). This would mean that the equalization of Warsaw districts and schools had no significant effect on children's cognitive performance. At first sight our data – especially the results concerning the role of schools – seem to corroborate the radically formulated theses of American researchers (Coleman, 1966; Jencks et al., 1972). They claim that any of the child's benefit from school depends mostly upon his/her initial level of intellectual functioning, and consequently, that any differences in school facilities and curricula are of no importance for his/her school achievement level.

It is our belief, though, that our results should not be interpreted as evidence of the worthlessness of stimulation provided by the urban and school environment. They only point to a paradox produced by the equalization and unification of living conditions and schooling. Making the school in an urban district equal for everyone, and not taking into consideration the children's individual needs and abilities, has no particular influence neither on their intellectual development nor on levelling differences between the more and the less gifted or disadvantaged children.

By thrusting the same curriculum and schooling conditions upon all children, the essential principle of the psychology of learning, pertaining to individual differences, is neglected. An unreflective adherence to the rule of equality of all people and the resulting belief that children should respond in the same way to the unified curriculum and schooling conditions may lead to harmful consequences for the children themselves, since they do not receive the type of schooling most efficient in their case. This involves an inefficient allocation of state budget resources for education: even providing a genuinely egalitarian allocation, those who have no special needs receive too much, while the ones who need much more receive too little or for a too short time. Another example is the low efficacy of a large-scale project, Headstart, in stimulating intellectual development of pre-school children (Clarke, 1984).

In more recent studies, not only were some more sophisticated indices of school functioning used (e.g. teacher-student relations, individualization of teaching process and style), but also various other measures of school achievement and adjustment besides IQ were taken into consideration. The obtained data suggest that school may be an important factor in stimulating general (and not only cognitive) development of children and contributing to their better social adjustment (Rutter et al., 1979; Minuchin, Shapiro, 1983).

In the first Warsaw study only rough statistical data served as indices of urban districts and school quality, and the child's cognitive performance was assessed only in terms of his/her scores on intelligence tests. Therefore, it is hardly surprising that the relationship between the school and ecological factors (measured by means of not too sophisticated methods), the children's test performance turned out to be rather weak, and that parental socio-economic status was found to be the best predictor of the child's cognitive performance level.

Stage II

In order to understand the nature of the relationship between parental socio-occupational status and the children's mental performance an attempt was made to seek phenomena that were, on the one hand, important for the child's cognitive development, and on the other hand, either resulting from or associated with the above-mentioned familial status. Thus, the object of our interest was the family and intrafamilial processes – including the family's interaction style, child-rearing methods, system of values and participation in cultural events. It has been our belief that the socio-cultural specifity of families belonging to different socio-occupational strata is crucial for comprehending differences in the children's intellectual functioning. It is generally known that working-class families differ from these of white-collar workers in respect of child-rearing methods, aspirations and attitudes concerning education, their value systems or participation in cultural events, etc. (cf. Bronfenbrenner, 1970; Bernstein, 1970; Smith Blau, 1972; Kohn, 1969; Kohn et al., 1990).

Thus, Stage II of the Warsaw study (Firkowska-Mankiewicz, Czarkowski, 1982) was focused on seeking intra-familial, psycho-socio-cultural correlates of the social structure which might contribute to the interpretation of the relationship between parental socio-occupational status and the children's mental performance. The sample under study consisted of over 1000 children selected by certain criteria from the cohort tested in stage I. It was a non-proportional stratified sample, where the children's mean score on the WISC was 87.6 (SD = 18.3) in the lowest stratum, and 128.8 in the highest (SD = 10.3). The research techniques administered individually to the child and his/her family included, amongst others, an extensive psycho-social interview with the parents (concerning the child's development in early childhood and at school age, the family's child-rearing methods, emotional climate, organization of household chores, participation in cultural events, and parental system of values) as well as a battery of psychological tests with the Wechsler Intelligence Scale for Children (WISC).

Among the psycho-socio-cultural variables which we refer to here were: frequent talks with the child; answering his/her questions; parental participation in cultural events together with the child; and good emotional climate in the family. These variables were found to be equally correlated both with the children's mental performance and with their parent's socio-economic status. Thus, without an additional analysis it was difficult to infer whether the variables in question had an independent effect on the child's cognitive performance, or whether the associations were apparent only, and would disappear if the effect of parental socio-economic status was controlled.

In order to dispel these doubts, the sample under study was divided by parental occupation into two subgroups, non-manual (N = 375) and manual workers (N = 330), and by IQ level into three subgroups: low, xIQ = 91.6, N = 224, medium, xIQ = 106.7, N = 304 and high, xIQ = 124.1, N = 247. The relationship between the psycho-socio-cultural variables and the children's mental performance level was analysed separately with each of the two subgroups. It should be noted that neither percentage of working mothers nor proportion of children attending kindergarten differed significantly in both groups. Some of the obtained results are presented in Table 2.

Table 2. Significance of association between selected psycho-socio-cultural variables
and intellectual achievement level in children of non-manual workers

Variables	SES	Significance of association with the WISC scores
Answering the child's questions	Non-manual	NS
	Manual	p < 0.10
Frequent talks with the child	Non-manual	NS
	Manual	p < 0.05
Good familial atmosphere	Non-manual	NS
	Manual	p < 0.05
Accompanying the the child at cultural events	Non-manual	p < 0.10
	Manual	NS

Source: Firkowska-Mankiewicz, Czarkowski, 1982

As can be seen, the majority of analysed associations between psycho-socio-cultural variables and the children's IQ disappear within the white-collar workers' subgroup, while some of the correlations remain at or approach the statistical significance level in the blue-collar subgroup. The only correlation consistently and distinctly present in both socio-occupational subgroups was that between the mother's estimated intellectual functioning level and the child's mental performance.

The results may be regarded as a clear exemplification of the hypothesis about the necessary minimal level of environmental conditions and stimulation, provided both by the family and social milieu. If the child's habitat is below the necessary minimum, almost any improvement of his/her living conditions or enrichment of the repertory of stimulation important for cognitive performance aids his/her intellectual development, activating hitherto unused resources inherent in the genotype. On the other hand, above this threshold any further increment in the range, intensity or number of environmental stimuli does not result in an automatic, linear rise of the child's cognitive performance level. The latter, undisturbed by the environmental deficits, develops at its own pace, within the limits determined by the child's genotype.

On the grounds of such a hypothesis (cf. Jensen, 1969; Clarke, 1984) it is understandable why a number of factors which in principle should aid the child's cognitive development exert no such effect in the subgroup of Warsaw white-collar families (in which the necessary minimum in respect of living conditions and intellectual stimulation seems to have been attained), while simultaneously the effect in question can be observed in the working-class families, particularly in the ones in which the hypothetical minimum has not yet been reached.

It can be hoped that, with improvement of living standards and social culture growth up to and even above the postulated minimum, both as regards extrinsic environmental factors and intrafamilial variables (or, in other words, when the equal start conditions are attained), resources inherent in genotypes will be fully exploited in children's cognitive development.

A second postulate will then remain to be fulfilled, emphasizing unrestrained social mobility in accordance with these potential resources. The postulate in question was successfully realized in Poland in the fifties, owing to the genuinely previous schooling system, which allowed gifted parents of our subjects to move freely within the social structure. This is evidenced e.g. by the fact that, in the white-collar subgroup, there is a high percentage of parents coming from rural areas or having a working-class family background. However, the process has been considerably slowed down in later years, which is reflected for example in the differentiated educational aspirations concerning children of parents representing various socio-occupational strata. Answering our question about the education level they believed to be attainable for their children, parents in the blue-collar subgroup indicated a level significantly lower than did the white-collar parents (although their children's intellectual abilities were objectively the same, as assessed by means of test methods).

The result suggests a loss of confidence in the real accessibility of the highest education levels for blue-collar workers' children, even gifted ones, as well as the existence of psychological barriers on their way to social rise.

That the psychological barriers result from an increasingly marked revival of institutional barriers is evidenced for example by the decreasing percentage, year by year, of manual labourers' and farmers' children enrolled in secondary schools, colleges and universities (Jarosz, 1981). It is also evidenced by the percentage of children with the above-mentioned family backgrounds referred to special schools for the mentally handicapped – this percentage is higher than it should be on the grounds of these children's actual mental performance level (Firkowska-Mankiewicz, Czarkowski, 1986).

Stage III

The above-mentioned problem of genetic determinants of intelligence was the object of research in Stage III of the Warsaw study.

An attempt was made to estimate the role of biological and social factors in the determination of children's IQs (Wald et al., 1978). The traditional analysis of family resemblance and of correlation between parents and children is not very fruitful since it is difficult to separate biological and cultural determinants: most children are being reared by their biological family. In order to find another reference system it was decided to use the family set method introduced by Schull and co. (1970). The idea of the family set consists in studying at the same time the index case, his or her sibling, the first cousin and an unrelated control. The sibs have one half of common genes, first cousins share one eighth of their genes in common, while the coefficient of relationship with an unrelated control equals zero. The complements of these coefficients may serve as measures of genetic distance. Mathematical aspects of the family set method were analyzed by Rodriguez (1976).

Two hundred index cases who had both a sibling and a first cousin born from 1961 to 1965 and living in Warsaw were selected from the study population. An unrelated control of the same sex as the index case was also randomly selected. The basic Raven's scores were used, without correction for age. The results are presented in Table 3.

Table 3. Coefficients of correlation between members of 200 family sets in raw scores on Raven test

Persons compared	Coefficient of relationship	Correlation in Raven scores
index-sibling	0.500	0.448 ± 0.057
index-cousin	0.125	0.152 ± 0.069 *
sibling-cousin	0.125	0.143 ± 0.069 *
index-unrelated	0	- 0.139 ± 0.070 *

* Not significantly different from 0.

The results suggest that genetic factors play a significant role in the determination of children's intellectual performance. The heritabilities were estimated by means of formulas developed by Rodriguez (1976). The latter were, however, modified to hold an index of parental SES constant. The correction was used since the original technique tends to overestimate the genetic component of variance. The correction may deflate the estimate. For instance, correlation between the index and sib yielded an estimate of heritability 0.896; after introducing the correction the estimate was 0.665, with 95% confidence limits of 0.429 – 0.923. The index-sib correlation yielded the lowest error of the estimate.

The estimates obtained in this study are not discrepant from other studies (Rao et al., 1976, Loehlin et al., 1975, Scarr, 1981, Clarke, 1984).

It should be noted that, under the theory, the proportion of common genes between a parent and a child or between sibs is 0.5. As regards additive traits, however, there is an assumption of random mating. If the mating is assortative then the correlations in question become $1+m/2$. Penrose (1944) estimated m as 0.5. If this value is accepted, the expected sib-sib correlation will be not 0.5 but 0.75. Parental IQs were not examined in the study but the correlation between both parents education was rather high (0.69). On the other hand, these values are for phenotypic resemblance and not necessarily for genotypic correlation. Rao et al. (1976) thought that from the genetic point of view it should approximate zero. If the genotypic correlation is equalized with the phenotypic one, there remains much room for environmental variation.

It should be noted that Rao et al. (1976) suggest that there is an age-dependent difference in the estimated genetic component of IQ variance in children and adults. It may be as high as 0.67 in children but much lower in adults (0.21). This indicates that environmental influences during the maturation process may be quite important.

Taking these data into account it seems justified to conclude that even if the genetic component of the variation in cognitive performance is substantial, the role of the environmental portion of variation, which can be more easily influenced, is extremely important.

Summarizing briefly the results obtained in the three stages of the Warsaw study, it should be said that equalization of schooling and ecological environmental conditions has not only failed to level differences in mental performance of children from families of varying socio-economic status, but has even made the differences in question more salient. These differences may be to some extent ascribed to positive psycho-social influences in the process of socialization, aiding cognitive development, but only in the case of families in which the minimum of stimulation necessary for mental growth has not been attained (i.e. in Warsaw working-class families). If the minimum has been attained or exceeded (which seems to be the case for Warsaw white-collar families), positive socializing influences do not result any more in a linear increment of test scores. It may be assumed, then, that in blue-collar families, inferior in socio-economic and cultural status, an improvement of living conditions as well as enrichment of the milieu with new stimuli may discernibly influence the children's mental performance, modifying – as the Clarkes say (Clarke, 1984) – the disadvantageous social trajectory of their development, while in the case of children of white-collar parents cognitive development may to a greater extent follow the biological trajectory determined by the genotype.

Thus, another paradox emerges as a consequence of equalising environmental conditions: namely, with a decrease of environmental differentiation, individual differences in cognitive development more and more reflect the differences in genetic equipment. This is particularly the case when equalising environmental conditions occurs at a relatively high level, i.e. when all members of a given community are provided with good living standards and social institutions do not hinder educational and social mobility. Under such circumstances the individual's genetic potential may be fully realized, while in a disadvantageous milieu the developmental chances are limited (cf. Dobzhansky, 1973; Scarr, 1981).

However, before we start seeking the causes of social and educational failures of social policy in an unequal distribution of genes, it is necessary to answer honestly the question of whether the social policy has really (and permanently, not only temporarily as it was in Poland) eliminated the numerous psychological, cultural, material and institutional barriers and impediments for the development of children from lower social strata.

The Warsaw study was carried out in the seventies. There have been considerable changes since that time. In 1989 the sociopolitical and economic system changed. Poland became the first country in Central and Eastern Europe to discard the system of real socialism and move towards a democratic state and market economy. With all these changes, an increase in ecological and educational differentiation of the society is to be expected. Social and educational policy must, therefore, take into account these trends and meet these challenges, to counteract any excessive stratification and stimulate the family educational resources.

References

Bernstein, B. (1970) The role of language, in Edge, D. (ed.) *The Formative Years*, New York: Schocken Book, 52–60.

Bronfenbrenner, U. (1970) Socialization and Social Class Trough Time and Space in Tumin, M. M. (ed.) *Readings on Social Stratification*, New Jersey: Prentice Hall, 204–226.

Clarke, A. M. (1984) Early Experience and Cognitive Development, in Gordon, W. E. (ed.) *Review of Research in Education* (11), 125–157.

Clarke, A. M., Clarke, A. D. B. (1958) Eds. *Mental Deficiency: The Changing Outlook*, London: Methuen.

Coleman, J. (1966) *Equality of Educational Opportunity*, HEW.

Dobzhansky, T. (1973) *Genetic diversity and human equality*, New York: Basic Books Inc.

Eysenck, H. J. (1979) *The Structure and Measurement of Intelligence*, Berlin, Heidelberg, New York: Springer-Verlag.

Firkowska. A., Ostrowska. A., Sokolowska. M., Stein, Z., Susser, M., Wald, I. (1978) Cognitive Development and Social Policy, *Science*, 200, 1357–1362.

Firkowska-Mankiewicz, A., Czarkowski, M. (1982), Social Status and Mental Test Performance in Warsaw Children, *Personality and Individual Differences*, Vol. 3, 237–247.

Firkowska-Mankiewicz, A., Czarkowski, M. P. (1986) Srodowisko spoleczno-kulturowe a zdrowie (na przykladzie uposledzenia umyslowego) (Socio-cultural environment and health – example of mental retardation – in Polish) *Studia Socjologiczne*, 3 (102), 199–200.

Flynn, J. R. (1987) The mean IQ of Americans: massive gains from 1932–78, *Psychological Bulletin*, 101, 171–191.

Jarosz, M. (1987) Intergenerational Trends in Deprivation and School Careers, In Ferge, Miller, S. M. (eds.) *Dynamics of Deprivation*, Aldershot: Gower.

Jencks, Ch. et al. (1972) *Inequality: A Reassessment of the Effect of Family and Schooling in America*, New York: Basic Books Inc.

Jensen, A. R. (1969) How much can we boost IQ and scholastic achievement, *Harvard Educational Review*, 31, 1–123.

Kohn, M. L. (1969) *Class and Conformity – A Study in Values*, Hamewood, Illinois: The Dorsey Press.

Kohn, M. L., Naoi, A., Schoenbach, C., Schooler, C., Slomczynski, K. M. (1990), Position in the Class Structure and Psychological Functioning in the United States, Japan, and Poland. *American Journal of Sociology*, Vol. 95, No. 4, 964–1008.

Loehlin, J. C., Lindzey, G., Spuhler, J. N. (1975) *Race differences in intelligence*. San Francisco: W.H. Freeman and Co.

Minuchin, P. P., Shapiro, E. K. (1983) The School as a Context for Social Development, In Mussen (ed.) *Handbook of Child Psychology*, Vol. IV., Socialization, Personality and Social Development, Hetherington, E. M. (vol. ed.), 197–274.

Penrose, L. S. (1944) Mental illness in husband and wife: a contribution to the study of assortative mating in man. *Psychiatric Quarterly Supplementum* 18, 161.

Rao, D. C., Morton, N. E., Tee, S. (1976) Resolution of cultural and biological inheritance by path analysis. *American Journal of Human Genetics*, 28, 228–242.

Rodriguez, A. (1976) A Monte Carlo simulation of the family set approach to estimate heritability. Unpublished Ph. D. Thesis, University of Texas School of Public Health, Houston, Texas.

Rutter, M., Manghan, B., Mortimor, P., Ouston, J., Smith, A. (1979) *Fifteen thousand hours: Secondary schools and their effects on children*, Cambridge, Mass.: Harvard University Press.

Scarr, S. (1981) *Race, Social Class, and Individual Differences in IQ*. Hillsdale, NJ: Erlbaum.

Schull, W. J., Harburg, E., Erfurt, J. C., Schork, M. A., Rice, R. (1970) A family set method for estimating heredity and stress. *Journal of Chronic Diseases*, 23, 89–92.

Smith-Blau, Z. (1972) Maternal aspiration, socialization and achievement of boys and girls in the white working class. *Journal of Youth and Adolescence* (1), 35–57.

Sokolowska, M., Firkowska-Mankiewicz, A., Ostrowska, A., Czarkowski, M. (1978) *Sprawnosc umyslowa dzieci w swietle czynnikow spoleczno-kulturowych* (Mental performance of children in the light of sociocultural factors – in Polish). Warsaw: Institute of Philosophy and Sociology, Polish Academy of Sciences.

Wald, I., Stein, Z., Susser, M., Sokolowska, M., Firkowska-Mankiewicz, A., Ostrowska, A., Czarkowski, M. (1978) Environmental and Genetic Influences in Mental Development. The Warsaw Study. Paper presented at the XIV International Congress of Genetics, Moscow.

A selection of the Clarkes' publications

Clarke, A. D. B. and Clarke, A. M. (1953) How constant is the IQ? *Lancet*, ii, 877–880.

Clarke, A. D. B. and Clarke, A. M. (1954) Cognitive changes in the feebleminded. *British Journal of Psychology*, 45, 173–179.

Clarke, A. D. B. and Hermelin, B. F. (1955) Adult imbeciles: their abilities and trainability. *Lancet*, ii, 337–339.

Clarke, A. D. B., Clarke, A. M. and Reiman, S. (1958) Cognitive and social changes in the feebleminded – three further studies. *British Journal of Psychology*, 49, 144–157.

Clarke, A. M. and Clarke, A. D. B. (Eds.) (1958) *Mental deficiency: the changing outlook*. London: Methuen. 2nd edition, 1965; 3rd edition, 1974, also published by The Free Press. See also Clarke, A. M., Clarke, A. D. B. and Berg, J. M., 1985.

Clarke, A. D. B. and Clarke, A. M. (1959) Recovery from the effects of deprivation. *Acta Psychologica*, 16, 137–144.

Clarke, A. D. B. Clarke, A. M., and Brown, R. I. (1960) Regression to the mean – a confused concept. *British Journal of Psychology*, 51, 105–117.

Clarke, A. D. B. and Clarke, A. M. (1960) Recent advances in the study of early deprivation. *Journal of Child Psychology and Psychiatry*, 1, 26–36.

Clarke, A. D. B. and Blakemore, C. B. (1961) Age and perceptual-motor transfer in imbeciles. *British Journal of Psychology*, 52, 125–131.

Clarke, A. D. B. and Cookson, M. (1962) Perceptual-motor transfer in imbeciles: a second series of experiments. *British Journal of Psychology*, 53, 321–330.

Clarke, A. D. B. (1963) *Inaugural lecture: Science and behaviour*. University of Hull Publications.

Clarke, A. D. B. and Cooper, G. M. (1966) Age and perceptual-motor transfer in imbeciles: task complexity as a variable. *British Journal of Psychology*, 57, 113–119.

Clarke, A. M., Cooper, G. M. and Henney, A. S. (1966) Width of transfer and task complexity in the conceptual learning of imbeciles. *British Journal of Psychology*, 57, 121–128.

Clarke, A. M., Cooper, G. M. and Clarke, A. D. B. (1967) Task complexity and transfer in the development of cognitive structures. *Journal of Experimental Child Psychology*, 5, 562–576.

Clarke, A. M., Clarke, A. D. B. and Cooper, G. M. (1967) Learning transfer and cognitive development. In Zubin, J. and Jervis, G. (Eds.) *Psychopathology of mental development*. New York: Grune and Stratton.

Clarke, A. D. B. (1968) Learning and human development – the 42nd Maudsley Lecture. *British Journal of Psychiatry*, 114, 1061–1077.

Clarke, A. M., Clarke, A. D. B. and Cooper, G. M. (1970) The development of a set to perceive categorical relations. In Haywood, H. C. (Ed.) *Social-cultural aspects of mental retardation*. New York: Appleton-Century-Crofts.

Clarke, A. M. and Clarke, A. D. B. (1973) Mental subnormality. In Eysenck, H. J. (Ed.) *Handbook of Abnormal Psychology*. London: Pitman.

Clarke, A. M. and Clarke, A. D. B. (1976) (Eds.) *Early experience: myth and evidence*. London: Open Books. New York: Free Press.

McAskie, M. and Clarke, A. M. (1976) Parent-offspring resemblances in intelligence: theories and evidence. *British Journal of Psychology*, 67, 243–273.

Clarke, A. D. B. and Clarke, A. M. (1977) Prospects for prevention and amelioration of mental retardation: a guest editorial. *American Journal of Mental Deficiency*, 81, 523–533.

Clarke, A. M. and Clarke, A. D. B. (1977) Sir Cyril Burt. *Bulletin of the British Psychological Society*, 30, 83–84.

Clarke, A. M. and Clarke, A. D. B. (1977) Problems in comparing the effects of environmental change at different ages. In McGurk, H. (Ed.) *Ecological factors in human development*. Amsterdam: North-Holland Publishing Co.

Clarke, A. D. B. (1978) Presidential address: Predicting human development: problems, evidence, implications. *Bulletin of the British Psychological Society*, 31, 244–258.

Clarke, A. M. and Clarke, A. D. B. (1979) The cardinal sin. *Nature*, 282, 150–151.

Clarke, A. M. and Clarke, A. D. B. (1979) Early experience: its limited effect upon later development. In Shaffer, D. and Dunn, J. (Eds.) *The first year of life: psychological and medical implications of early experience*. Chichester: John Wiley.

Clarke, A. M. and Clarke, A. D. B. (1980) Comments on Professor Hearnshaw's 'Balance sheet on Burt'. In Beloff, H. (Ed.) *A balance sheet on Burt. Supplement to the British Psychological Society Bulletin*, 33, 17–19.

Clarke, A. D. B. and Clarke, A. M. (1981) 'Sleeper effects' in development: fact or artefact? *Developmental Review*, 1, 344–360.

Clarke, A. M. (1981) Adoption studies and human development – the 13th Hilda Lewis Lecture. *Adoption and Fostering*, 104, 17–29.

Clarke, A. M. and Clarke, A. D. B. (1981) Problems of applying behavioral measures in assessing the incidence and prevalence of severe mental retardation in developing countries. *International Journal of Mental Health*, 10, 76–84.

Clarke, A. M. and Clarke, A. D. B. (1982) Intervention and sleeper effects: a reply to Victoria Seitz. *Developmental Review*, 2, 76–86.

Clarke, A. M. (1982) Developmental discontinuities: an approach to assessing their nature. In Bond, L. and Joffe, J. M. (Eds.) *Facilitating infant and early childhood development*. Hanover, NH: University of New England Press.

Clarke, A. M. (1982) Psychology and education. *British Journal of Educational Studies*, 30, 43–56.

Clarke, A. D. B. and Clarke, A. M. (1984) Mental subnormality in childhood and adulthood. In Gale, A. and Chapman, A. J. (Eds.) *Psychology and Social Problems*. Chichester: John Wiley.

Clarke, A. D. B. and Clarke, A. M. (1984) Constancy and change in the growth of human characteristics. *Journal of Child Psychology and Psychiatry*, 25, 191–210.

Clarke, A. M. (1984) Early experience and cognitive development. In Gordon, E. W. (Ed.) *Review of Research in Education*, 11, 125–157.

Clarke, A. M., Clarke, A. D. B. and Berg, J. M. (1985) (Eds.) *Mental deficiency: the changing outlook*. 4th edition. London: Methuen; New York: Free Press.

Clarke, A. M. and Clarke, A. D. B. (1986) Thirty years of child psychology: a selective review. *Journal of Child Psychology and Psychiatry*, 27, 719–759.

Clarke, A. D. B. and Clarke, A. M. (1987) Research on mental handicap, 1957–1987: a selective review. *Journal of Mental Deficiency Research*, 31, 317–328.

Clarke, A. M. (1987) *Early experience and the life path – the Sixth Vernon-Wall Lecture*. Leicester: British Psychological Society.

Clarke, A. M. and Clarke, A. D. B. (1988) The adult outcome of early behavioural abnormalities. *International Journal of Behavioral Development*, 11, 3–19.

Clarke, A. M. and Clarke, A. D. B. (1989) Invited editorial: The later cognitive effects of early intervention. *Intelligence*, 13, 289–297.

Clarke, A. D. B. (1991) A brief history of the International Association for the Scientific Study of Mental Deficiency. *Journal of Mental Deficiency Research*, 35, 1–12.

Clarke, A. M. and Clarke, A. D. B. (1992) How modifiable is the human life path? *International Review of Research in Mental Retardation*. In press.

Clarke, A. M. and Clarke, A. D. B. (1992) Variations, deviations, risks and uncertainties in human development. In Carey, W. and McDevitt, S. (eds) *Prevention and early intervention: individual differences as risk factors for the mental health of children*. New York: Brunner/Mazel. In press.

The contributors

J. M. Berg, Professor Emeritus, Faculty of Medicine, University of Toronto. Director of Biomedical Services and Research, Surrey Place Centre, 2 Surrey Place, Toronto, Ontario M5S 2C2, Canada

Janet Carr, Regional Tutor in the Psychology of Mental and Multiple Handicap, Department of Psychology, St. George's Hospital Medical School, University of London, Cranmer Terrace, London SW17 ORE

Don C. Charles, Emeritus Professor, Department of Psychology, Iowa State University

Stella Chess, Professor of Child Psychiatry, New York University Medical Centre

Robert Fawcus, Professor of Clinical Communication Studies, City University, Northampton Square, London EC1V 0HB

Margaret Fawcus, Director of Undergraduate Studies, Department of Clinical Communication Studies, City University, Northampton Square, London EC1V 0HB

Anna Firkowska-Mankiewicz, Assistant Professor of Health Sociology, Institute of Philosophy and Sociology, Polish Academy of Sciences, Warsaw.

Masud Hoghughi, Honorary Professor of Psychology, University of Hull, Director of the Aycliffe Centre for Children, Copelaw, Newton Aycliffe, Co. Durham DL5 6JB

Helen Koller, Principal Associate, Albert Einstein College of Medicine, New York, New York 10461

Edgar Miller, Clinical Psychologist, Department of Health and Social Security, London

Peter Mittler, Professor of Special Education and Director of the School of Education, University of Manchester, Manchester M13 9PL

Doria Pilling, Research Fellow, Rehabilitation Resource Centre, City University, Northampton Square, London EC1V 0HB

Stephen A.Richardson, Professor Emeritus, Albert Einstein College of Medicine, New York, New York 10461

Michael Rutter, Professor of Child Psychiatry, Honorary Director Medical Research Council Child Psychiatry Unit, Denmark Hill, London SE5 8AF

H. Rudolph Schaffer, Professor of Psychology, University of Strathclyde, Glasgow G1 1RD

Alexander Thomas, Professor of Psychiatry, New York University Medical Centre

Barbara Tizard, Emeritus Professor, Thomas Coram Research Unit, Institute of Education, 27 Woburn Square, London WC1H 0AA

Ignacy Wald, Institute of Psychiatry and Neurology, Warsaw, 02–957

William Yule, Professor of Applied Child Psychology, Institute of Psychiatry, University of London, Denmark Hill, London SE5 8AF